Convicts in the Colonies

Convicts in the Colonies
Transportation Tales from Britain to Australia

Lucy Williams

PEN & SWORD
HISTORY
AN IMPRINT OF PEN & SWORD BOOKS LTD.
YORKSHIRE – PHILADELPHIA

First published in Great Britain in 2018 by
Pen & Sword History
An imprint of
Pen & Sword Books Ltd
Yorkshire - Philadelphia

Copyright © Lucy Williams, 2018

Hardback ISBN 9781526718372
Paperback ISBN 9781526756312

Typeset in India by Vman Infotech Private Limited

Printed and bound in the UK, by TJ International Ltd.

Pen & Sword Books Ltd incorporates the Imprints of Pen & Sword Books
Archaeology, Atlas, Aviation, Battleground, Discovery, Family History, History,
Maritime, Military, Naval, Politics, Railways, Select, Transport, True Crime,
Fiction, Frontline Books, Leo Cooper, Praetorian Press, Seaforth Publishing,
Wharncliffe and White Owl.

For a complete list of Pen & Sword titles please contact

PEN & SWORD BOOKS LIMITED
47 Church Street, Barnsley, South Yorkshire, S70 2AS, England
E-mail: enquiries@pen-and-sword.co.uk
Website: www.pen-and-sword.co.uk

or

PEN AND SWORD BOOKS
1950 Lawrence Rd, Havertown, PA 19083, USA
E-mail: Uspen-and-sword@casematepublishers.com
Website: www.penandswordbooks.com

Contents

Acknowledgements

Writing this book has been yet another exciting chapter in my own history. As with any undertaking, I have accumulated a significant debt of gratitude along the way.

This book would not have been possible without my involvement in the Digital Panopticon project. Since 2014 it has been my privilege to spend my days working with convict records and tracing the lives and journeys of Australia's convicts. I have been phenomenally lucky to count as my colleagues some of the leading academics in the history of crime, punishment and convict transportation. The opportunity to discuss transportation with Barry Godfrey, Tim Hitchcock, Hamish Maxwell-Stewart, Deborah Oxley, Robert Shoemaker, Richard Ward and Emma Watkins, and to learn from their collective wealth of knowledge, has been invaluable. They each have my enduring thanks and admiration. Nell Darby too has provided much food for thought when it comes to discovering and writing convict histories. She has always been generous with encouraging words and helpful suggestions, for which I am very grateful. Any mistakes or omissions remain my own.

I would like to thank the National Library of Australia and the State Library New South Wales for providing some of the images in this book. Special thanks also to the Tasmanian Archives and Heritage Office, and the exceedingly helpful and patient staff at the State Records Office of Western Australia. Both online and in person these institutions go above and beyond to help researchers from around the world access our unique shared history. Special thanks to the Female Convict Research Centre in Tasmania, and the countless individual researchers across Australia with who I have discussed convict lives, particularly Dr Ruth Mann, who pointed me in the direction of the Ford sisters.

I am incredibly fortunate to have a tribe of supportive friends who are ever understanding of my need to cancel plans or disappear behind a stack of books for months at a time, and who are always still waiting when I finish a project. Sara Fisher and Kate Hales have both offered encouragement at regular intervals when I was most in need. I am lucky to have them. As usual, Mike McGibney deserves a special mention, for offering support, encouragement, and gentle mockery on an almost daily basis, even in a year full of his own adventures and challenges.

As always, my biggest thanks go to my husband Lorin, first mate on this voyage of endeavour, who kept me on course and provided safe harbour when the sea was roughest.

Introduction: The Lives of the 'Lagged'

I'll put it at once into a mouthful of English. In jail and out of jail, in jail and out of jail, in jail and out of jail. There, you got it. That's my life pretty much, down to such times as I got shipped off ...

I've been done everything to, pretty well – except hanged. I've been locked up, as much as a silver tea-kettle. I've been carted here and carted there, and put out of this town and put out of that town, and stuck in the stocks, and whipped and worried and drove.

Abel Magwitch tells his story in
Charles Dickens' Great Expectations (1862).

In the last four years, I have spent almost every day banished beyond the seas, out of time and out of place, in convict Australia. At least a part of every day anyway. This book is a collection of tales I found there. I trawled through the lists, records, and hundreds of names of the men and women whose (mostly) ordinary lives were suddenly upended when they were loaded onto a boat and shipped across the world. In doing so, I could not help but be transported alongside them. As I waded through hundreds of documents I had a front row seat to watch as most of them disembarked at the other end, and as their fates unfolded in Britain's farthest, and yet most familiar, penal colonies. I was with the First Fleet when they deposited a ragged horde of early settlers on the beaches at Botany Bay, and with the final ship as it pulled into Fremantle harbour to disembark its human cargo at the end of an astonishing era.

Such a journey could not help but inspire me to find out more about a fascinating eighty-year history. Between 1787 and 1868, approximately 168,000 convicts from Britain and Ireland were sent to Australia. There are many histories of convict Australia out there. Histories that trace the social, economic, and political background of the system, and similarly its impact on both sides of the world. There are books that offer a detailed insight into specific colonies, time periods, or particular groups. Whether your interest lies in juveniles, female convicts, or those sent to labour in chain gangs, you'll find a rich and satisfying history available. The more I learn about convict transportation the more I realise what an impossible task it would be for a single book to do justice to almost a century of history, three huge colonies, and so many individual experiences. Luckily, this book has more modest intentions – to tell a collection of tales of those transported to Australia. It was whilst immersing myself in the wider history of Australia's penal colonies that I came across the very first one. A man called Isaac Comer.

Isaac was thirty-four when he was sentenced at the Somerset Sessions in Bath, in April 1844, to be transported for a term of fourteen years. Isaac's crime was not the most glamorous. He was guilty of receiving stolen goods. Nor was his criminal record the most inspiring. He had one previous conviction for the same kind of offence, had served five months for an assault, and three weeks for a bout of drunkenness which had seen him dishonourably discharged from the army. He was single, with no children that he knew of, and had been born in the town of his conviction.

Isaac was transported to Van Diemen's Land aboard the *Lord Auckland* just a few months later, alongside more than 230 other convicts. Isaac wasted no time getting into trouble in the colony – as did many convicts. Isaac was in fact so troublesome that his record of offences, written down in large leather-bound conduct registers, spilled over two pages, whilst his neighbour in the following entry had just a few scrawled lines taking up no more than an eighth of a single page. Isaac was given his Ticket-of-Leave (a document that effectively granted him parole in the colony) in 1857, and continued to offend with remarkable persistence until his sentence finally expired in 1868, long after the penal colony had stopped accepting convicts. Not even his freedom was enough to ensure his good behaviour. Isaac seemed to have an uncanny knack of finding trouble, and the police for finding him. As soon as he stepped out of line, each and every time, it seemed, he was identified and linked with his long history of offending.

Isaac's bad luck, it transpired, was on account of him being a marked man. Not figuratively, but literally. Covered from head to toe in tattoos, the police could make no mistake when they apprehended Isaac Comer. In July of 1871, the Hobart *Mercury* reported:

Yesterday, a prisoner named Isaac Comer, who has a string of convictions against his name quite appalling, but who after a long prison life has been at liberty since 1857, has his body nearly covered with marks indelibly tattooed into the skin. The following almost incredible list of such marks, should, we imagine, leave no doubt as to his identity should it at any future time be required:

On his right arm – man smoking a pipe: S.C.; woman with glass; jane bell; woman and man smoking a pipe; R.C.; glass and jug on table; man; C.C.; sundry stars; a half moon; man and woman hand in hand; sun, woman with glass: W.M.; woman with glass; mermaid and sun. On the back of his right hand - anchor; crucifixion; J.B.; J.C.; and seven stars. A ring on the middle finger of right hand. On his left arm – Highlander; man with hat in his hand arm in arm with a woman; B.J.C.; blue square; turkey-fowl; J.C.; J.B.; sun crown; anchor (upside down); crucifix; anchor; sun; woman; crucifixion; sun; half moon; 9 dots; heart and darts; and shears. Bracelet on left wrist; 21 dots; 7 stars; an anchor; 5 hearts; A.J.B.; and sun on back of left hand. Ring on each finger of left hand. On his breast – ship; mermaid; hull of a ship; 2 men sparring. On his right thigh – woman; 7 stars; crucifixion; sun and moon. On his left thigh – man smoking a pipe; mermaid with comb and looking glass; 7 stars; a woman with a dove in her hand; man hanging from a gallows; man and ladder. There is also a ring round belly. Seven stars; 2 rings; an anchor inside his legs, besides marks on other parts of his body.

His convict description noted that those additional tattoos were in fact 'seven stars, two rings, and an anchor' on his 'yard' – otherwise known as his penis. Such markings were rarely a random accumulation for artistic purposes. Tattoos like Isaac's were the story of a life. Triumphs and tragedies, employments, meaningful relationships, gang affiliation, religious beliefs and criminal records, all inked onto the skin. Isaac's conviction in Bath, and his long list of crimes in Van Diemen's Land, suddenly became just part of a fascinating and complex story. One which perhaps nobody but Isaac would ever know. Isaac was one of a kind, and so was his story. The same is true of every one of the tens of thousands of convicts who arrived in Australia. Convicts like Isaac who journeyed beyond the seas together shared many experiences. A large proportion of them could doubtlessly find much in common with at least some of their fellow prisoners. But with crimes as diverse as picking a handkerchief from a pocket, and murder, committed by everyone from destitute elderly women, to middle-aged gentleman swindlers, and young children barely tall enough to see out of the dock at their trials, the best way to start exploring convict journeys is through as many individual tales of transportation as we can.

In the following pages, readers can travel through this unique system of punishment all the way to the Australian colonies, through the stories of the men and women who found themselves transported. This is not a comprehensive investigation of the workings of the system of transportation, nor a thorough history of each of the colonies. Instead, it is a collection of tales about convicts and their journeys of transportation. They are fascinating micro histories of individuals who experienced one of Britain's most notorious punishments, which together let us explore the process of transportation and life in the penal colonies. The aim of this book is to tell the stories of convicts themselves – which in turn often shed a surprising amount of light on the system they were a part of – by bringing together the varied and disparate sources that their lives left behind.

Where do we sail, and who will we meet?

Australia was not the first of Britain's penal colonies, nor the last. In the late eighteenth and early nineteenth century, the British Empire covered huge swathes of the globe. British subjects from around the world might face penal transportation. At the same time as Britons were travelling to Australia, Britain had penal settlements in Bermuda, Gibraltar, Singapore, India and elsewhere besides. Britain's global penal estate incorporated not only criminal convicts, but political prisoners, military prisoners and colonial prisoners from around the world. This book focuses on just some of those journeys: tales of transportation from Britain (and Ireland) to the Australian penal colonies.

The penal history of Australia, even between 1787–1868, is bigger than we might first expect. Through a collection of tales of those transported from Britain, we will visit New South Wales, Van Diemen's Land (now Tasmania), and Western Australia. These were the three main British penal settlements in the country. However, convict transportation to Australia was accompanied by a history of convict transportation throughout Australia too. There was a failed attempt to establish a penal colony in Victoria, and a band of unlucky convicts made their way to Moreton Bay in Queensland. Free settlers in the early days of the Swan River colony in Western Australia might find themselves sentenced to transportation if they committed a serious crime, and sent to Van Diemen's Land. Although we will not have the opportunity to follow these journeys, it is important to remember that convict transportation was, at its core, a system of removing 'undesirable' individuals from one place, and depositing them in another. This did not always end when convicts washed up in Australia.

There are tens of thousands of individual stories of those who were transported. Within that number there are stories for every decade, every colony, and almost every conceivable convict experience. Yet not all stories are equally accessible. Convict histories are based upon convict records, newspaper entries, letters, diaries, memoirs, scraps of paper and notes in margins. Scattered breadcrumbs of information from which we must make a path. The earlier into history we venture, the more scattered, and often the less filling, those breadcrumbs become. Swathes of records from certain colonies or time periods have been lost, damaged, and destroyed over time, meaning the permanent loss of some convict stories. Other convicts arrived in the colony and passed their time in the convict system quickly and quietly, leaving little record afterwards. As such, the most comprehensive convict narratives which generated the most records and have survived to our own time fall into three categories: convicts who escaped or attempted to escape the colonies; convicts who achieved success or fame after their sentence; and those who failed to thrive, dipping in and out of institutions until they died. Examples of each can be found in the following chapters.

Stories of those transported from London are, admittedly, overrepresented here. This is in no small part due to the wealth of convict lives revealed over the course of the Digital Panopticon project and the fantastic repository of online records for those convicted in the capital. Londoners were not the biggest group of the transported – the Irish, Scots, and those from Lancashire also numbered significantly amongst the thousands sent to Australia. Yet, not all archives are equal, and good stories rely on good records. Wherever possible the experiences of convicts from around the UK are considered, as are the breadth and diversity of those experiences.

I am, primarily, a social historian of women, crime, and deviance. Recapturing women's stories, so often lost or underplayed in the historical narrative, is no less important in the history of transportation to Australia than it is anywhere else. I have, wherever possible, included as many stories of the activities and experiences of female transportees, so essential to both the convict system and the building of modern Australia. However, as with prosecutions and punishments at home in Britain, transportation to Australia was overwhelmingly dominated by men. The proportion of male convicts transported during the period 1787–1853 was far greater (around ¾ to women's ¼), and men also endured an additional fifteen years of transportation after 1853, to which women were not subjected. With only a few exceptions, it was men and boys who endured the horrors of the hulks and the terrifying sites of secondary punishment such as Norfolk Island and

Port Arthur. So, while transportation is a joint story of the men and women who had their lives irrevocably altered when they were torn from home and shipped beyond the seas, their narratives may well dominate separate sections of this book.

All of the stories related here are based on original records. From criminal trials and ships' registers that tell us the where and what of crime and punishment, to census entries, letters, and newspaper articles that provide us with the personal details that so often help to explain an individual's actions and experiences. Gaps have been filled in through the writings and testimony of the men who operated the convict system, from guards that sailed with them, to the men who oversaw their sentences in Britain and Australia. Unusually, some of the convict narratives here are based on the correspondence or memoirs of former convicts themselves, who already recognised the historical significance of what they had experienced, and who wrote down their thoughts and stories for posterity. Some of the stories here are not being told for the first time, but the tales of famous and exceptional convicts are no less valuable for the retelling; the same can be said for the stories of ordinary convicts whose tales are new.

As with any history, we must take stories where we find them, and treat what we find written as fact, unless evidence or healthy scepticism tells us otherwise. We cannot be certain that everything memoirs, letters, and newspapers reported was true, just as we cannot be sure that they were false. Nothing in these stories has been fabricated. Whilst contemporary quotes have been edited to reflect modern spelling and grammar, the content of these quotes has not been altered. I have stuck, as closely as possible, to telling as detailed an accounts as any single paper trail allows. If I had access to the material, I've incorporated it into the convict lives here. We can never know for sure what motivations caused men and women to act, nor how they felt about their experiences. Using my knowledge of the period, places, and criminal justice system, I have in some cases made suggestions for the most likely scenarios which saw certain lives play out as they did, but we cannot know for sure. One of the joys about history is being able to decide, when faced with the evidence, if you agree with others' suggestions.

Victims and villains

Offending histories are always tricky to tell, especially histories that focus on the lives and experiences of offenders as well as their crimes. Having looked at the life histories of hundreds, if not thousands, of offenders over the last decade, I remain convinced that the history of offenders is more often than not one of disadvantage, prejudice, poverty, and trauma. The history of transported convicts is no different.

Between 1787 and 1868 the British justice system was in flux. It moved away from the barbaric 'bloody code' of decades past, through the experiment of its penal colonies in Australia, to the advent of the convict prison system that we may recognise today. However, despite debates about penal practice, reform, and prisoner welfare which played a significant role in this era, the British justice system remained faithful to some central principles. Throughout this period, criminal justice overwhelmingly valued property over people. Although murder remained a capital crime, assaults, wounding, and rape could all be punished with a few months or a year in prison, while the theft of a pocket watch could earn an offender ten years of transportation. Most of those transported to Australia as convicts were not serious violent offenders, but rather property offenders, who by today's standards had committed fairly inconsequential thefts. British criminal justice also often operated as a tool of the ruling elite to control and oppress the poor.

The overwhelming majority of those who found themselves sentenced to transportation were working-class people. Those living in poverty often had greater cause to stray outside the bounds of the law in order to provide for themselves. Furthermore, prejudice from the governing class meant surveillance and efforts at apprehending offenders were more focussed on capturing poor law-breakers. This meant that working-class individuals were both more likely to commit need driven crimes, and more likely to be caught. They were also more likely to be convicted than their affluent peers should they appear in court. Working-class people would always face a middle or upper-class judge, and juries were always composed of a group of property owning men. As we might expect with such a class divide, those operating the criminal justice system could be predisposed to feel outrage on behalf of victims like themselves, or offer the benefit of the doubt to defendants of their own social standing over those of a lower social class. The bulk of those transported to Australia were sentenced and sent before the reforms of the mid-nineteenth century took place – reforms which began to think differently about age, gender, and rehabilitation. As such not only the poor and destitute, but also the very young, were sent to Australia with little consideration. Children as young as eight could face a full criminal trial, and children as young as eleven and twelve arrived in the penal colonies where they served time alongside adults in the convict system.

During the period of transportation, thousands of men, women, and children, most of who were guilty of little more than small thefts, were processed through a brutal system. The weak, the young, the vulnerable, the innocent alongside the guilty, those unable to prepare a defence, those who had suffered a miscarriage of justice, and most of all those whose greatest misfortune was to be poor and in need, were packed onto ships and exiled. They travelled for months in dark and dirty ships where disease or disaster might kill them. They were at the complete mercy of their fellow convicts and the men who guarded them. They were torn from their families, friends, possessions, homes, and everything they knew. These individuals, defined totally by their convict status, had years of forced labour ahead of them in the colonies. They lived in penal settlements where failure to comply might mean a flogging, a reduction of diet, or confinement alone in the dark for days on end. When freedom came, there was no assistance to migrate home to Britain, and most had to build new lives in the colony in which they had been deposited. Those transported between 1787–1868 were victims of the convict system, as were their families who lost mothers and fathers, brothers and sisters, children, husbands and wives. They were victims of a system of forced migration and forced labour. Victims of a criminal justice system that protected the property owning classes at the expense of the poor. Transportation was a physical, psychological, and social trauma from which some never recovered.

However, just because we accept that the British justice system could be socially unjust, and that transportation was a traumatic experience for which we may feel sympathy, it does not follow that all offenders were likeable or sympathetic characters. It is easy enough to feel compassion for a twelve-year-old pickpocket who may not have realised the high stakes of his endeavour until it was too late, or the destitute mother who paid a heavy price for stealing food for her starving children. We do not have to look far into records of transportation to find such stories, or to rationalise such offenders as victims of an oppressive and uncaring criminal justice system. It is much harder to feel this way about a rapist or a murderer, or those who abused children, defrauded the vulnerable, or used violence to rob, intimidate, and maim. These offenders too numbered amongst those sent in chains to Australia. Yet transportation to Australia was no more fair, safe, or pleasant for unlikable offenders convicted of terrible crimes than it was for victims of circumstance and prejudice convicted of relatively minor offences. Our perspective on the justness of a system of punishment should not change on a case by case basis.

Real convict men and women had real victims, from whom they stole, or whom they hurt or exploited. Not all of these victims were affluent gentlemen who could afford to lose the odd pocket watch. Many victims were just as poor, and just as vulnerable as the convicts who were transported. For the family of a murder victim, it must have been poor consolation to know that the perpetrator was heading to Australia, where they would obtain freedom, and perhaps prosperity, within a decade. Or reading in the papers that the man who raped you, or the woman who burgled your house, had been sent to a colony which was experiencing a gold rush, as many victims must have. Most of us interested in the social history of crime and punishments should, and do, feel sympathy for the victims of crime whose lives were damaged and disrupted through the actions of offenders. They deserve and will no doubt receive their own histories. But sympathy for one group must not cancel out sympathy for the other.

Amongst the convicts who landed in Australia, there were the guilty and the innocent, the desperate and the opportunistic, the good and the bad. However, the nature of the crime they committed, the victim of that crime, and their individual character made little difference to the impact of transportation of their lives. Whoever an offender was, and whatever they had done, the wait to sail could still be interminable, the voyage dangerous and disease ridden, and life in the colonies unfamiliar, dislocating, and hard. Convicts were in all but a few cases torn from their lives and loved ones, usually never to return. Even for those who claimed they wanted to go to Australia, there was no choice about it, and certainly no option to change their minds once they arrived – if they ever did. Transportation was a system which cost some convicts their lives, and exposed others to levels of brutality unthinkable in modern society. Being transported, and forced to labour thousands of miles from home, was a traumatic experience; the psychological, physical, and social impact of this system of punishment could last a lifetime. Even stories of convict success in Australia do not serve to prove that the overall practice was positive. In the following pages the trauma caused by the transportation of convicts to Australia is often referred to, and the stories of convicts have been presented with that in mind. However, at no point should a wish to better understand their experiences and the impact of transportation on their lives be read as a lack of sympathy for the victims of their original crimes or subsequent offences. The terms of 'victim' and 'villain' can be reductive and unhelpful in the history of offending – a complex and multifaceted topic. If tales of transportation teach us anything, it's that convicts could be both, simultaneously, interchangeably, and intermittently.

The cost of convicts, and the European history of Australia

The eight decades of convict transportation to Australia had many costs. Aside from the inevitable financial burden of starting what was effectively a new country, there was a substantial human cost to the endeavour, such as the emotional cost to the convicts torn from home, and their families left behind. The very lives of those sent to Australia in bondage might have become forfeit, whether on the treacherous voyage, or as they faced starvation and danger in the fledgling colonies. Even after the colonies were established, danger, disease, and neglect took yet more lives.

Without a doubt, however, the biggest cost of the British colonisation of Australia was to the lives, lands, and culture of the indigenous peoples of the country and surrounding islands. Every convict settlement (or free settlement for that matter) displaced numerous indigenous communities. In settling land that had been previously used by nomadic peoples, British colonialisation cost lives and irreparably damaged the cultures of indigenous Australians north, south, east, and west. The prejudice and persecution bought to Australia by settlers echoed down the generations, and has continued to affect the lives and life chances of Aboriginal people into the twenty-first century. These histories should be, and need to be, told. They are being told by members of affected communities, and scholars who have dedicated their careers to understanding this dark part of British history. But these histories are being told slowly. Both in volume and international attention, histories of Aboriginal Australia are overshadowed by the European history of the country.

It is impossible to completely separate the stories of British convicts in Australia from those of Aboriginal peoples. Convicts had violent clashes with indigenous Australians, they settled on their land, and committed crimes with and against them. The history of British relations with indigenous peoples, and those peoples' experiences living in and around Australia's three main penal colonies, does not appear here. This is no reflection on the significance of this history, or its importance. Its absence here is a reflection of the fact that the subject deserves to be more than a footnote in another history of the British colonies, and I have neither the knowledge nor skill to do it justice in these pages.

Beyond the seas

This book, full of tales of transportation, is ultimately about convict journeys. In the following five chapters you'll find stories of men, women, and children whose lives were touched by transportation.

The first chapter is set where all convict journeys began, in Britain. It traces the legal journeys that convicts might take through the justice system, the crimes which warranted a sentence of transportation, and a complex post-sentencing system full of so many twists and turns that all manner of people ended up in Australia, or got left behind. There you'll find stories of those who escaped the noose to make it to a penal colony, who endured the horrors of the hulks, and even those who died before boarding a ship.

Chapter two looks at the convict voyage itself, and the many perils that awaited those who boarded a convict vessel. Chapters three, four, and five offer stories of those sent to the three main penal settlements of the period: New South Wales, Van Diemen's Land and Western Australia. In these chapters, you'll find a mix of stories which follow convicts as they progressed through the convict system, flourished in a brave new land, or failed to thrive. I hope they will be as enjoyable and interesting to read as they were to write.

Now, nothing is left but to begin our own journey, into history and beyond the seas.

Chapter 1

Sentencing, Selection, and the Wait: Pathways to Australia

If transportation to Australia were a television drama, scenes would cut in quick succession as our convicts progressed through the criminal justice system and from Britain's docks, to sandy beaches at the other side of the world. The judge would bang his gavel, sentence some poor soul in the dock to be transported for the term of their natural lives, and the screen would cut to the day they hustled in chains aboard a vessel to begin their voyage. But the lives of convicts, and certainly British justice, was not as neat as centuries of creative licence would have us believe. Far from being the final word in a convict's fate, the passing of sentence was but an early step in a long and twisting journey with few guarantees of a new life in the colonies.

From the courtroom, a convict might endure years of incarceration at home before being selected for a voyage. That's if they ever were. Not every convict sentenced to transportation during our period arrived in Australia. At different moments during the life of the Australian penal colonies, as few as thirty per cent of convicts sentenced to transportation actually arrived in Australia. Even at its height, only around seventy-five per cent of sentenced convicts arrived. Particularly earlier in the period, but as late as the 1860s, there were a range of alternate fates that might await our transportees.

This chapter, before those that will take us across the world, examines some of the fundamental questions about some of the most famous prisoners in British history. Who were the men and women sentenced to be transported and what crimes had they committed to warrant such justice? We'll look at the alternative fates that claimed convicts as they made their way from court to port, and gain a little insight into what a sentence of transportation meant to the men and women on the receiving end.

The worst of the worst?

When transportation meant a voyage across the Atlantic to the American colonies in the seventeenth and early eighteenth centuries, the sentence was often greeted with relief. During these centuries, the worst crimes (and often even the seemingly insignificant) would be punished with a long drop at the end of a short rope. Transportation might be used for those whose crimes were minimal, for first time offenders, or for those who through mitigating circumstances managed to avoid execution. However, somewhere in the few decades between American transportation and the new colonies in Australia, public perception, and that of convicts themselves, shifted. In its earliest years, transportation to Australia was often portrayed as the fate that awaited the worst and most wretched of criminals.

The poor reputation of transportation to Australia was not based on the calibre of convicts alone. In the late eighteenth century, as the First and Second Fleets set sail, life in Australia was a much more uncertain prospect than America had been, and the land a greater unknown. Not to mention the damage done to the reputation of penal transportation by the disastrous British experiment in West Africa just a decade or so before. However, the idea of transportation as the fate awaiting the most villainous and wicked of criminals remained long into the nineteenth century, after most immediate dangers had passed. Until, that is, positive reports of life in the antipodes began to trickle back from former convicts, and the system, no longer a deterrent, began its slow closure, one penal colony at a time. Certainly, the idea of transport ships being packed with thieves and ruffians, prostitutes, drunkards, and murderers is one that has had a lasting impact on our own perception of penal transportation (Image 1). But how accurate is it? What crimes and what criminals warranted the sentence of transportation?

Undoubtedly, prostitutes, drunkards, gamblers, and brawlers all found their way across the seas as British convicts, but it was not these crimes that took them there. Crimes against public order, like drunkenness, breaking the peace, and prostitution were amongst the most common offences dealt with in British courts. However, these offences, tried by magistrates at Petty Sessions, did not carry serious sentences. Breaches of public order (unless part of riots which could result in the most extreme of sentences) were usually met with little more than a fine or a few days in a local lock up. Low level violent crimes – fights between neighbours, drunken brawls, and injuries caused without danger to life or the use of a weapon – were likewise commonly punished with a short term of imprisonment. It was only more serious 'indictable' crimes, heard at higher courts, for which a sentence of transportation could be passed. When prostitutes and drunks did find their way on board convict vessels, it was as a result of a connected offence. The drunkard whose intoxication ended in a fatal argument or accident, the prostitute who picked the pocket of the wrong customer. Whatever else transported convicts were in their lives at home and abroad, the convicts sent to Australia can be described rather reliably as thieves and swindlers, fraudsters, violent criminals, murderers and rapists.

Thieves, burglars, receivers, coiners, shopbreakers and fraudsters

Offenders convicted of property crimes made up by far the biggest proportion of those sentenced to be transported. Theft was the largest category of all property crimes and covered an enormous range of individual offences. All thefts could be tried as felonies, but the specifics of a trial and sentence usually came down to the particulars of the offence, such as the value of the theft, the location of the theft, and the manner in which the theft was carried out. The higher the value of the theft, the more likely it was that a felony charge would be brought. Until 1827 (forty years into transportation to Australia) thefts could be broadly divided into two categories, of 'petty' and 'grand' larceny.

Petty larceny was the charge brought for thefts under the value of a shilling. If defendants were lucky, this offence would be tried by a local magistrate rather than a higher court, meaning a summary conviction and an escape from more serious punishment. However, while it was never punishable by death, petty larceny could still be tried as a felony and carry a sentence of transportation if the context of the crime was thought to warrant it. In 1825, Mary Edwards, a twenty-year-old Londoner, was found guilty of stealing twelve yards of ribbon. The value of the ribbon was only sixpence, but the manner of the theft – in which she worked with an accomplice – saw her sentenced to be transported for seven years.

Grand larceny was a felony charge used in cases of theft over the value of a shilling. Not only did a conviction for grand larceny warrant a sentence of transportation, it could also carry a sentence of death. Although capital sentences were uncommon as grand larceny denoted a theft with no aggravating circumstances such as violence or breaking into private property. Fourteen-year-old Ann Maloney committed grand larceny when in February 1822 she stole a coat (valued at eight shillings) from Ann Richardson, a lodger in her mother's house. Ann pawned the coat and took the money. She, like Mary Edwards, received seven years of transportation. After 1827, both these categories of theft were replaced by 'simple' larceny, a category of offence which removed the one shilling barrier between the two former offences. This resulted in all thefts without aggravating circumstances constituting the same offence. After the Criminal Justice Act was passed in 1855, an increasing number of simple larceny cases were tried in lower courts, making them no longer eligible for transportation. This change came too late for the more than 150,000 individuals that had already been shipped to New South Wales and Van Diemen's Land.

Other than generic larcenies, there were many other ways of stealing that ended with a sentence of transportation. Any theft in which violence was used, such as highway robberies, were automatically felonies, and eligible to receive capital (death) sentences. However, as the eighteenth century gave way to the nineteenth, executions were usually only carried out in cases of murder. William Challinor, a nineteen-year-old from Staffordshire, was sentenced to ten years transportation when he was found guilty of beating pensioner William Graham about the head on the night of 17 June 1847, and stealing from him a silver watch and chain. Burglary was another aggravating circumstance which immediately placed even thefts of small value in line for a sentence of transportation. In a society in which the sanctity of home was absolute, breaking and entering private premises, or stealing from a private home, even if the said property was empty at the time, was a serious offence. Thomas Allen and his family were away from home in May 1837 when Edward Rodwell broke into their house in Shouldham, Norfolk. Rodwell took a few razors and a microscope from the empty house, but when apprehended was sentenced to be transported for fourteen years. Pickpocketing, shoplifting, and thefts by servants were popular forms of theft for women and children, who often lacked the physicality for offences like robbery with violence or breaking and entering, which also end in a sentence of transportation.

A litter of other property offenders were sentenced to transportation too. Receiving stolen goods, for which Ikey Solomon was indicted, cementing his place in both history and literature, (see Chapter four) and feloniously disposing of the same could both carry sentences of transportation. Producing and uttering counterfeit currency, especially coins, was a royal offence, again technically worthy of a capital sentence, which saw many shipped across the seas. There was also a range of what we would now call 'white collar' crimes, for which a number of educated upper and middle-class felons, like James Hardy Vaux, (see Chapter three) were transported. Those who embezzled, committed frauds and large forgeries ensured that a surprising social mix of convicts made transport lists.

Violence, murder and mayhem

Theft might have been the most common offence which saw offenders sentenced to transportation, but it was violent and sensational crimes which helped shape transportation's fearsome reputation and captured the popular imagination. Yet the proportion of offenders sentenced to transportation for violent crimes was tiny when compared to the number of property offenders. Cases of rape very rarely made it to eighteenth and nineteenth century courts and those that did often ended in acquittal due to lack of evidence. Convictions for rape, depending on the parties involved and the circumstances of the case, might end in a few months' imprisonment for the perpetrator, or transportation. The outcome heavily depended on how the judge interpreted the severity of the case. Rapists were a minority of those sentenced to transportation, but as the period wore on sexual offences against children were treated with increasing severity by the courts. In the 1850s and 1860s especially, those convicted of sexual offences against children were increasingly given sentences of transportation, and shipped out to Western Australia. Other violent offences such as murder, and manslaughter, serious assaults, and wounding (assaults in which a weapon was used) could all, technically, be met with a sentence of transportation, and some were. James Baird and James Meikle were both convicted separately at the same Fife Sessions for an 'assault to the danger of life', and were punished with seven and nine years of transportation respectively. However, even acts of violence that we would consider significant today were often tried at summary courts, resulting in short terms of imprisonment. Those acts of violence thought serious enough to be felonies often skipped lower punishments and proceeded straight to the death sentence.

Dead men… sailing

Murder, manslaughter, and other forms of unlawful killing or serious wounding remained the only crimes still continuously eligible for capital sentences throughout the period. Yet even by the late eighteenth century, large volumes of hangings were waning, and transportation provided a suitably serious, but non-lethal, alternative to the death penalty. As such, convicts of this nature were far more common in the Australian colonies than they had been in previous penal colonies. Some of those on trial for murder or manslaughter might be found not guilty on account of insanity, but for those found guilty and in possession of their full faculties, it was far more likely that they would initially face a black-capped judge who sentenced them to hang. At the same time, however, in many capital cases, mercy was later recommended, and convicts were brought back to the courtroom and offered pardons on the condition that they be transported for a term of between seven years and the rest of their natural lives. Thus, a significant proportion of those in the 'transportation pool' who left court and began their wait for a voyage actually received transportation as a secondary sentence.

Elizabeth Hinchcliff, a fourteen-year-old London servant, poisoned her mistress and two of her mistress's lodgers with arsenic in September 1810. She was not successful in killing them, but for the attempt alone she was sentenced to death. Elizabeth was recommended by the jury to mercy on account of her young age. She later had her initial sentence commuted on the condition that she be transported for life, which she was. She sailed on the *Minstrel* to New South Wales in May 1812. Francis Fernandez, a twenty-year-old sailor, joined Elizabeth on board the *Minstrel*. He had been tried at the same court as Elizabeth the following year, in May of 1811, charged with stabbing John Clare and Thomas Day with the intent to kill them. Fernandez was sentenced to death, but given mercy two months later on the condition that he be transported for life.

Of course, the above are only broad categories of offences commonly punished by transportation. In the cities, towns, and villages of Britain and Ireland, in their houses and streets, their pubs, shops and alleyways, there were at any given moment all kinds of crimes and misdemeanours for which men and women might eventually find themselves living on the other side of the world. The eighty years in which transportation to Australia occurred spanned a period in which justice and punishment was evolving. Transportation spanned a period which saw the iconic threat of the gallows and savage punishments of the bloody code diminish, and the modern prison system emerge. Likewise, no two crimes, and no two criminals were quite the same, and from high treason to pocket picking, the subjective way in which courts dealt with offenders meant individuals could never be entirely sure of what the outcome of their trial would be.

Subjective sentencing

Even though they changed as the decades rolled on, the rules for sentencing convicts at British courts during the transportation era were fairly clear. Some crimes were eligible for a sentence of transportation, and some were not. Under the right circumstances, a death sentence could be substituted for one of transportation. Judges knew their trade, and stuck, fairly rigidly, to matching up particular offences with their prescribed tariffs. Yet crime alone was not the only factor judges had to consider in passing a sentence. In some cases it could be as much about who a convict was as about what they had done when it came to sentencing. Age, criminal record and personal circumstances could all impact how well a defendant fared in the dock.

Offenders old and new

When it came to property crime, having previous convictions of a similar nature greatly increased a convict's likelihood of being sentenced to transportation. The knowledge of a previous conviction could be used in the court as proof that the defendant was a bad character (just the kind Britain wanted shipped from her shores forever). A criminal record might also be interpreted by the judge as a sign that more lenient punishments like short terms of imprisonment, admonishments and fines had not been effective in teaching an offender a lesson. An 'old offender', as defendants with criminal pasts were often termed in the dock and the press, was twice as incorrigible as a first timer and could expect less mercy when it came to their sentence, even in cases where the value of their crime was relatively low. The young, who in less than a century would face special institutions for juveniles rather than the full force of adult justice, could be 'old' offenders during this period, with recidivist children as young as eleven and twelve regularly sentenced to be transported. At the Bristol Quarter Sessions of summer 1832, ten defendants under the age of twenty were sentenced to varying terms of transportation for a range of seemingly small offences.

George King, aged sixteen, and Edward Storer, aged fifteen, were charged with stealing a single silk handkerchief from a Mr G. Hillhouse at a market. Storer was sentenced to twelve months of imprisonment with hard labour, but King, 'being an old offender', was sentenced to seven years transportation. George's previous offences, though not listed, were likely to have been minor, but even a single teenage transgression might have been enough to seal his fate. Likewise, Thomas Player, a youth of just fourteen, was found guilty of stealing a handkerchief on Bristol bridge. Also known to the court as an old offender, Player was sentenced to fourteen years' transportation. Within a year, Thomas had sailed for Van Diemen's Land, where he lived for the rest of his life, in all likelihood having few memories of the country that cast him out as a child.

George Evans, a boy of just eleven, was given seven years' transportation for the theft of a half crown. A child of George's age could usually expect some mercy from the court but, unluckily for him, George had appeared at the previous Quarter Sessions a few months earlier to answer for a similar offence. Notably, George Evans received no recommendation to mercy, making it unlikely his sentence would be commuted. John McCafrey, aged twelve, was found guilty of stealing a handkerchief from John Harris and 'though so young, [had] been repeatedly before the magistrates'. In the dock John seemed to fare better than George. He was initially given a sentence of transportation, but the court 'said this sentence was passed upon him in mercy, as he would be placed on board a vessel set apart by government for the reception of juvenile offenders, where he would be taught a trade'. Given the conditions on such training ships, it is difficult to say which of the boys ultimately had the better fate. In contrast, 49-year-old Joseph Mapstone, whose embezzlement of ten shillings from his employer, was a crime far greater in value than the half crowns and handkerchiefs taken by the children who appeared in the same dock, was given twelve months of imprisonment with hard labour for the crime. Joseph was an adult, but he was also a first-time offender.

Of course, more adults were transported than children. Not only were grown offenders likely to receive less sympathy in court, but adults also had far more opportunity to amass a string of criminal convictions before committing the crime that would ultimately see them transported. What the Bristol Sessions of summer 1832 show us is simply that there was no consistent collection of factors guaranteeing a sentence of transportation. Age and criminal history could be important, gender and class could also play a role. The crime itself might be the deciding factor. Any one of these factors might count more or less for an offender, depending on the court, the judge, the year, and the social context of the time and offence. That said, defendants were often more aware of the law and the processes of the court than we give them credit for. Some offenders would have weighed up the potential consequences of their actions, and the reception they could expect in court, prior to committing an offence. An adult offender with several previous convictions for property crime, found guilty of burglary, or picking a pocket in the early nineteenth century, could have been fairly certain that a sentence of transportation would be forthcoming.

So, we know that those sentenced to transportation were, broadly speaking, between the ages of fourteen and seventy, probably with previous convictions, found guilty of property offences. We know that a good proportion of violent criminals were added to this number when they accepted a lesser sentence of transportation in order to escape the noose. Unbeknown to these convicts, however, was that their day in court was just the first step on a long and winding road that would see them, and the others that shared their fate, confronted with a series of decisions, opportunities, and mandates that could see them end up anywhere but Australia.

I beg your pardon

Even in the eighteenth and nineteenth centuries, convicts had the right to appeal their sentences. Some were lucky enough to have the aid of legal counsel to do so, but even those with no such resources were allowed to petition the Home Secretary for a remittance of their sentence. Pardons were the primary official method through which convicts escaped transportation. The grounds on which a convict could appeal for a pardon were manifold, as were the reasons for which one might be ultimately granted (although these could differ for a single case). Likewise, the condition on which a convict received their pardon could depend on age, sex, former character, and the context of the crime, not to mention the wider social and political climate of the era.

A Free Pardon was the lottery win of judicial mercy. A Free Pardon released a convict almost immediately, with no need for further punishments, and (usually) no conditions for their release. Pardons of this nature were, understandably, rare. A Free Pardon might indicate doubts over the veracity of the initial conviction, or the acknowledgement of a miscarriage of justice in which legal counsel was unavailable or denied. Otherwise, a full pardon could be granted in cases in which extenuating circumstances meant that it was in the penal estate's interest to release a prisoner. A small number of female prisoners might be granted a full pardon due to pregnancy, or a large number of dependent children. Whereas adult men might be most likely to receive a full pardon in the case of ill health. Just a handful of full pardons were recommended for convicts tried each year. At the Old Bailey in 1797 for example, just five full pardons were recommended. One of the lucky recipients was thirty-five-year-old Thomas Bull, who had been convicted in January of that year for stealing a half crown and three shillings from William Tilt. After a long and protracted trial, Bull was found guilty and sentenced to transportation for seven years. However, by the following month, he had been recommended to a full pardon, on account of the fact that 'the judge had doubts on the case and took advice from twelve judges who thought the conviction was bad.' Meanwhile, first time offender Francis Evans was recommended to a full pardon of his seven year sentence due to the fact that he was given no time to prepare a defence as 'the time elapsed between indictment and trial was 2 hours'. Evans' case was further bolstered by the good character and offer of a job he received from a previous employer.

Other recipients were in considerably worse shape when their Free Pardon arrived. John MacDonald, a former soldier of good character who had served more than ten years in the West Indies, was sentenced to be transported for seven years after the theft of a watch. After conviction, while waiting in Newgate Gaol, MacDonald appealed for a pardon, citing his previous good character and service, but was recommended to freedom ultimately because he was 'very ill in Newgate and in a very short period he most probably will terminate his existence'. MacDonald was granted his pardon so that he could live out the remainder of his life outside prison walls, and, more importantly, outside the state's responsibility.

Far more common a form of mercy was the Conditional Pardon, which reduced or mitigated a sentence after imposing certain conditions. Sentences of death could be remitted if a convict agreed to be transported instead, but sentences of transportation too could be remitted, meaning that just a few months after trial, a number of convicts initially bound across the seas to Australia found themselves heading elsewhere. In the first decade of Australian transportation, the British criminal justice system experimented with a small number of cases of 'self transportation'. A few male convicts (there is currently no evidence that the same offer was made to women) were given the opportunity to take themselves away from Britain for the term of their sentences; they might also be asked to provide a small sum of money to ensure that they did not return until the sentence expired. Very little is known about what then happened to these men, where they went and what became of them. With limited powers of surveillance, it is not clear how far they would have needed to travel, or indeed how likely they were to be apprehended if they returned before their sentence expired. Self transportation was banishment in all but name, a form of punishment used in Britain since at least the sixteenth century. There is very little evidence as to why certain Australian convicts were recommended for this kind of pardon, or why the practice ceased.

Pardoning records do give us a few rare glimpses into the cases of men recommended for self transportation, like John Hetherington. Hetherington had stolen, along with his accomplice William Willis, printed linen with a value of five shillings. Both men were convicted and sentenced to seven years of transportation. Of the two men, only Hetherington was recommended by the prosecutors to mercy. After serving two years at hard labour on board a prison ship, Hetherington applied for a pardon on the grounds that he was a first time offender, he had not committed a violent crime, and that he was intoxicated at the time of his offence. Hetherington stated that 'he was willing to transport himself to Charles Town, South Carolina, where he has friends' in place of going to 'Botany Bay'. The judge recommended he do so until the final five years of his sentence were expired, and that he provide sureties to the court that he would not return before this date. We do not know whether Hetherington made it to America, but whatever his fate, he never arrived in Australia.

Relatively few convicts were trusted to transport themselves, but some offenders facing a voyage to Australia were given a reprieve on the condition that they take steps to ensure their future good conduct. This kind of pardon was predominantly granted to young, first time offenders, who might gain the mercy of the court by proving they had productive employment waiting for them outside of the penal establishment. Nineteen-year-old apprentice Henry Stephens was granted a pardon on the condition that he returned to his master's service and fulfil the rest of his indenture there. His master was willing to provide a cash guarantee of Henry's good behaviour. George New, just a few years older than Henry and from a respectable Wiltshire family, had the remaining part of his seven-year sentence remitted due to his contrition and the offer of employment as a labourer on release.

For female convicts whose options for employment were more limited, a Conditional Pardon might entail undergoing a short term of imprisonment, or paying a small fine and providing sureties for future good behaviour. Poverty and having young dependents often featured prominently in the cases made by female convicts for why they should not be sent to Australia. Being responsible for dependents was taken seriously as reason to pardon both male and female convicts, and women, more than men, could often claim sole responsibility for young children. As with the case of Free Pardons, Conditional Pardons on the grounds of poverty and family responsibilities were in no small part down to the pragmatism of the authorities. Transporting a convict mother with several young children not only placed the cost of their care at the feet of the state, but was often lamented as a cause of further crime and disorder. Children orphaned by the transportation of a parent and breadwinner might well become the teenage pickpockets who filled a transport vessel just five or ten years later. In May 1807, twenty-one-year-old Hannah Gorman was convicted of stealing boots, shoes, pillowcases and handkerchiefs from Richard Willis when she worked for his family as a wet nurse. Hannah had two young children at the time of the offence, and a husband serving abroad in the Royal Navy, leaving her totally responsible for her family. Mercy was granted to Hannah in recognition that a dispute with her employer had led to him withholding her wages, supposedly causing Hannah to steal his items in recompense. Not only had Hannah's poverty prevented her from engaging any legal counsel at her trial, but since her confinement in Newgate, she had fallen ill. A judge recommended her to mercy 'in view of her young age and having two infant children to look after while her husband is away'. Hannah was recommended for release once she had served six months of imprisonment. Hannah's transportation would have been a disaster for her entire family, leaving her children vulnerable, and possibly necessitating that her husband give up his employment to fill the gap she left. The state had little practical option but to pardon those who would otherwise prove a burden at home, or abroad in the colony. Sarah Roberts, another pardoned convict, was 'a widow with four children' found to be 'in a deplorable state of health'. She was pardoned on these grounds as she was unlikely to survive seven years in Australia, and the last thing the fledgling colony needed was responsibility for four orphaned children.

A number of histories have provided evidence to suggest that, at least in the early decades of transportation, only young, healthy, and preferably unmarried women were wanted for the colonies. By the time most pardons were processed, many burdensome convicts had already served months or years of their sentences waiting to be transported, and thus the conditions of their sentence mitigation had already been served, allowing them to leave prison as if they had Free Pardons. Of course, in all pardoning cases, if the convict reoffended, mercy was unlikely to be forthcoming a second time, and an additional sentence might be all the heavier for the failure to observe conditions from a previous remittance.

The fate of convicts hoping for mercy was not only down to their own circumstances, background, sex, health, and opportunities for employment. Rates of mercy and the options for pardons fluctuated significantly over the eighteenth and nineteenth centuries. The likelihood of convicts receiving some kind of mitigation for their sentences was also shaped by the needs of the British Empire. In times of war especially, young male convicts were simply too valuable to send to obscurity across the world. In the early decades of transportation, when military pardons were most prominent, the British were facing threats from nearby neighbours (from the French revolution, to the Napoleonic wars) as well as wanting to expand the Empire abroad. This not only created a need to boost numbers in the British forces, but also left Britain with a reduced number of transport ships with which to take convicts abroad. In some years, the Home Secretary was left with a choice of putting men to work for the interest of empire, or leaving them to stagnate in British prisons. Thus, many young healthy men were pardoned on the condition that they enter the army. Previous experience serving in the army or navy could be a significant factor in an application for mercy. Convict William Hunt, for example, could claim a record of good conduct from more than six years of service in the '2nd Life Guards'. He was pardoned six months into a seven-year sentence to serve in the West Indies. Experience was not a prerequisite however, and many younger men were pardoned on little more than a willingness to enlist. Abraham Bolton, a boy of just fourteen, made an application to be pardoned due to his willingness to serve in the navy and was recommended to mercy on the condition that he do so.

For those who feared the uncertainty of transportation, the prospect of a pardon must have felt like a bright light at the end of a dark tunnel. There were certainly prisoners throughout the country who advocated as strongly as possible for any kind of remittance. For others though, for whom applications were made, or who were offered remittance as a matter of course, the King's Mercy (as pardons were often referred to) was of little interest. Justice was not only something which happened to passive men and women with no say in their own fates. Even before they stood in the dock, some convicts had such strong ideas about what a sentence of transportation meant that they were unwilling to have a legal process take such an important decision out of their hands.

Refusing the Royal Pardon

Transportation divided opinions, between lawmakers and penal experts, and amongst convicts themselves. It is a topic that still challenges historians today by presenting a story of two halves. Some saw the trip to Australia as an opportunity for a new and better life. Not only is there evidence to suggest that some offenders committed crime with the intention of being transported, as in the tragic case of Maria Hoskins (see Chapter two), some fought bitterly to make sure that their sentences of transportation were instigated.

Mary Black, an orphaned girl of nineteen, was sentenced to be transported in 1812 having perjured herself by falsely identifying a man named James Kennedy in a grand larceny trial. Mary was young; it was a first-time offence. When her case came before the judges for evaluation, she met many of the criteria common for a Conditional Pardon. A judge recommended Mary to mercy based on her previous good character and a standing offer of employment on release. The application was made not by Mary, but on her behalf. Mary did not want such mercy, or a sentence of imprisonment, or a fine, which would return her in short order to the life she had in London. When questioned, it was reported that Mary 'speaks strongly against mercy'. She wanted to be transported. Mary got her wish. No mercy was forthcoming, and she was transported to New South Wales aboard the *Wanstead* the following year.

For other convicts, transportation was a fate worse than death. It was especially so in the early years, when the First Fleet faced a journey into the unknown, and subsequent convicts faced a perilous voyage, starvation, and harsh discipline in the colony. For some, even up to the very last ship, transportation was an unhappy fate, tearing them from their families and all they knew. For some capital convicts facing the gallows, the offer of transportation was no mercy at all, and they refused. Refusing a pardon to trade death for transportation was not a common tactic, so great was the risk that death might be forthcoming. Yet, cases in which convicts did speak out provide a fascinating insight into perceptions of the punishment at the time, not to mention the relationship between convicts and the justice system changing their lives.

There were those that refused mercy purely as a point of principle, protesting their lack of guilt and suggesting that to accept mercy was tantamount to admitting punishment was deserved, and so refused any mercy as a statement of innocence. George Hyser was convicted of highway robbery in May 1787. The highway robber was much reviled in eighteenth century England, and for stealing the sum of four shillings, George was sentenced to death. In September of that year, he was offered the King's Mercy. He would not hang if he would agree to be transported for seven years. Hyser rejected the offer. When bought up to face the court and respond to his pardon, he said 'I return his majesty many thanks, but as I must leave my native country for a thing I am innocent of, I should rather have my former sentence, if I may have a proper time to make my peace with my Maker.' Hyser was warned that if he persisted in refusing, his execution would be ordered immediately. But refuse again he did, repeating only his request to be given time to make his peace with God. George was taken from the court to a condemned cell, to await his imminent execution. However, only two months later, George sailed with the Second Fleet for New South

Wales. Perhaps Hyser had a change of heart when the hour of his execution drew near, or perhaps the state decided it was not good practice to let convicts have a say in their own disposal. Ultimately, no evidence survives to indicate how Hyser avoided execution not once but twice, if he survived the journey, or how he fared once he arrived in Australia. His case is intriguing, but far from unique. At the same court in the same month, Thomas Newby refused a pardon on condition of transportation. Protesting that he was innocent, and as such transportation would be nothing but submission to a 'state of slavery', he wished, he stated 'to resign my life among my friends and relations.' William Davis stated 'death is more welcome to me than this pardon' and Thomas Messenger 'I would rather die.'

Fear may have been a significant motivator in convicts' refusal of transportation when it was offered as a pardon. Just over five years before the First Fleet sailed, a gaggle of unlucky convicts had arrived in West Africa. Many had died of malaria shortly after landing, whilst some of those who survived the initial onslaught of disease were sent out into the wild to fend for themselves. Some starved, and others met their deaths through accident, animal attack, or at the hands of hostile locals. It is hardly a surprise that this disastrous penal experiment coloured how ordinary men and women, many of whom would have never stepped foot outside of Britain before, felt about colonial exploration and settlement. Even after the First Fleet had made ground in Australia, rumors of starvation, hostile indigenous tribes, and even cannibalism filtered back to Britain, leaving some convicts feeling that they would rather face the familiar gallows at home than risk a less clean death in a strange land. When offered the royal pardon in return for transportation for life in 1792, Thomas Jones replied that he 'would rather die than go to sea to be starved to death'. For others, refusing to be sent out of sight and out of mind was not only a decision born of fear. It could be a personal one, borne out of solidarity and frustration; it could also be a surprising political statement.

In February 1788 Sarah Cowden, Sarah Storer and Martha Cutler were brought up in the Old Bailey on a charge of highway robbery. Their victim, Henry Solomon, maintained that he had being going about his business in Whitechapel in June that year, when he was accosted by three or four women at the end of an alley. Solomon testified that the women made use of obscene gestures and 'very bad expressions' and pushed him into a passage that led into a house. Solomon was ushered into a small room and thrown down onto a bed, where with two women restraining him, a third took over fourteen guineas from his person. When the ordeal was over, he was let up and told to go about his business. Solomon and a number of other witnesses, including a policeman, were able to identify the three women on trial. Despite all protesting their innocence and claiming police brutality, all three women were found guilty. The sentence passed down to them was death. Cutler, Cowden, and Storer were all returned to custody to await their fate.

Over one year later, which the women would have passed in the cramped and unsanitary confines of the local gaol, they were bought back to court with other convicts to be pardoned. Each woman was offered a pardon, granting her respite from the gallows on the condition that she submit to being transported to New South Wales for life. At first, all of the women declined, citing various reasons. Sarah Cowden was first to speak, and protested that she had been wrongly convicted saying only, 'No, I will die by the laws of my country; I am innocent, and so is Sarah Storer; the people that had the money for which I was tried, are now at their liberty, therefore I will die by the laws of my country before ever I will go abroad for my life.' Sarah Storer likewise refused her pardon and protested her innocence. There were other women there too, also refusing to be transported. Sarah Mills stated 'I would rather die than go out of my own country to be devoured by savages.' Mary Burgess also declined to live as a convict, testifying 'I had rather go to my former sentence [death]; I had rather die than leave my child and husband behind me; I am very willing to die; I will die before I leave my poor child in a strange place.' Two more women protested ill health should prevent them, having languished for several years in gaol awaiting sentence. Those who refused were returned to gaol and told they must prepare to die.

Two months later, Cowden, Storer and Cutler were brought again to the court, and asked a second time to accept a pardon. Martha Cutler, given time to dwell on the alternative, readily accepted her pardon when it was offered again in June of that year. Cowden and Storer, however, remained defiant. Both women held fast and told the court they would choose death rather than face life on the other side of the world, wrongly convicted. Sarah Cowden was the first to answer, and she attempted at first to bargain with the court. She stated 'I tell you what: I am willing to accept whatever sentence the King passes upon me, but Sarah Storer is innocent, I would not care whatever sentence I went through; I will accept it if that woman's sentence is mitigated.' Cowden was warned that the question required either acceptance or rejection, and that she would be given no say in any other case but her own. A second time she gave the same answer, she would only accept if her friend was set free. A third time Cowden stated that she could never accept unless Sarah Storer's sentence was mitigated. The court was in uproar. To have the King's justice challenged, and by a woman of such lowly station, was a scandal. Cowen was warned that mercy was not a thing to be 'trifled with' and that if she refused, she would be taken from the court to face execution the next day. She confirmed she was ready to die, and that she hoped that in meeting God, she would have 'more mercy shown me than ever I had at this bar'.

Cowden and Storer were taken back to gaol under the threat of execution within the next few days. They waited, and saw the hour of their executions come and go. Their very public refusal to accept a pardon, not once, but twice, placed the court, the Home Secretary, and even the King, in a difficult position. The state was, in general, reluctant to hang women in the later eighteenth century, especially for property crimes. Both of the women were young (Cowden was only twenty), and had no records of previous conviction. Hanging them would be met with a mixed public reaction, in a tumultuous decade which had seen the loss of the American war, the Gordon riots, and other civil unrest. Yet the women's refusal to accept mercy meant that pardoning Storer and Cowden anyway made the state look weak at a time it needed to appear strong. By the end of June 1789, both Cowden and Storer had been quietly pardoned – without another appearance in court, and presumably without their consent.

Both women were taken on board the *Lady Juliana* convict ship which sailed immediately for New South Wales, arriving the following year. Yet Cowden and Storer remained true to their word and refused to be transported, somehow escaping from the moored vessel before it set sail. This would most likely have entailed somehow making it over the side of the ship and into the water undetected, before making it back to dry land. Such a feat was not common amongst even able-bodied male convicts, let alone women. Nothing more is known of Sarah Storer, who, if she survived, made her way back to the obscurity from which she had come. Sarah Cowden returned to London, perhaps in the company of the friend for whose freedom she had fought so bitterly.

Sarah established a life for herself, having two children and gaining work in the silk industry. Three years after escaping the ship, while at work she was spotted by chance by the man who had delivered her on board the *Lady Juliana*. Returning from transportation, which Sarah had technically committed when she escaped the ship, was a felony. She was taken back to the Old Bailey, and sentenced, again, to death. Luckily, in the intervening years, Sarah had worked hard to cultivate a reputation for 'honesty and industry'.

She was able to call five witnesses to testify to her good character. The jury once again recommended her to mercy. Sarah had a final factor in her favour. She was pregnant. Two months later, in December 1792, Sarah Cowden was released from gaol as a free woman, having escaped two death sentences and emerging victorious in her refusal to be banished beyond the seas.

Gaining a conviction for the right kind of crime, at the right sort of time, was an essential part of the journey from Britain to Australia. But a sentence alone was not enough. A convict might successfully navigate the pardon process to have their sentence altered to either obtain or escape transportation. Yet even when all judicial processes were exhausted, a convict could still not count their place in the colonies as a sure thing. For most, once their final sentence had been agreed, another stage lay between them and embarking for the colonies. A long wait in which good health, good conduct, and good luck could make all the difference when it came to arriving in Australia.

The wait

Once a sentence of transportation was confirmed, the pathways of male and female convicts diverged. Female convicts were much smaller in number. This meant both less competition for space on board convict vessels (which tended to have single-sex convict passengers) and saw a greater demand for women in the colonies. After the First Fleet had established a settlement, there was usually good work to be found for convict women, not to mention their desirability as wives and helpmeets to Australia's growing population of free male convicts. Unless detained by ill health, or other undesirability (see below) female convicts rarely faced the same agonizing wait and uncertainty of their male peers. The often short length of their delay between sentencing and sailing also meant it was not necessary to find special accommodation for female convicts. As such, one of the most iconic features of the Australian transportation era, England's dreaded floating prison ships, the hulks, were the plight of male prisoners. Inside these vessels, many lost years of their lives, or even life itself.

The floating prison ships, made most famous by Dickens' chilling description of Abel Magwitch in *Great Expectations*, were something unique to the period of transportation to Australia (Image 2):

A fearful man, all in gray, with a great iron on his leg. A man with no hat, and broken shoes, and with an old rag tied round his head.

A man who had been soaked in water and smothered in mud, and lamed by stones, and cut by flints, and stung by nettles, and torn by briers; who limped and shivered, and glared, and growled.

Magwitch seemed to Pip on their first encounter to be a devil, and little wonder when he came from such a hell. The horror with which the hulks were recalled by all who knew them have seen them occupy a particularly significant place in British penal history, second only to the whippings, brandings, pillory, and stocks of the bloody code in terms of brutality and fearsome reputation. Their origin, however, was a matter of pure practicality.

When the American war of independence stopped the easy flow of convicts out of Britain, it caused a crisis in the ancient and creaking prison system. Gaols, lock ups, and prisons only ever intended to house those awaiting trial, or for a short term before punishment, were now being used as mass storage for those facing years of bondage and who had nowhere else to go. What Britain lacked in space and infrastructure, it made up for in its abundant waterways and shipping power. The idea of using decommissioned naval and colonial vessels as 'overspill' incarceration was made law by an Act of Parliament in 1779. The Act stated:

For the more severe and effectual punishment of atrocious daring offenders, be it further enacted, that, from after the first day of July one thousand seven hundred and seventy-nine, where any male person ... shall be lawfully convicted of grand larceny, or any other crime, except petty larceny, for which he shall be liable by Law to be transported to any parts beyond the seas ... shall be punished by being kept on board ships and vessels properly accommodated for the security, employment, and health of the persons to be confined therein, and by being employed in hard labour in the raising of sand, soil, and gravel from cleansing, the river Thames, or any other river navigable for ships of burthen.

It is ironic that the hulks were initially enshrined in law this way, specifically for the purpose of providing the 'security, employment, and health of the persons confined therein', as every contemporary record left to us by those who endured the hulks, or those who witnessed them, suggest that these vessels provided nothing of the sort. While it is true that prisoners on the hulks were set to hard and dangerous labour in way of employment, accounts of poor rations, unsanitary conditions, ill health, violence and mistreatment were rife.

The first hulks were moored in the River Thames at Woolwich in London, an area already usefully a military stronghold. The *Justitia* was a ship previously used by the East India Company and the *Censor* a retired frigate. In the coming decades, many more were introduced throughout the country, with hulks stationed at Deptford, Chatham, Gosport, Plymouth, Portsmouth, Sheerness, and even Cork in Ireland. Some were more notorious than others, with a few, like the *Defence*, and *Warrior*, allowing visits from journalists and social observers, who recorded their conditions for posterity (Image 3). Sixty years after their introduction, at the time of the 1841 census, a snapshot of the hulk population on an ordinary day was captured. The population of prison hulks in England was more than 3,500 men. Ten years later, with the advent of the modern convict prison system, the notorious hulks had begun to fall out of use, although there was still a population of more than 1,800 men living in squalid conditions on these floating prisons. By 1861, just six years before the final convict vessel, the *Hougoumont*, sailed for Western Australia, more than 1,300 prisoners were still held on the hulks, awaiting their fate. During the course of eighty years, the hulks played home to thousands of prisoners. No accurate records of the rates of death or disease on these vessels remain, but their terrible reputation enshrined in contemporary fiction, newspapers, political debates, and eyewitness accounts paints a vivid picture of their awful conditions.

Most of the prisoners sent to the hulks were Englishmen who had come through the English justice system. Irish, Scottish, and Welsh convicts were held in prisons in their own countries until they travelled to meet up with a convict vessel as it prepared to sail. As noted above, women were almost entirely exempt from life in the hulks (the legislation specifically providing for 'male person', rather than 'convicts'. There were a few exceptions to this. The *Dunkirk* prison hulk at Plymouth in the late eighteenth century, for example, held four of the famed convicts who escaped from New South Wales in a rowboat in 1792 (see Chapter three). Mary Broad, often hailed as the heroine of the adventure, was confined on the *Dunkirk* alongside James Cox, James Martin, and the man who would become her husband on arrival in Australia, William Bryant.

Although women were largely exempt from the horrors of the hulks, children were not. In the earliest years of transportation to Australia, boys as young as twelve and thirteen might find themselves confined below decks with the population of adult male prisoners. This practice was only halted later in the nineteenth century amongst concerns of the abuse and corruption of juveniles by older hardened prisoners. From the 1830s, juvenile training ships and special juvenile hulks, like the *Euryalus,* separated the child prison population from the rest. However, whether the material conditions on such vessels were any more preferable is questionable. By the 1850s and 1860s, special juvenile reformatories had replaced adult punishments for many children. The abuse of children by adult prisoners on the hulks was a particular concern. Even though inmates were guarded closely by officers throughout the day, at night officers would retire, and convicts were locked below decks in open 'wards' where prisoners slept side by side in hammocks.

The evil hulks permitted in allowing the free association of convicts with minimal supervision from guards; this was a major criticism levelled time and again at the regime. In the emerging convict prisons of the nineteenth century, Millbank, Pentonville, and later, Portland, great care was taken to ensure a tightly monitored reformative regime, where prisoners were given limited opportunity to interact with one another lest the hardened criminals instruct the new arrivals in the ways of criminality, or old convicts plot nefarious activities to undertake upon release. The hulks had no reformative agenda, and left prisoners free to plot, plan, socialise and trade with one another. The bullying of certain inmates by others was not unknown, and there was little that could be done to prevent acts of violence or sexual assault under such conditions. Social commentator Henry Mayhew noted:

> It is very clear that forty or fifty men cannot be crammed into one side of a ship's deck, put together upon works, and swung elbow to elbow in hammocks at night without finding ample opportunity for free conversation.

James Hardy Vaux (see Chapter three) was confined on the hulks for around one year at the beginning of the nineteenth century, after his sentence was passed. He recalled the hulks as a dangerous, unhappy place, where the weak were preyed upon and violence was common. He wrote:

> If I were to attempt a dull description of the miseries endured in these ships, I could fill a volume; but I shall sum up all by stating, that besides robbery from each other, which is as common as cursing and swearing, I witnessed among the prisoners themselves, during the twelvemonth I remained with them, one deliberate murder, for

which the perpetrator was executed at Maidstone, and one suicide; and that unnatural crimes are openly committed.

In his later memoirs Vaux recalled the horror of arriving on a hulk for the first time:

> I now had a shocking scene to contemplate; and, of all the shocking scenes I had ever beheld, this was the most distressing. There were confined in this floating dungeon nearly 600 men, most of them double-ironed (bound by iron shackles at the hands and feet); and the reader may conceive the horrible effects arising from the continual rattling of chains, the filth and vermin naturally produced by such a crowd of miserable inhabitants, the oaths and execrations constantly heard among them; and above all, from the shocking necessity of associating and communicating more or less with so depraved a set of beings.

Above all else though, it was the conditions in which prisoners were forced to live and work that drew most criticisms to the hulks, and has been their enduring legacy into the modern age. The notoriety of the hulks was such that, writing more than fifty years after their closure, Beatrice and Sydney Webb wrote in their 1922 history of the English prison system:

> Of all the places of confinement that British history records, the Hulks were apparently the most brutalizing, the most demoralizing, and the most horrible. The death rate was appalling, even for the prisons of the period.

The mortality rate on the hulks was high. In their earliest years of use, around one in every five inmates succumbed to disease, infection, or exhaustion. The hulks were dark, dank, and squalid. They had no fixed sanitation (waste was dealt with by buckets pitched over board) and a lot of stagnant water. Rats and lice were rife, as was disease amongst convicts who already had their immune systems further degraded by hard physical labour and poor diet. It is small wonder that cleanliness became an integral part of the daily regime. Prisoners were expected to wash before dressing in the morning, and after work at night. Each deck was cleaned daily, and guards and officers doused the surroundings in lyme. Yet not even repeated cleanings were enough to protect inmates against rats, lice, and disease. Mayhew wrote of a conversation he had with a guard who remembered the hulks of the early nineteenth century in all of their squalor. The man 'well remembers seeing the shirts of the prisoners, when hung out on the rigging, so black with vermin that the linen positively appeared to have been sprinkled over with pepper'.

Charles Couzens, a local of Milford Haven in Pembrokeshire, was convicted at a military court for threatening the life of a senior officer in 1839. He was given a sentence of ten years transportation. Couzens was taken first to Millbank Prison, where he was processed into the convict system, before a short time later being transferred to the *Justitia* hulk. He, with a number of other military prisoners, was set to washing the clothes of the hundreds of convicts present on the ship. He remembered:

> The greatest inconvenience experienced in this branch of the department was occasioned by the filthy state of the shirts from vermin, which, on some, literally swarmed, and every place in the wash-house, from long usage, was in the same state. This was truly most dreadful and repulsive.

Despite having been captive for several months in a military prison, and having been inducted to convict life at Millbank, Couzens wrote that it was only after he arrived on the hulk and was placed in leg irons that he 'first experienced in its full force the misery and debasement of my position'. Couzens' part of the cell contained around twenty inmates, with some estimated to be as young as twelve.

Even in the hospital ships, set up to take the most sickly and contagious prisoners out of the main hulk population and provide them with comfort and respite, conditions could be dire. During his visit at Woolwich, Mayhew noted:

> Even so late as 1849, we find the *Unité* hospital ship at Woolwich, described in the following terms:- 'in the hospital ship, the "*Unité*", the great majority of the patients were infested with vermin; and their persons in many instances, particularly their feet, begrimed with dirt. No regular supply of body-linen had been issued; so much so that many men had been five weeks without a change; and all record had been lost of the time when the blankets had been washed; and the number of sheets was so insufficient, that the expedient had been resorted to of only a single sheet at a time, to

save appearances. Neither towels or combs were provided for the prisoners' use, and the unwholesome odour from the imperfect and neglected state of the water closets was almost insupportable. On the admission of a new case in the hospital, patients were directed to leave their beds and go into hammocks, and the new cases were turned into the vacated beds, without changing the sheets.'

Vaux could not bring himself to describe the conditions below decks, noting only 'I shall not attempt to describe it; but nothing short of a descent to the infernal regions can be at all worthy of a comparison with it.' Few outside their immediate families mourned for sick and dying convicts. Those who did not survive their time on the hulks were discarded in unmarked graves in the marshland a short way from shore.

If convicts proved healthy enough to survive the disease and vermin, they had to further contend with poor diet. The food made available to convicts was cheap and of poor quality. The contractors who provided it wanted to maximise their profits, and few cared enough about prisoners to protest. Vaux wrote:

Their provisions being supplied by contractors, and not by government, are of the worst kind, such as would not be considered eatable or wholesome elsewhere; and both the weight and measure are always deficient. The allowance of bread is said to be about twenty ounces per day. Three days in the week they have about four ounces of cheese for dinner, the other four days a pound of beef. The breakfast is invariably boiled barley of the coarsest kind imaginable; and of this the pigs of the hulk come in for a third part, because it is so nauseous that nothing but downright hunger will enable a man to eat it. For supper they have, on banyan [naval term for vegetarian] days, burgoo [similar to an Irish or mulligan stew, but with no meat], of as good a quality as the barley, and which is similarly disposed of; and on meat days, the water in which the beef was boiled is thickened with barley, and forms a mess called 'smiggins', of a more detestable nature than either of the two former!

Vaux may have found the diet all the harder given his relatively privileged background, but many ordinary prisoners had cause to complain of their meagre fare. Even official accounts of convict dietary provisions show that the diet for prisoners waiting on the hulks was basic. Enough to sustain them for their heavy labour, but no more. Fresh vegetables were rare, meaning debilitating scurvy was a constant possibility. Breakfast consisted of cocoa and bread. Lunch was meat, potatoes, and bread, and dinner more bread accompanied by soup, meat and potatoes on some days, or a pint of gruel on the rest. Those on the punishment diet received just one pound of bread a day, and water, and invalids had a pint of gruel and bread thrice a day. Mark Jeffrey, a famed transportee to Van Diemen's Land (see Chapter four) claimed that above all else, it was the terrible rations on board the hulk at Woolwich, and the constant lack of sufficient nourishment, that drove him to commit the assault that saw him transported for life.

Looking back on his experience many years later, Mark devoted more time to his access to food on the hulks than any other aspect of life there; he wrote 'Oh what a period of misery I went through at Woolwich! … Starvation, misery, and want beset me on every side. Day after day my life was horrible and I cursed existence.' His complaints were always the same, that the food was not enough to sustain adult men carrying out hard labour: 'half a pound of bread per meal and two or three ounces of meat per diem – a substantial repast indeed, for a man of my size and stamina to subsist upon!'

Part of the problem, according to Mark, and many other observers, was the regime on the hulks was subject to corruption and abuse by staff and inmates alike. The hulks were a strange combination of the squalid and corrupt eighteenth century gaols which had come before, and the strict regime of the modern convict prisons that followed. The hulks arguably had the worst of both: the punitive nature of incarceration and hard labour, and the corruption which allowed wealthy prisoners to buy better treatment and provisions. Mark remembered:

> There was a system of swindling carried on at the hulks that my readers will scarcely believe. Certain of the prisoners of the better classes – 'flash chaps' I called them – who obtained money secretly from their friends, were permitted to purchase extra food, and this was actually deducted from the supplies of the poor unfortunate men who were not in a position to buy, with the result that they were in a state of semi-starvation!

Time on the hulks took its toll not only on the physical health of prisoners, but on their mental health too. Prisoners were isolated from everyone they knew. While friends and family were permitted to visit prisoners on the hulks, they were not permitted to board the vessel, having instead to pull alongside it on a separate boat. Visits were kept short in duration. James Vaux recalled 'If a friend or parent has come 100 miles, they are not allowed above a ten minute interview; so that instead of consolation, the visit only excites regret at the parties being so suddenly torn asunder.' Convicts on the hulks were not automatically entitled to write or receive letters, and even when they were permitted this privilege, letters out were scrutinised, censored, and suppressed. This left convicts with virtually no way to access help if they were being victimised, or to raise awareness if their complaints about the regime or their treatment were ignored by hulk officers.

When not at work, convicts ate and slept on board the ship. Accommodation for convicts was placed on each deck of the vessel where large cages 'very like those in the zoological gardens' ran along either side of the boat from one end to another with a corridor between them. Convicts on the hulks were confined like livestock. How far up the boat a convict was housed, and thus his proximity to light and fresh air, was, as with everything else, determined by penal class. The better a convict's perceived behaviour, the more privilege (what little there was on the hulks) he would enjoy. The caged sections in which convicts hung in hammocks quarters provided no privacy and no personal space; convicts were visible to each other or to guards at all times.

The labour carried out by most convicts resident on hulks was hard and dangerous dock work (there were of course also those assigned work to ensure the smooth running of the system – cooking, washing, serving, cleaning). Convicts would load and unload vessels that docked nearby, they would transport heavy goods such as timber and stone to and from vessels. They would repair and clean military ships. Those men moored on the Thames were put to work clearing sand, gravel, and soil from its shores to improve its navigability. Convict men worked alongside free labourers, under threat of punishment if they refused to comply. The labour carried out by convicts was not only a way of keeping a captive population occupied, and weary from hard physical activity, reducing the likelihood of revolt, it was also hugely valuable to the British government, saving thousands of pounds per year in the employment of free labour. Prisoners did accrue a small sum each week of their confinement, though even for the highest class of convicts, this was mere pence, rather than the shillings their work would have received on the open market. The sum of their earnings would only be made available to them after discharge, if they could evidence good conduct. By the mid-nineteenth century, unlucky convicts on the hulks might find themselves engaged in breaking and removing stones (quarry work that later became a staple of the regime at Portland prison), and removing mud or gravel from the dockyard and rivers – a task that could never be completed.

The convict day began at 5.30am when the prisoners had to rise and ready themselves for the day. At 6am followed a brief breakfast, before the men had to return to clean their quarters. By 7.30, each man had arrived at the destination of his labour and begun work, which continued until noon, when each convict had an hour of respite while they took lunch. Depending on the time of year, convicts would carry out another three or four hours of labour, before returning to the boats to wash and prepare for the evening meal. After the meal, around two hours of evening occupations such as religious services, education, or the mending of items took place. The final roll call would then be taken, and the men were in bed for lights out at 9pm in the summer, and 8pm in the winter. The next day, the routine would begin again. There were no deviations, and no exceptions. Those that refused to labour would be placed in solitary confinement on the lowest deck, and placed on a penal diet of bread and water until they complied (See Image 4).

The routine of the hulks, and the class system which convicts were expected to navigate, replicated the regime many would face if they ever made it to Australia. The hulks were in this way a proving ground for the next stage of punishment. However, for a significant number of male convicts, there was no other stage. For one reason or another, a convict might be consigned to serve his entire sentence on the hulks. The Ticket-of Leave system was in operation on the hulks as well as the colonies, but there is evidence to suggest that hulk convicts often served a larger proportion of their sentence before a ticket was issued, than did their peers in Australia. Whether it took ten months or ten years, the misery of hulk life only came to an end when a convict had served their time and gained release, or when a convict was finally selected to board a transport vessel. By the time such a selection was made, inmates were often glad of the chance to be anywhere else, even Australia. Charles Couzens, despite having only spent a comparatively short six weeks living on the hulks, wrote of how welcome news of imminent transportation could be:

> Such a prospect of immediate release from the unvarying routine and monotonous drudgery of hulk life was a source of general and unfeigned satisfaction, although at the sacrifice of their home, country, and kindred to many of them; and the event was hailed as the happiest occurrence which could possibly take place.

Joseph Morrell was sentenced to seven years transportation for the theft of a copper kettle in 1784. Joseph was a recidivist and known to associate with a network of thieves. Joseph was considered 'dangerous to the public' and even a judge admitted that transportation was 'the very best way of disposing of him'. There was only one problem: with the American War of Independence lost, and the colonies there closed, there was nowhere to send him. Australia would not start accepting prisoners for another three years, and so Morrell was confined to wait, in limbo, on the hulks. When Morrell was offered the opportunity to go to Australia, in 1789, he was overjoyed at the prospect. Morrell stated:

> I wish to speak a few words; I have been here six years for transportation, since I was sent to gaol; and I went to Woolwich; I suffered such hardships, that I made my escape; since that, I have been three years in this gaol; I hope I shall not go on board any more hulks; I accept my sentence very freely, only not to send me on board the hulks.

The joy with which news of imminent transportation could be greeted only serves to reinforce the squalor, deprivation, and danger of life on board the floating prisons.

A would-be Houdini on the hulks

Not all convicts were content to wait out their sentence on the hulks, hoping that their ship would figuratively, and literally, come in. Philip Dixon had already served several shorter terms of imprisonment when he was convicted of housebreaking at Chester Assize in 1847. He was sentenced to fifteen years of transportation, and transferred immediately to the *York* hulk at Portsmouth, where he spent almost two years under monotonous routine, fierce discipline and hard labour.

In September 1849, the *North Devon Journal* reproduced Dixon's account of his escape from the hulks. Dixon's statement is testimony to the poor conditions on such ships, the multiple barriers that prevented more convicts from making a bid for freedom, and the price of making a failed escape:

> I was removed with nine more out of about 1400 prisoners to Portsmouth, to the *York* Hulk. Here I remained for nearly twenty

months. During this time I saw fourteen convicts so severely flogged that the flesh came from the backbone, and were immediately sent out to work again with the rest of the convicts, all for bad behaviour. On one occasion I was present when a convict of the name of Hatter murdered our guard, James Connor. I seized the mallet out of his hand at the time, but it was too late – the poor guard was dead. For this Hatter was tried at the Winchester Assizes, condemned, and hung. I was still very unhappy, and while many of my fellow sufferers were fast asleep in their hammocks, I was thinking of my poor wife and children, and contriving in my mind how I could make my escape from that place. I was, in the daytimes, working on the gun wharf, and there I picked up a file. I concealed it under my sleeve and brought it in. The following night, when all was still and quiet, I began filing the bars of the port window of the ship, but dare not to do much at the time lest I should be heard. The next night I did the same. I generally embraced the opportunity of working at this when the tide might be coming in and the wind made noise, so that the guard should not hear me from the quarter deck. When I had finished a certain portion of my filing I filled it up with Brown Soap, which was the colour of the paint on the bars. I found I could not get on so well as I wished at night, so I concealed myself under the hammock on Thursday evening, when all the prisoners went to chapel. During this time I did a great deal of work towards getting the iron bars from my window; I had them all finished on the ninth night; I got up about twelve o'clock, to get through the window and jump into the sea, but the tide was going out at a very rapid pace, and the wind was so very high that I was obliged to give it up for that night. I was, as I suppose, seen by some of the prisoners putting in the soap the next morning, and as I came up on deck I was stopped by one of the officers; one of them went down into my ward and found the iron bars had been cut; they brought me before the Captain and they put a pair of cross irons upon me; I kept them on, and worked in them and slept in them for three months. They then shifted me to the dock yard, where they thought I should be more secure; but I knew better, for after my irons were taken off, I resolved a second time to make my escape, for I could not forget my poor wife and children; they were constantly before my mind. I was determined to get some clothing out of some of the men-of-war ships, which were in the dockyard. In this I succeeded, and got a shirt, a cap, a handkerchief, and an old pair of trousers. I concealed them in my own cell, one by one, at different times, and kept them in my hammock until I could find an opportunity of making my escape. I got up one morning about three o'clock, and dressed myself with the clothes I had stolen, and put my convict's dress over them. At the time we mustered, which was always about seven o'clock in the morning during the winter, the guard searched me and I passed. I got into the boat and was again detected, and was called onto the quarter deck, and was stripped naked. I was again ironed and put into the black-hole [solitary confinement]. And was kept there 14 days and nights upon a pound of bread a-day and plenty of water. Seven of these days I did not see daylight, but the other seven days I was allowed to exercise an hour in the day. After the expiration of these 14 days I was brought out of the black-hole and when I got on deck I, for the first time in my life, fainted. The irons were kept on me. I was then under the doctor's care for about three weeks. After this I went to work as usual with about 20lb weight of iron upon me for [a] full three months. During this time my wife came to see me. I was cut to the heart on account of her great distress of mind, she wept bitterly when she saw the heavy irons upon me, and told me that both she and her children were almost in a state of starvation, as the parish would not allow sufficient to support them. I thought to myself, when I saw her, 'I will try again to make my escape for her sake and for the sake of my dear children.' I could not rest night nor day on their account. After having seen her I became more desperate and determined than ever. I was again set to work in the dockyard with light irons. I resolved on a plan one night, although I had several guards to pass, and a very long way to swim.

Consequently on the following night, when we had left off work to go into the small boat, which always took us from our work to our ship, the *York*, which was on the 25th of November, instead of going into the boat, I ran up to the piles under the jetty, up to my middle in water, where I remained for about an hour and a half. When the boat was pushed off to return to the hulks I heard the guard say 'where is Dixon?' I hear one of them say 'He has done us at last, for he is not here'. When they came on shore they were over my head and again exclaimed 'He has done us!' They asked one of the soldiers whether he had seen one of their men, and he answered, 'no'. All this time I was in the water. I was afraid to use my file to take off my irons, lest the soldiers above me should hear me. Presently, the drum on board the *Victory* was beaten as is usual. I then began to use my file, and got my irons off. As soon as it became dusk (it was very foggy) I began to strip. I uttered a few words in prayer, and cast myself into the water. The tide was coming in very strongly. I went at a very rapid rate, and had to pass by a guard on board the [ship] *Illustrious*, and several other guards higher up the harbour. After I had been on the water about a quarter of an hour, I heard a gunshot; after this, several more had been fired. I thought they were all coming to me. I then thought it was all up with me; I was alarmed; but I believe the firing was only in consequence of the Queen having visited Portsmouth that day, and they were taking down the standard. I was so much terrified with the shooting that, when I passed by King George's yacht, I fastened myself to one of the buoys; it was, however, so very cold that I was obliged to let go, and plunged again into the great deep. I ultimately landed at Porchester Castle, a distance of about five miles from the dockyard. When I got out of the water I was almost exhausted, and was forced to lie down for a considerable time, as I had nearly lost the use of my arms. I then started off naked; I think it must have been about 9 o'clock p.m., and travelled on some distance. When I heard the footsteps of some one, and it struck me it was one of the guards on the Portdown-bridge, where a file of soldiers are always kept. I returned back again and went over a small hill, at the bottom of which was a small river about as wide as the Dee. I swam across this river, which I found much more cold than the sea. I went over hedges and ditches quite naked until it was daylight. I then got into a pigsty and covered myself with straw, and remained there until night with no food or drink, and several thorns in my feet. I then started off again and travelled at night until I got to a farmhouse and made my way into the stables, where I found an old mock frock, which I gladly put on me. Here I remained all day. This was the third day I had no food. Going over Epsom racecourse I saw a policeman. I turned down a lane before he could see me, and got into a cottage where I found an old woman. I begged for mercy and pardon. She took me to the fire and gave me a pair of stockings, a cap, and a pair of old shoes. I travelled on, but was so much fatigued that I was obliged to go on to a house and beg for a bit of bread. I got some with some cheese. On my way onwards I saw a man with some cattle going to London. I helped him to drove the cattle, and he gave me 4 ½ d., being all he had. I wanted a nights' rest and went to a lodging house on the road. I asked the woman how much my lodgings would be? She said 4d. I had only then one halfpenny left; with this I bought some apples. I went to bed and had a good night's rest, and started off early next morning for London.

Unbelievably, Dixon made it to London, relying only on the kindness of strangers and the opportunity to raise funds by completing odd jobs along the way. Once in London, Dixon made contact with a former convict, who took pity on him and gave him clothing and ten shillings with which to start his life as an escaped man. Dixon left London, travelling on foot to Oxford, Banbury, and Warwick, walking along the canals. As Dixon progressed, he supplemented the money he had made by hawking along the road, and sent word to his wife to meet him in Wolverhampton. Though he reunited with his wife, their children were being kept by the parish at Chester, and they were unable to regain custody of them, drawing Mrs. Dixon, and then Dixon himself, back towards the city in hopes of fetching them. The local police had been made aware of these circumstances, and were patrolling the nearby towns in search of Dixon, forcing him to move around different towns in the Marches, hoping to avoid detection. Dixon made his way to Aberystwyth and found work, obtaining leave after a few weeks to fetch his wife and children from Chester. He travelled through Wales with a fellow hawker, but upon stopping in the market town of Bala, and committing an assault, Dixon was quickly apprehended by the police and taken into custody.

He was held in Chester Castle, and despite his best efforts his sentence was reinstated. Dixon became one of the first men transported to the penal settlement at Western Australia, on the *Mermaid* in 1850. There is little doubt that his transportation, separating him from his wife and children (reuniting with whom he made regular inferences was the primary object of his escape), would have grieved Dixon greatly. Yet without his attempt at escape, Dixon may well have been amongst the convicts who served out their entire sentence on the hulks – a fate many considered to be worse than transportation, or even death.

Selection

As both men and women waited, on hulks and in prison cells, to take the next step in their penal journeys, a serious of administrative cogs were turning.

Lists of names were being drawn up, 'bay drafts' to determine which lucky (or unlucky) few would be next to be loaded onto a transport vessel. What the testimony of prisoners languishing on the hulks, or women begging mercy from prison cells shows us, is that even after waiting for years, there was still no guarantee that a convict under sentence of transportation would ever leave Britain.

Unlike the other stages from sentencing to sail, through which convicts passed on their way to Australia, this final stage of 'selection' seems to have been conducted on the basis of a set of informal, and certainly unwritten, rules. The decisions as to who was sent to Australia and who was left behind were largely undocumented, leaving historians and researchers to ponder both the criteria that had to be satisfied, and the individuals in charge of making such decisions. One of the only written sources we have to indicate who was chosen, and why, comes from the testimony of John Henry Capper, His Majesty's Superintendent of the Hulks. Capper was called to appear before a parliamentary select committee in 1812, to give information on the process of transportation. Capper, occupying a senior position in the convict establishment, was not, of course, responsible for selecting individual convicts on a day to day basis. What he provided was the informal 'rules' on which selection decisions should be based. Capper outlined the process:

> When the hulks are full up to their establishment, and the convicted offenders in the different counties are beginning to accumulate, a vessel is taken up for the purpose of conveying a part of them to New South Wales. A selection is in the first instance made of all the male convicts under the age of 50, who are sentenced to transportation for life and for 14 years; and the number is filled up with such from amongst those sentenced to transportation for 7 years, as they are the most unruly in the hulks, or are convicted of the most atrocious crimes; with respect to female convicts, it has been customary to send, without any exception, all whose state of health will admit of it, and whose age does not exceed 45 years.

Youth was one of the primary criteria a convict needed to be selected, according to Capper. Women were in more demand in the colony than men, but their desirability reduced sharply when they were no longer of child-bearing age. Capper clarified:

> We generally confine it, as nearly as possible, about two-and-forty, and not more than five-and-forty; there have been instances where we have been imposed upon, where they wished to go, but we have brought them back.

When asked if the age restrictions of women were specifically in relation to child bearing, Capper denied it. The age restriction was 'with a view to the service of the country generally; but generally speaking, they are very young that go out, from London in particular'.

Capper may have been coy, or trying not to say the wrong thing in front of a powerful audience. However, in reality, women were really no less able to work at fifty-five than forty-five, and so the middle-aged restriction would seem strange if not related to child-bearing capacity. The colony had to be practical. They needed men and women of marriageable age for stability, and a growing population of young free-settlers if they were to thrive. An ageing population of former convicts would not be enough for prosperity. In the case of women, Capper stated 'there are not many fit to send there, many are not fit from old age, which would render them a matter of great burden to the colony'. Old women, in Capper's mind, had little use. While female eligibility may have been tied to reproductive capacity, male eligibility was tied to labour potential. Younger men with lives as working labourers ahead of them were preferable, and in selecting male convicts 'We seldom exceed the age of fifty; where a man is fifty years of age he is not sent.'

To stand a good chance of being transported, then, convicts needed to be young enough to be useful when they arrived. They also needed to have the stamina to survive the journey, and acclimatise when they arrived. Yet most offenders tended to be young, able-bodied, and relatively healthy anyway. Property crimes (not to mention the physicality of violent crimes) usually required some kind of strength or dexterity. The very young and the very old or infirm made up the minority of convicts sentenced to be transported (and not pardoned) in the first place. There was a surfeit of eligible convicts to pick from. So if they met the physical criteria, convicts could next be separated by sentence length and conduct. The longer the sentence, the more likely a convict was to be transported. The British penal estate did not have the infrastructure to house prisoners on a life sentence indefinitely. Even if there had been space to provide for a static prison population, it is highly unlikely that a convict could survive ten or twenty years on board a hulk or in a prison. Those on long sentences had to go, although it might be some time before they did. Convict William Eaton was thirty-four when he was sentenced to a term of life in 1851, but he spent more than a decade incarcerated in England before he was transported to Western Australia aboard the *Clyde* in 1863. The vast majority of convicts, however, were those on shorter sentences of seven years. When it came to this mass of convicts Capper noted:

> We have reference books where magistrates in the different counties inform us of the atrocious conduct in some acts they have committed in the respective counties, or from the conduct on board the Hulks, in attempting escape, and striking officers, and such like ... it is absolutely necessary for the safety of the Hulks to remove those who have been guilty of the most atrocious crimes.

Bad behaviour was, it seems, a good move for those hoping to escape the hulks. Those who attempted escape, or damaged a hulk (like Philip Dixon) or those that posed a danger to guards or other prisoners (like Mark Jeffrey) could be fairly certain of transportation. Although if this policy was intended to improve the safety on the hulks, it would perhaps seem counterproductive as many may have been tempted into bad conduct in the hopes of escaping the floating hell of life on board. Bad behaviour was also no guarantee of expediency for convicts with shorter sentences. A convict with good behaviour might be released from a hulk four years into a seven year sentence, while a disruptive convict might end up like John Brooker, who was sentenced to seven years at the Lewes Quarter Sessions in 1838, then incarcerated in Britain until he was transported to Van Diemen's Land aboard the *Marquis of Hastings* in 1842, only to die a few months after arriving in the colony.

Capper remained adamant that it was for their physical criteria, sentences, and conduct only that some convicts were selected and others were left behind. He denied that convicts were picked for transportation based on possible utility to the colony, although many subsequent studies have found that occupation may have been an important factor in selection, depending on which colony a convict was selected for and when they were sailing. There was also the matter of a convict's utility to the State. Pardon records show us that many were formally excused transportation to participate in military service, but there may also have been a less formal undocumented process by which convicts conducting particularly useful labour at home were not prioritised to be sent abroad. In Ireland for example, Capper admitted:

> The Irish Convicts have generally been sent with less selection than those from England; and this has arisen from the want of hulks, and other means of confining and employing them, which are here often substituted for transportation.

We don't have to look very far for examples of convicts who fit Capper's criteria. It is very likely that these broad guidelines were, in many cases, the foundations on which decisions of who was listed for transportation, and who was not, were based. That said, the convict system was huge, managing thousands of men and women at home and abroad, and at any one time collecting together hundreds of individuals for a single voyage. Although we can find evidence to support Capper's rules, in most voyages we do not have to look very hard for convicts who were transported in direct contradiction of Capper's guidelines.

Yorkshire born Snowden Dunhill was sentenced to seven years of transportation at the Lincoln Assize in 1823, at the age of fifty-nine. He spent less than one year on board a hulk, where his conduct was 'orderly' before he was transported aboard the *Asia*, arriving in 1824 at the age of sixty. Mary Beldon was forty-one when she was first convicted at the Old Bailey for a felony theft. Her trial in 1810 for multiple thefts earned her a sentence of death, later commuted to five years of imprisonment. She was fifty-one by the time she arrived back at the Old Bailey, again for a felony theft, and was sentenced to seven years of transportation. She departed England aboard the *Mary Ann* one year later at the age of fifty-two. There were further extremes. Irishwoman Mary Cregan was tried in Limerick and served two years of her sentence in Dublin before being transported to Van Diemen's Land at the age of seventy in 1841. Newport born Charles Biffon was sentenced to life at the Shropshire Quarter Sessions in 1835 for horse-stealing, and transported to Van Diemen's Land the following year at the age of eighty-six, while two years earlier, eighty-seven-year-old John Steward had arrived in New South Wales aboard the *Hive*.

Those making the final decisions as to who boarded a ship bound for Australia, and who remained behind, had a number of undocumented factors to consider. Capper claimed that the preference of convicts was never taken into account when drawing up lists for sail, but there are multiple cases in which convicts advocating for transportation got their wish, to say nothing of the rumours that wealthy or influential convicts were able to bribe their way on or off transport lists if they found a willing clerk. The requirements for transportees also changed over time. Each of the three main penal colonies had their own needs and requests to factor in. Western Australia in particular had a set of criteria for convicts which by the end of the period were being completely ignored by the British penal administrators (see Chapter five). What's more, after 1853, transportation as a category of punishment had been abolished and replaced with penal servitude, leaving a large mass of male convicts for whom the Home Secretary and administrators could choose either imprisonment or transportation at will. Even without changes to legislation and colonial interference, there were practical concerns which could boost or damage the likelihood of transportation.

Health was an important factor when it came to transportation. If a convict fell ill at any time, up to and including when they arrived on the convict vessel, they could be discounted. With the restrictive rations and close confines convicts experienced on the voyage, mortality was a serious concern. Beginning a journey with a ship full of the weak or sickly was almost guaranteed to end in disaster. Poor sanitation in crowded gaols and hulks saw many otherwise healthy convicts incapacitated and even dead before they could be transported. James Hardy Vaux wrote of his own experience of the dreaded 'gaol fever' in Newgate prison:

> About a month after the close of the session, the gaol being unusually crowded with prisoners, a most dreadful contagion, called gaol fever, made its appearance, and spread so universally throughout every ward and division of the prison, that very few escaped its attack. I was one of the first to contract it, and was immediately carried to the infirmary, or sick ward of the prison, where I only remember having my irons taken off, and being put to bed; for the same night I became delirious and was so dreadfully affected, as to continue insensible for three weeks, during which time I had no knowledge of my parents or of any other person who approached me; and the fever raged in such a degree, that I was obliged to be bound in my bed, in order to refrain me from acts of mischief ... numerous were the unhappy persons who fell victim to this dire disease.

While some of those who fell ill awaiting a voyage to Australia were officially pardoned, most were not. They were simply passed over when it came to selection. Inmates in prison sick wards or aboard the hospital ships were not even considered for a voyage. Those who died before their chance for selection came are rarely recorded in surviving records. The answer as to why such a significant proportion of those sentenced to transportation never arrived may lie in histories of ill health. Unfortunately medical records for the poor and criminal in the eighteenth and early nineteenth centuries are few and far between. We do know that some convicts could find themselves struck down within days of departing on a voyage. Twenty-one-year-old Mary Davis was sentenced to seven years of transportation in 1793, and six months later was transferred aboard the convict ship *Surprize*, ready to sail to New South Wales. With just a few days to go, Mary developed a case of lock jaw, and was removed back to Newgate. Returning to prison and her eventual release, after coming so close to embarking for Australia, must have been a cause of significant relief or disappointment for Mary.

Time and place are perhaps some of the most important, yet least explored, factors that made the difference when it came to selection for transportation. Convicts were assigned to wait in hulks or prisons depending on space. It was convenient to house London and home counties prisoners on the hulks at Woolwich, but not always possible, and if there was space in Plymouth, that was where they would go. A prisoner tried at the Birmingham Sessions one month might find themselves confined in Sheerness, another month in London. Unbeknown to convicts, the hulk on which they waited, and the day, week, or month at which they arrived there, might elevate or reduce their chances of sailing, or at least impact how long they had to wait. Convicts seemingly indistinguishable by any other criteria other than where they were held could receive radically different outcomes.

The same unwritten decisions that determined whether a convict was transported or not also controlled which ship they were sent on board, and ultimately what colony they arrived in. There was significant overlap between the colonies of New South Wales and Van Diemen's Land, and even a small overlap between the last years of transportation to Van Diemen's Land, and the first convict arrivals in Western Australia. Convicts of the same age, health, crime, sentence, and year of embarkation could find themselves at totally different colonies with no explanation. At the Old Bailey on 31 October 1792 thirty-eight men were sentenced to be transported. Thomas Poore, a twenty-six-year-old former mariner from Exeter who stood five feet and three inches tall, was taken from court to the *Stanislaw* hulk at Woolwich. John Harrison, a thirty-nine-year-old thief and labourer, just an inch taller than Poore, was taken on board the *Prudentia*, also moored at Woolwich. Both men waited for four years before they were taken aboard the convict ship *Ganges* and shipped to Australia in 1796. However, Richard Powell, a twenty-two-year-old labourer and pickpocket, the same height as John Harrison, who was tried on the same day, at the same court, and who received the same sentence, was taken on board the *Lion* hulk at Portsmouth. Powell was never transported. He received no pardon, and no records indicate that his behaviour or health set him apart from Poore or Harrison. The only quantifiable difference was in where they waited for a ship to come in.

The decisions made by administrators when it came to selecting convicts for a voyage often produced transports that contradicted not only the official narratives of who was transported and why, but that also seem to challenge the idea of a single set of concrete rules altogether. Ships were full of the young and old, the skilled and unskilled, the weak and the strong. Transports were made of the well behaved, and the worst and most dangerous prisoners, of those on long sentences and short, and virtually all kinds of felony offenders. Transports might keep together, or separate forever, friends and kin convicted of a joint offence, or dozens of convicts tried at the same place on the same day. The chaos of the selection system must have left many convicts awaiting to learn their fate frustrated, confused and, above all, powerless to navigate the process with any certainty.

Conclusions

In fiction, some histories, and especially in the popular imagination, there had been a tendency to think of transportation as a quick fix. A sentence handed down for the slightest infraction, a swift and dreadful punishment that saw convicts at home one day, and sent to Australia 'lagged for life' the next. Yet far from being as neat as those nicely edited scenes in which offenders move from court to colony in rapid succession, transportation was actually a long drawn out process. A series of multiple episodes in which the plot of a convict's penal journey had the ability to twist and turn, and during which some characters joined the cast, and others exited before the story's conclusion.

There were no certainties when it came to transportation. A sentence could be changed, and less formally a whole range of criteria had to be satisfied before a convict was granted a place on a convict vessel. The sex, age, and occupation of a convict could be all important when it came to which decision was made. The young, skilled, and healthy were in demand in the fledgling colony. Yet it was not all that mattered. A convict might also need to be in the right place and right time as a ship came in, another factor over which they had almost no control. Illness was the ever-present spectre, in prisons and gaols, and especially on the dreaded hulks, which could rob a convict of their chance to sail away, and in many cases, of their very life.

There will have been convicts for whom the lottery process that occurred after an initial conviction was a blessing. Pardons, space, selection criteria, and even illness could all save an unwilling convict from being transported, a punishment many feared. However, it could also be a frustrating delay to those eager to escape their former lives. For those who did make it through sentencing, selection, and a wait that could last years, one final hurdle still remained between them and Australia. The voyage.

Chapter 2

Disease, Danger, and Death:
The Voyage to Australia

Convicts might have to wait years as legal and administrative procedures took their course from the point of sentencing, and even then, we've seen that there was virtually no way to guarantee that any one individual would be selected to sail to Australia. However, those who managed to commit the right kind of crime, at the right time, have their offence heard in front of the right judge, and navigate successfully through the pardon system, were in with a chance. If they managed not to die in the squalid conditions of hulks and prisons, or to contract an illness or incapacity at the wrong time, if they could prove themselves young, or fit, or useful, their likelihood of making it to Australia further increased. Even then, luck still had a role to play. Those held in the right place, at the right time, as prisons reached capacity, and a ship was preparing to sail, would one day wake to the news that they were to prepare to transfer. The guards might come for them weeks or just days later, attaching chains to their hands and feet, and marching them to the waterside, where they would then be brought on board a transport ship.

Making it on board the ship was just another step in a difficult journey. Before convicts could arrive in Australia, and take their chances in the convict establishment, we often forget that first they had to make it across the world. For those in Britain, Australia still feels like a distant land – most accessible only to those willing to undertake long-haul flights that last all day. Even in the relative safety of commercial air travel, arriving on the other side of the world can feel like a momentous journey not without its risks. Our modern notions of distance and travel, though, can do little to help us understand what that same journey from Britain to Australia felt like for the convicts facing it two centuries ago. When boat was the only method of travel, the voyage took months, and there was hope, but no guarantee, of reaching Australia alive.

The voyage itself could take anywhere between three and nine months, depending on the size and condition of the vessel sailing, the weather and wind, and the stops that a ship needed to make *en route*. Ships might stop in Spain and its islands off the coast of Africa, at Brazil's Rio de Janeiro, and at South Africa, on their way to Australia. These ports provided a vital lifeline for taking on board fresh water and food, cleaning the ship (poor sanitation below decks quickly led to filthy conditions and sickness), and allowing the non-convict passengers some respite on dry land before continuing onward. Depending on the state of the ship, the crew, and the convicts, these stops might take just a few days, or many weeks. If infection and illness was rife, many captains preferred to wait in port for the health of the ship to return, rather than risk the final leg of the journey to Australia with contagion aboard and nothing but the open sea ahead of them.

During the eighty years in which transportation operated, more than 168,000 men and women were taken across the world during the course of approximately 800 separate voyages. An average of around seven ships, carrying hundreds of convicts each, sailed from Britain and Ireland every year. Of course, transportation was a system of fits and spurts, rather than a steady trickle of convicts to Australia. In the initial phase of transportation, there could be a year or more between voyages, and in the final fifteen years, fewer than forty ships sailed, taking under 10,000 men to Western Australia. By contrast, during the height of the system in the 1820s and 1830s, with two thriving colonies to the east and south of the country taking in convicts, dozens of voyages occurred year in and year out. The shipping of convicts across the world was also subject to global economic and political forces. Times of war – the Napoleonic conflicts at the beginning of the nineteenth century for example – saw vessels and troops from the convict establishment commandeered for war work, and even the convicts themselves put to 'better' use. With so many factors at work to even get convicts on board, it is little surprise that the individual convict experiences of sailing across the seas were as variable and changeable as the weather on which the endeavour depended.

However, there were a few common practices which lasted throughout the convict era. Wherever possible male and female convicts were transported on different ships. This precaution was taken in order to promote the safety and order amongst both groups. Female convicts were obviously considered vulnerable to the harassment of male convicts, and it was not unknown for both male and female convicts to have violent altercations over spurned advances, jealousies, or rivalries for the attention of a convict of the opposite sex. Nevertheless, on some ships a small number of convict women were required to undertake domestic duties, like laundry; or logistics made it necessary to take groups together.

The practice of sending a convict's family with them on a voyage was not particularly common. Arrangements could be made for a (usually male) convict's family to follow them on a separate ship, or after the convict had obtained their Ticket-of-Leave in the colony at the discretion of the authorities. Yet, sending wives alongside their husbands on the same ship was thought to have the potential to cause 'a degree of jealousy on the part of those men who are obliged to be separated from the others, on account of their wives, and (in point of morality) the inducement on the part of the others to get at those women'. Female convicts were in some cases permitted to take young children with them. This was a pragmatic, rather than merciful, step by the colonial authorities who wished to make the convict transition to life in Australia as smooth as possible with minimal burden to the British state. Children under the age of four years could accompany their mothers (only in rare cases over this age), whereas children aged five and upwards with no one else to care for them could be put in parish institutions at home.

All convict voyages were not created equal. The conditions of a voyage, the provisions for convicts, and the attention paid to their wellbeing was highly dependent on the period in which they sailed, the captain and crew, the weather, and the law. While the overwhelming majority of convicts did arrive in Australia and live to tell the tale – or serve their sentences, at least – this was by no means a certainty. Voyages suffered from many of the same issues that caused complaint in British prisons and on the hulks. Convicts were stored below decks in cramped and squalid conditions, in the dark, with limited access to light and fresh air. There were limited opportunities for exercise and the diet could be poor. Sanitation was an issue. In such conditions, illness and death were a very real concern. The convict ships faced additional worries. They carried a hostile cargo who, if conditions allowed, might mutiny at any turn. Unlike the boats moored safely on British shores, convict vessels faced the terror of the open seas where the weather itself could kill, and help could be days away.

Disease and degradation

First-hand accounts of how convicts experienced the voyage to Australia are few and far between. Universal education in Britain did not begin until after the cessation of transportation and so the literacy of many convicts was limited. Furthermore, so was their access to even the most basic provisions on board a convict ship, let alone materials for writing, which was a privilege preserved for ship's officers. Even if convicts arrived in the colonies and managed to acquire writing materials, their minds were often too full of the sights, sounds, smells, and experiences of a strange new land to think it worth recalling too much of the dull months below decks in a ship.

Margaret Catchpole, a horse-thief originally from Suffolk (see Chapter three), was one of a number of female convicts transported upon the *Nile* in 1801. Margaret's letters to friends and relations back in England are a fascinating and detailed account of early New South Wales through the eyes of an ordinary convict woman. Margaret's descriptions could be vivid and engaging, but in her first letter back home after arrival in the colony, she only noted a few lines about a journey that had taken more than half a year:

> We are all well – Barker is alive, but she was very much frightened by the roughness of the sea – she used to very often cry out "I wish I was with my dear Mr. Stebenes [the prison doctor to whom Margaret was writing] for I never shall see Ipswich no more" – but she is much the same as ever ... On the voyage I was tossed about very much indeed, but I should not mind if I was but a coming to old England once more.

Margaret wrote nothing of the provisions made for convicts, the conditions below decks, or the treatment of convicts by the seamen on board. Confronted with the bright wilderness of Sydney and the bustle of the colony, all she could recall of the journey was that the seas were rough, and some of her companions were afraid.

Introduction to a convict ship could be a brutal and disorientating affair. James Hardy Vaux recalled his own arrival aboard the *Minorca* in 1801:

> Having entered the ship, we were all indiscriminately stripped (according to indispensable custom) and were saluted with several buckets of salt water thrown over our heads by a boatswain's-mate. After undergoing this watery ordeal, we were compelled to put on a suit of slop-clothing. Our own apparel, though good in kind, being thrown overboard. We were then double-ironed, and put between decks, where we selected such births, for sleeping, &c.

The salt water and destruction of clothes on arrival was likely to be less of a seafaring custom, and more an attempt by the crew to stop the spread of disease and parasites, both known to be rife in the prisons and hulks of Britain and Ireland. Salt water would have provided limited disinfectant properties, but was all the crew had to hand to protect themselves, and give the new arrivals on board the best chance of beginning the voyage clean and healthy. For more than a decade before James Vaux boarded his own ship, convict voyages had been plagued by high mortality and horrendous conditions.

When the First Fleet set out in 1787, the men and women who made up its human cargo may have been so preoccupied with concerns about what would happen when they reached their destination, that they had little time to fear the journey they were about to embark upon. However, those who had charge of them knew only too well the toll long journeys in captivity could have on a human cargo. British ships had hundreds of years of experience transporting those in bondage around the world. Not only did they carry transportees to America and Africa, but also generations of enslaved people, thousands of whom had found their lives forfeit on torturous journeys across the world. Despite being heavily loaded with supplies, and confident of their route across the world, the voyage of the First Fleet to Australia carried all the concerns of human shipments that had gone before, and was considerably more ambitious. No expedition had ever attempted to take so many so far. The intention was to land them in New South Wales healthy and ready to build a new outpost of empire. The outcome of the attempt was far from certain.

To the delight of all involved, mortality on the voyage of the First Fleet was low. Months of government planning and naval precision had paid off when more than 1,000 convicts on board the First Fleet of six convict vessels (accompanied by five other naval and supply vessels) arrived to found a fledgling colony. The *Alexander, Charlotte, Friendship, Lady Penrhyn, Prince of Wales,* and *Scarborough* convict vessels carried between 1,000 and 1,500 convicts when they departed from Portsmouth in May 1787. The precise number remains subject to ongoing debates, but records indicate that around at least 1,300 of that number arrived safely in New South Wales. Rough estimates suppose that fewer than 100 convicts died on the first voyage. The loss of 100 lives is by no means insignificant, but for an untested voyage, with captive passengers in the late eighteenth century, a fatality rate of less than one in ten remains impressive, especially when we consider the fate of many of those who came afterwards.

With hundreds more transports to be made over the next decades, the British government could not devote the time and resources they had given to the First Fleet to each and every one. Once the safe arrival of the first colonists in Australia had been assured, future transports were tendered out to private contractors, relieving the British state of a large part of the complex and tiresome logistics of convict transportation. As is often the case when government endeavour is left in the hands of private contractors, the cost of each shipment now had to accommodate a profit for private businesses. Whilst the ultimate cost to the British state was little changed, the experience for convicts became much worse. In order to maximise their return, corners were cut by private contractors when it came to ensuring the welfare of their human cargo.

The scandal of the Second Fleet

Just as with prison fatalities and deaths before voyage, there were certain prisoners who were less likely than others to make it to Australia alive. When questioned about deaths on board convict ships, John Hunter, former Governor of New South Wales, maintained that the majority of those who died on board were 'very old people and infirm when they embarked; very unfit to be sent on such a voyage'. However, after the arrival of the Second Fleet of convict ships at Sydney in 1790, and more in the decade that followed, it became apparent that it was not only the weak and vulnerable succumbing to illness and death on the voyage.

Some of the early ships used to transport convicts, especially those like the *Scarborough* and *Surprize* in the Second Fleet, were not originally intended for human cargo. The holds in which prisoners were held were dark and cramped, damp from seeping water and lack of ventilation, not to mention from stagnant pools of filthy water. Hundreds of warm, unwashed bodies were crammed together below decks without adequate sanitary provision to clear away the daily ablutions of convicts, or the vomit of those who did not fare well at sea. The smell of the convict hold must itself have been truly nauseating. These conditions alone were enough to encourage the rapid spread of diseases like typhoid fever and dysentery, and the spread of vermin like lice. Added to the insanitary conditions was a second threat to convict life – poor provisions. Convicts were given only meagre rations to sustain them through the voyage, and provisions were severely lacking in any fresh fruit or vegetables. Scurvy and malnutrition took hold of men and women whose immune systems were already weakened from months or years of imprisonment.

Prisoners spent most of their time in irons below decks (chains which rubbed away at the skin and could easily cause deadly infection) primarily for security reasons. The government had stipulated that the convicts should be allowed up onto the top deck daily, and cleaned at regular intervals, but once a ship was at sea, there was very little way of ensuring these measures were taken. A foiled mutiny on board the *Scarborough* was said to have heightened fears about allowing convicts freely up on deck on this and other vessels. Lieutenant-Colonel David Collins of the Royal Marines wrote of the arrival of the *Surprize* and *Neptune* convict ships and offered some details of conditions on board in his *An Account of the English Colony of New South Wales from its first settlement in January 1788 to August 1801*, published in 1804:

> The masters, who had the entire direction of the prisoners, never suffered them to be at large on deck, and but a few at a time were permitted there. This consequently gave birth to many diseases. It was said that on board the *Neptune* several had died in irons; and what added to the horror of such a circumstance was, that their deaths were concealed, for the purpose of sharing their allowance of provisions, until chance, and the offensiveness of a corpse, directed the surgeon, or some one who had authority in the ship, to the spot where it lay.

Of the more than 1,000 convicts sent out on the *Neptune, Scarborough*, and *Surprize*, fewer than 800 arrived in Sydney alive. On the *Neptune* alone, approximately 160 of 500 convicts died on the voyage. A huge proportion of those who did make it to shore were in a dire state of ill health. Their clothes and meagre possessions were burned in the hope of stopping the spread of infection, but many more would die on the beaches and makeshift hospital beds of the fledgling colony. Collins recalled the arrival of the ships to Australia:

> They had the mortification to learn that the prisoners in this ship [*Surprize*] were very unhealthy, upwards of one hundred being at that time on the sick list on board. They had been very sickly also during the passage, and buried forty-two of their unfortunate people. A portable hospital had most fortunately been received by the *Justinian*, and there now appeared but too great a probability that they would soon have patients enough to fill it, for the signal was flying at the South head for the other transports and they were expected to be in as unhealthy a state as that which had just arrived.

On the evening of the 28th the *Neptune* and *Scarborough* transports anchored off Garden Island, and were warped into the Cove on the following morning. Nor were they mistaken in their fears of the state in which they might arrive, as by noon the following day, two hundred sick had been landed from the different transports. The West side afforded a scene truly distressing and miserable; upwards of thirty tents were pitched in front of the hospital (the portable one not yet being put up); all of which, as well as the adjacent huts, were filled with people, many of whom were labouring under the complicated diseases of scurvy and dysentery, and others in the last stage of either of those terrible disorders, or yielding to the attacks of infectious fever.

The appearance of those who did not require medical assistance was lean and emaciated. Several of these miserable people died in the boats as they were rowing on shore, or on the wharf as they were lifted out of the boats; both living and the dead exhibited more horrid spectacles than had ever been witnessed in that country. All this was to be attributed to confinement, and of the worst species, confinement in small space and in irons, not put on singly, but many of them chained together.

The company Calvert, Camden, and King of London had been given the contract for the Second Fleet. They were supposed to be paid £17 for every convict they received on board the ships. That sum was to provide payment for the company, and to fund the acquisition of everything a convict required during the voyage. This system, which paid for convicts as they embarked rather than arrived safely, and saw every day of provisions for them eat into earnings, created a toxic system where the dead were more valuable than the living. George Barrett, an observer of the disastrous Second Fleet, noted:

It appeared that some of the captains had very much abridged their unfortunate passengers of the allowance stipulated by government for their subsistence; and this inhuman practice had been carried to such an extent in some of the ships, that it appeared many had been literally starved to death.

There is little to suggest that those manning the convict vessels were intentionally starving and killing their cargo. Rather, that the systems put in place by the British government to facilitate private contractors promoted the casual neglect of hundreds of men, women, and children, some of whom paid the ultimate price for private profit. There was an inquest into the conditions of the convict vessels that allowed such high mortality of convicts. Yet, no-one involved in the transportation of the Second Fleet was held accountable under law for the deaths, disease, and degradation suffered by the convicts on the voyage.

Unbelievably, the same contractors were engaged for the Third Fleet, a transport of eleven vessels carrying more than 2,000 convicts the following year. George Barrington sailed to New South Wales aboard the *Active* just one year after the voyage of the Second Fleet. He immortalised the journey in his memoir *A Voyage to Botany Bay*. Barrington noted that once on board he and his fellow convicts were required to wait for several weeks before sailing while other prisoners were loaded, the crew acquired, and provisions for the long voyage secured on board. When the ships set out, they experienced a period of rough weather before making it to the calm waters on the open sea, progressing towards Australia at what George estimated to be 'about seven miles an hour'. The conditions aboard had altered little since the disaster of the previous year. George wrote:

> My fellow prisoners, to the amount of upwards of 200, were all ordered into the hold, which was rendered as convenient as circumstances would admit, battens being fixed for and aft for hammocks which where hung seventeen inches apart from each other; but being encumbered with their irons, together with the want of fresh air, soon rendered their situation truly deplorable.

Whilst there was considerable public outrage at such a senseless loss of life, and sympathy for the inhuman conditions endured on board, when news of the Second Fleet returned to Britain the government had more practical concerns. New South Wales, still lacking basic infrastructure and steady agriculture, needed healthy new colonists to build and plough and grow. Sending convicts who died on the way, or arrived sick, indigent, or emaciated did nothing but deprive and burden an already struggling colony. In the years following the atrocious conditions of the Second Fleet, the government put in place measures to ensure greater survival. But change was slow to take hold and mortality still high. For a decade after the arrival of the Second Fleet in Australia, conditions on some convict vessels continued to be dire.

Between 1795 and 1801, 385 of the 3,833 convicts transported – around one in ten – died on the voyage. This was, of course, an improvement on the very worst examples of convict voyages, but still too high considering the young and supposedly 'healthy' nature of most convicts selected to sail. It was only in the nineteenth century that conditions began to drastically improve. Between 1801 and 1812, there was a considerable improvement in convict life-chances compared to previous years. Only fifty-two of 2,398 transported convicts died on their way to the colony. A rate of just one in forty-six.

John Hunter was one of many expert witnesses called to give testimony by the 1812 Select Committee into transportation. He confirmed the pot-luck nature of early convict journeys, stating, 'There were some ships particularly attentive to convicts, and others equally careless'. Hunter testified that throughout the transportation period the root cause of convict deaths on a voyage was always the same, 'the convicts being confined, and being badly taken care of'. Hunter made an example of one ship in particular in his testimony. The *Hillsborough*, sailed from Portsmouth in 1798 and arrived in New South Wales in July of 1799, almost a decade after the Second Fleet had sailed. The conditions aboard the *Hillsborough* showed how little had changed.

Three hundred convicts had embarked aboard the *Hillsborough*. Approximately a third of them died on the journey, and a few more died soon after being delivered to the colony. The *Hillsborough* sailed under the old system under which contractors received payment for convicts embarked rather than safely arrived. As such, Hunter reported, 'I believe that occasioned carelessness with respect to their health' and 'the consequence was they lost such a number of men it was astonishing'. When Hunter testified to the Select Committee, he was recalling events more than a decade later, allowing him to talk relatively dispassionately about the voyage. Hunter did, however, write to the Duke of Portland in 1799 as the *Hillsborough* arrived in Sydney:

> The *Hillsborough* transport arrived yesterday, in which had been embarked three hundred convicts, but I am sorry to say that such had been the mortality on board that ship two hundred and five only were landed here, and of that number six are since dead; most of them must for a time be placed in the hospitals ... These people have been put on board this ship with a miserable mattress, and one blanket, and the clothes only in which they embarked, not a supply of any kind to land them here in, and those worn on board the ship are not fit to be taken on a shore ... I will direct every means to be used for preventing the gaol fever (which I understand to be the principal malady) from being introduced into our hospitals.

It was suggested by some that the transport had been doomed from the start, not only due to poor conditions, but also in part of the fact that sick convicts from the overflowing prisons of London had been loaded onto the ship. Five of the convicts supposed to be transported aboard the *Hillsborough* were offloaded at the request of officials before the boat left England due to ill health. But many more carrying the same illness remained and an infection had taken hold, some witnesses testified, shortly after the ship left port. Missionaries who joined the *Hillsborough* for the voyage to the Cape of Good Hope reported the conditions of convicts below decks:

> About two hundred and forty of these miserable creatures were chained in pairs, hand to hand or leg to leg, in the orlop deck, to which no light could find admission except at the hatchways. At first the darkness of the place, the rattling of the chains, and the dreadful imprecations of the prisoners, suggested ideas of the most horrid nature and combined to form a lively picture of the infernal regions. Besides, in a short time, a putrid fever broke out among the convicts, and carried off no fewer than thirty-four of them during the voyage to the Cape of Good Hope. The state of the prison was now loathsome beyond descriptions.

After the disaster of the *Hillsborough*, and the numerous other voyages on which lives had been lost through negligence, the British government eventually required that any transport vessel had to contain a ships' surgeon, whose duty would be to ensure convict health. From the early nineteenth century:

> The owner of the vessel provides a surgeon, who undergoes examination at Surgeon's Hall and the Transport Office. He is instructed to keep a diary not only of the illness on board but of the number of convicts admitted on deck; of the scraping of the decks, cleaning the births, and general treatment of the transportees. The sick are to be visited twice daily, the healthy once. He is ordered to take the greatest precaution against infection, and to fumigate the clothes of those taken to the hospital. He has not only the power to use medicines, but also the stores, if any sick be in want of greater nourishment.

Each surgeon was paid a bonus of around ten shillings for each live convict that arrived in the colonies – ensuring his maximum motivation that convicts arrive alive and healthy. Although surgeons had the power and the desire to administer to convict's needs, the ships' masters and captains continued to outrank them for more than a decade, sometimes overriding surgeon's orders, against the interest of convicts. By 1815, surgeons were given total authority on all disciplinary and medical matters, as well as the hygiene of the ship. Financial motivation was, it appeared, one of the surest ways to guarantee convict safety. At the same time as surgeons were placed on board ships and offered a bonus for healthy convicts, payments to private contractors were renegotiated. Payment was changed to cover only living convicts who arrived in Australia. These alterations dramatically changed the experience of convicts sailing to Australia. They had access to better medical care and provisions, and more care was taken in their clothing, cleanliness, and access to fresh air and exercise. From approximately 1815 until the end of transportation in 1868, the measures put in place to protect convict cargo saw transportation voyages become some of the least dangerous of all seafaring passenger ships. A remarkable fact when one considers the premise on which they were based, and the truly hellish conditions in which early settlers were knowingly permitted to sail.

Danger and disorder: mutiny beyond the seas

With such awful conditions on board some vessels and the neglect of convicts' basic needs for sanitation, fresh air, and exercise, it is no surprise that the glowing embers of discord amongst convicts below decks could be easily fanned into a flame. Convicts considerably outnumbered the crew on any vessel and often had cause to protest, but outright mutinies were rare. Convicts might lack organisation or opportunity to carry out a plan, or might find themselves betrayed by one of their number who got cold feet. Moreover, the penalties for insurrection were severe. Some of those responsible for the earlier voyages to the colonies suggested that the limited access to the top deck given to convicts was due to fears of mutiny. Ebenezer Kelly was a midshipman aboard the *Hillsborough* and recounted how only a few were brought up at a time, and always restrained:

> According to law, when the prisoners behaved themselves, they were single-ironed and allowed to go on deck in gangs, part in the forenoon and part in the afternoon were brought up and chained to a large chain which ran from mast to mast; they looked very much like a string of beads.

The prisoners on this voyage had planned, according to Kelly, a mutiny. Though one of their number, an educated prisoner called John Holmes (a Londoner sentenced to seven years in July 1797), betrayed the plan in writing to the captain. The prisoners were discovered to have already removed their irons in preparations, and after a brief standoff with the crew, the convicts were again brought to order and placed in chains. Many of those involved were flogged for their trouble. Kelly wrote 'Some received fifty, some three hundred, and one man five hundred, lashes, instead of hanging as the captain had threatened.' Captains and ships' masters were entitled to hang mutineers without trial, and without appeal, such was the danger they were thought to pose to the entire ship. George Barrington claimed to have witnessed a failed insurrection on the *Active* for which 'two of the ringleaders were instantly hung [*sic*] at the yard–arm, and several others severely flogged at the gangway'. Several other convicts and crew testified to even more cruel and unusual punishments for would–be mutineers; however, the accuracy of such accounts is hard to verify.

With the stakes so high and the likelihood of success so low, it is little surprise that there were only a small number of successful mutinies. However, the few reported incidences of successful passenger uprisings on the way to Australia give us an insight into the extremes possible on a convict voyage. Mutinies were a reminder to everyone, from convicts to captain, and audiences on both sides of the world, of the precarious nature of power and control on a convict ship. Mutinies illustrated just how easily order could fall apart at the seams.

Not all mutinies saw convicts and crew on opposing sides. Some convicts refused to take part in mutinies and found themselves sharing the fate of the crew that were overthrown. Some sailors, tired of poor pay and worse conditions shuttling convicts back and forth across the world, threw their own lot in with mutineers, joining their former prisoners in roving and raiding on the seas.

The mutiny that took place aboard the *Lady Shore* when she sailed from England to New South Wales in 1797 became the stuff of Australian legend. In the century and a half that followed the mutiny, the tale of the *Lady Shore* appeared from time to time in the press, usually as a romantic tragedy, or tale of swashbuckling adventure. In reality, it saw a group of convicts caught in the middle of a series of events driven by geo–political antagonisms between Britain and her near neighbour France.

On board the *Lady Shore* were almost seventy female convicts, guarded by fewer than thirty crew. Alongside the convicts were almost sixty soldiers from the New South Wales Corps; while amongst their number were a small collection of German, Spanish and French political prisoners, and male capital convicts reprieved on the condition that they spend the rest of their lives in service in Australia. The captain, a man named Willcox, asked that the transport be delayed. Evidently, with so small a crew, he felt a horde of sailors and foreign military men made the journey more dangerous and vulnerable to mutiny than the usual consignment of pickpockets, housebreakers, and animal thieves. Wilcox was overruled, and the ship pulled out to sea.

Newspapers reported that after several weeks, when the ship was a matter of days from Rio de Janeiro, the French prisoners and a number of others rose in the night, convinced their only means of escape was to seize the ship and flee into South America. The captain and two other members of the crew were killed after the French seized the sentries' weapons, and control of the ship. The female convicts were placed under guard and told they would be shot if they attempted to intervene. After a successful mutiny, aided by other political prisoners and some of the men on board, the remaining passengers were informed that they would face harsh reprisals if they attempted to take back control of the ship, or collude with British soldiers. A number of the crew with their wives and children were given rations and navigation equipment and cast away in a longboat. The *Lady Shore* arrived at Montevideo in Uruguay a short time later, and was allowed to make port by the Spanish, who considered the French to be political refugees. The convict women were offloaded from the ship, and turned over to the authority of the Spanish. Little is known of their experiences other than that some of them were passed on to be servants in the city.

For some of the women on the *Lady Shore*, the mutiny would have been a lucky escape. Mary Howarth had been sentenced at the Warwick Assizes in 1793 to a term of transportation for life. She had already waited almost four years to sail, and would have faced several more in the penal colony before becoming eligible for a Ticket-of-Leave. Life as a servant in South America may have been a preferable alternative to those like Mary who faced long sentences, or who dreaded life in a fledgling and undeveloped colony. For others like Hannah Anderson, Sarah Lewis and Susannah Keys, who had already served three years of their seven year sentences, life in Uruguay with little means of return to England must have seemed like a hard bargain. Inevitably some women settled and prospered, living happy lives in South America. Others faced misery. While work as servants in Montevideo may have been little different from the indentured servitude they would have faced through assignment to free settlers in New South Wales, few documents do justice to the terror and brutality that may have coloured their experience. Unlike life in a penal station, the women would have faced a strange land with little knowledge of the Spanish language. They would have been perceived as foreigners by the state, and experienced the alienation and disadvantages that accompanied that status. Unlike life in the convict system, the women had no mechanisms for complaint, and no automatic right to release. From the moment of the ship's capture, the women would have been vulnerable to exploitation and sexual violence. Some thrived, some survived, and others did not. The convict women of the *Lady Shore* are some of the most famous and most successful mutineers of the Australian convict period. All without having, or even wanting, to mutiny at all.

The threat of mutiny did not end with safe arrival in the colony. The voyages of convicts bound for Australia were not always over once they disembarked in one of the major penal colonies. Serious offenders, disruptive prisoners, or those convicted of secondary offences in the colonies could all be sent on to sites of secondary punishment. Getting to these islands and small remote parts of the mainland required another voyage on the same ship, or a new one. Although the journeys were much shorter than those from Britain to Australia, conditions might be no better, the crew might prove more skeletal, and attention to the safety of the convicts and the voyage might grow more lax. One of the most notorious convict mutinies took place in 1829, as a small group of convicts made their voyage to the much feared Macquarie Harbour.

In August of 1829, thirty-one convicts, a captain and around ten crewmen set out on the *Cyprus* from Hobart to Macquarie Harbour penal station. The convicts – runaways, secondary offenders and disruptive prisoners – were to be deposited there for the remainder of their sentences. The *Cyprus* also carried crucial supplies for the penal station, which struggled to provide enough food for its inhabitants. Macquarie Harbour was renowned as a place of physical and psychological hardship (see Chapter four). The only supplies came from the main colony by sea, with starvation an ever-present fear. Disease and malnutrition were rife, and discipline was hard. The men at the station faced regular floggings. Unsurprisingly, many of the men aboard the *Cyprus* were keen to avoid such a fate.

A few days into their voyage, the captain of the *Cyprus*, Lieutenant Carew, pulled into Recherche Bay, almost halfway between Hobart and Macquarie Harbour, to escape unfavourable winds. Carew took a small party of fellow officers ashore in order to fish. After some hours, the crew at the beach heard musket shots from the direction of the ship, and decided to return. In their absence, a small group of the convicts had easily overpowered the five crew left to guard them, and had seized control of the ship, injuring several men in the process. Ultimately, Carew, the crew who refused to join the mutineers, and any convicts who refused to be part of the mutiny, were abandoned on the beach in Recherche Bay, with no food or water, and no hope of finding their way back to Hobart through the treacherous and untamed interior of Van Diemen's Land. The castaways would have certainly died from exposure, thirst, starvation, or illness, had one of their number, John Popjoy, not managed to fashion a rudimentary raft and sail for help.

Meanwhile, William Swallow, George Davis, Alexander Stevens, John Beveridge, and William Watts (all serving sentences of fourteen years or life), along with Michael Harring, Robert McGuire, William Templeman, Matthew Parnell, Samuel Thacker, Leslie Ferguson (who would for a time become leader of the mutiny), John Lynch, James Jones, Charles Towers, James Chum, Thomas Bryant, John Denner, William Brown and James Camm sailed around the Pacific. The mutineers visited New Zealand and several Pacific islands, plundering along the way until landing at a Tongan island. Once there, Ferguson and six other convicts decided to stay, whilst Swallow took command of the vessel and set a course for Japan, then China. By the time they arrived near Canton, most of the convict mutineers had already departed, and the ship was intentionally wrecked on the Chinese coast. Here, the remaining convicts took on new identities, claiming to be survivors from another voyage, and booked passage home to England in early 1830.

By the time they arrived, however, their identities had already been ascertained by another mutineer who had returned to Britain and confessed the story. The mutineers were placed on trial. Watts and David, considered the ringleaders, were sentenced to be executed. Large crowds gathered in December 1830, little more than a year after the mutiny, to watch them hang at Executioners Dock in London. Swallow, Stevens and Beveridge were transported back to Van Diemen's Land. Swallow, already under a life sentence, had lost little for the endeavour. He was delivered to Port Arthur, where he remained until his death a few years later.

Fantastical tales of mutiny and piracy on the high seas were few and far between. Far more common were plots or attempts to mutiny that were thwarted before they could succeed. No doubt, many more never progressed that far, the thought given up by convicts when faced with the overwhelming odds against them. We have little way of estimating how common plans to mutiny were amongst convicts. Many of the convicts eager to arrive in Australia had no wish to disrupt the voyage. Others being torn away from lives and loved ones felt anger towards the British government for condemning them to a state of near-slavery, and resentment towards the sailors and guards who facilitated the trip. Those undergoing the heaviest sentences – fourteen years or life – had more to mourn than most, and less to lose. While we have well documented cases of the few successful mutinies to take hold, who knows how many convicts lay in their dark and crowded bunks dreaming of overthrowing the crew above. How many groups of friends passed the monotony of life below decks sharing suggestions for seizing the ship, or fantasising about where they would sail when they did?

For some these preoccupations would have been deadly serious, for others, little more than daydreams to while away the hours. Either way, most convicts would have been too sensible of the punishments they would face for even suggesting an uprising to speak much of it at all. The captain and crew of a convict ship could not allow even the seed of the idea of a mutiny to take hold below decks, and anyone suspected of planning rebellion could face a restriction of rations, solitary confinement, heavy irons, and even a flogging. Even successful mutineers would face years on the run, always in the shadow of the hangman's noose. Members of the crew, especially those responsible for guarding convicts, had to be constantly vigilant for signs that discontent was turning into something more sinister. A single officer's watchful eye could be the difference between a failed plot and a successful mutiny.

In the summer of 1836, the convict ship *Captain Cook* pulled away from Cork, and headed out onto the open sea. Just a few days into the journey, John Pollen, the ship's hospital attendant and former army officer, was informed that a group of prisoners were planning to seize control of the ship. Most of the men involved in the plot had been, it was reported, transported before. They had no intention of returning to bondage in Australia. It is perhaps surprising that there were not more successful mutinies aboard convict ships. After all, the strength of numbers lay heavily in the convicts' favour. There were more than 200 male convicts aboard the *Captain Cook*, and a crew of fewer than forty men. According to the *Sydney Monitor*, the would-be mutineers of the *Captain Cook* planned to have the boatswain (a member of a ship's crew, and in the case of the *Captain Cook*, also a fellow convict) throw open the prison doors below decks, so that as many men as possible could rush the ship's crew. Meanwhile, convict ringleaders

Dogherty, Higgins, Hamilton and Murphy would lead a party of men tasked with incapacitating the guard. Reportedly, they planned that 'no mercy was to be shown'. Three sailors were to be retained to help them navigate the ship to their intended destination: America. When land came in sight, these sailors would be thrown overboard. The mutiny was planned for when the ship neared the equator.

Pollen reported what he had heard to the surgeon on board and other superiors, who dismissed the plot as nothing more than rumours. But Pollen watched as groups of convicts engaged in earnest and secretive conversation in the following days, and convinced the guards to place thirty-eight men in heavy irons in order to abort disaster. Several confessed to their plans, and the plot was confirmed. As the ship approached the Cape of Good Hope, talk of insurrection again began to swirl around the ship. The ringleaders of the original plot were convinced that if the rest of their convict fellows held firm to the plan, their own incapacity would not matter. The crew of the ship were already on high alert, and took the further precaution of chaining the convicts together, making it impossible for the plan to be carried out. They remained this way until they reached Sydney in November, when around half of the ringleaders were sent to Goat Island to carry out heavy labour in a prison gang. No doubt they were segregated so their malcontent would not take hold in the main convict establishment in Sydney.

At the mercy of the elements

Despite the physical dangers of a voyage, and the trauma of being uprooted into the unknown, not all convicts looked to the voyage with terror. As we have seen, some were relieved to join a vessel for little other reason than escaping from the condition of their confinement at home. Others greeted the day of arrival on board a convict ship with joy and excitement, knowing when they disembarked it would be in a land of new opportunity. The voyage was their gateway to a new and better life. This was particularly true from the 1820s onwards, after the difficulties of initial settlement were largely overcome and two successful colonies in New South Wales and Van Diemen's Land had been established. Some have even suggested that the end of penal transportation in 1868 was due, at least in part, to it no longer providing sufficient deterrent to convicts (see Chapter five). Not all convicts were as averse to the journey and the destination as we might at first expect.

In our haste to measure and chart the lives of convicts landing *en masse* in Australia, and to assess how effective this unique penal experiment was, we can often lose sight of the thousands of individual human journeys, emotional and physical, that were taking place. Journeys that represent the great injustice befalling those sent unwillingly miles from home as property of the state, the challenges faced by those who embarked, and most of all the hopes and heartbreak of those who begged to go but never arrived. Sometimes a single voyage reflects the emotional and historical complexity of transportation to Australia, and is a stark reminder of the dangers every man and woman faced when they stepped aboard a ship.

All aboard the *Amphitrite*

In late August 1833 the convict ship *Amphitrite* set out from Woolwich, bound for New South Wales. Officially, on board were 101 female convicts. A range of accounts also suggest that there were seven other convict women, and twelve of the convicts' children between the age of two and twelve. The female convicts came predominantly from London and Scotland although there were a scattering of women from other areas of Britain. They were aged between sixteen and sixty, and had sentences ranging from seven years to life. Luckily for these convicts, their journey through the justice system had been brief. Almost all of those on board the *Amphitrite* had been tried in 1833 and waited just a few months for departure. The women aboard the *Amphitrite* were in many ways indistinguishable from the majority of other nineteenth century female convicts. Those from Scotland were reportedly notorious recidivists, and from the details available of the London convicts, a good proportion of them were prostitutes. Most, if not quite all, of the women had been convicted of property crimes. Women like Mary Stuart and Charlotte Rogers, convicted of picking their customer's pockets and sentenced to fourteen years transportation.

We know some by their own admission were guilty, and others like Mary Hamilton, sentenced to a term of fourteen years, may have been innocent. In Hamilton's case even the victim of a robbery, Williams Carter, admitted 'I cannot say the prisoner is the person.' As a rule, female convicts on ships like the *Amphitrite* tend to leave very little in the way of evidence about how they felt about the sentences they were given. All we can do is imagine. Did women like Mary Brown, who ran a 'house of ill fame', and Charlotte Smith, a prostitute, who worked with her to rob a customer, feel relief when their death sentences were commuted to life in Australia? Were the women terrified and devastated, or like Caroline Ellis, seemingly indifferent? Ellis was overheard by a policeman speaking to a fellow inmate at the local lock up, herself a returned transportee, stating matter-of-factly that she supposed she 'should be transported this time'. There were others like Maria Hoskins, aged twenty-eight, who admitted in court that she wanted to be sent to Australia. Hoskins stole a watch from her land lady and pawned it. The landlady discovered the theft and asked for the pawn ticket so she might retrieve the property. Hoskins replied, 'No. I will not do that; I did it with the intention of being transported.' Hoskins refused to say where the watch was pledged until the landlady fetched a police officer to arrest her. She told the arresting officer, 'If you have any compassion on a female you will take me up – if you do not, I will do murder.' Hoskins, impoverished and desperate, saw the potential for a better life in Australia. Police Constable Richard Broderick testified:

> I took the prisoner; she said if she was not transported for this, she would commit something more heinous that would send her out of the country – that she had applied to Covent Garden parish for relief, and had been refused, and if she came across Mr. Farmer, she would drive a knife into him, and hang for him.

Hoskins was given what she desired, a term of seven years' transportation. She wasted no time in preparing for her trip. From Newgate prison, she made applications to the authorities so that she and her fellow convicts might be granted new clothes for their fresh start in Australia, and clean blankets for the voyage. Hoskins wrote that she and her fellow convicts were 'anxious to alter our way of living, and, by a strict adherence to the rules laid down for our future conduct, are in hopes partly to retrieve our reputations, which we have unfortunately forfeited'. Undoubtedly Hoskins' sentiments were in part a ploy to present her case for new clothes to the Sheriffs of the City of London. Yet given her seemingly earnest desire to be transported, it is likely that the prospect of arrival in New South Wales did feel like an opportunity to begin again in a new respectable life.

Tragically, like the other 100 known convicts on the *Amphitrite*, Maria Hoskins never reached her destination. The *Amphitrite* was caught in a severe storm off the coast of Boulogne, France, just days after departing from England. The captain declined to put into port, and instead tried to weather the storm on the open sea. The ship was driven onto the rocks, and the Captain dropped anchor, hoping that when high tide came, the ship would be lifted off. A French ship came out to give assistance, but with the crew in their quarters, packing clothing in preparation to leave the ship, few noticed.

Those that did were rumoured to have been persuaded not to accept the help of the ship, lest the convict women escape. As the situation worsened the convicts were kept below decks which, one crew member later testified, was six and a half feet under water. The women forced their way onto the deck of the boat, but were forced to wait there an hour and a half in the storm, with the captain and surgeon forbidding them access to the longboats (lifeboats). Far from helping the ship, as the tide came in the ship began to break apart. The captain gave the order for the crew to abandon ship and swim to shore if they could. Even competent swimmers would struggle in turbulent waters. Most of the convict women would have no experience of swimming, and would have been weighed down by the fabric of their convict uniforms if not the irons they wore. It is impossible to imagine the terror with which the convict women witnessed the scene unfolding before them, or their horror when they realised no help was to be afforded them. We can but wonder what those final hours were like for convicts such as Anne Lewis from west Wales, who spoke no English, and would have been unable to request help or follow instructions. The ship was completely destroyed, and every convict woman, every child, and all but three of the crew were drowned.

The *Amphitrite* was the first convict vessel to be lost since the start of transportation to Australia, and the first loss of a female convict transport. The loss of the ship was big news, inspiring ballads, paintings, and broadsides (Image 5). Much sympathy was felt for the position of the convict women, whose fate lay totally in the hands of the crew with whom they travelled. Although the wreck was occasioned by a storm, blame for the tragedy was placed at the feet of the senior officers on board who were felt to have allowed the women to die by declining help and refusing to let them go ashore. They did this, survivors testified, because the captain felt he lacked the permission to take convicts off of a vessel at any other port but Australia. The large loss of life from the wreck, made all the worse in the public eye by being almost entirely women and children, again drew criticisms as the product of a system in which convicts had been treated like cargo, rather than human beings.

Just two years later, the memory of the *Amphitrite* was revived when another convict ship ran into trouble off the coast of Australia. The *Neva* had left Ireland in January 1835 carrying 150 female convicts, thirty-three of their children, and a small number of free women and their children. Five months into their voyage as they neared Van Diemen's Land on the way to Sydney, the ship unexpectedly hit a reef and began to break apart. With no protocol for such an event, it was every passenger for themselves, no assistance was rendered to those unable to swim. As convicts and crew alike fought for survival, fights broke out and chaos ensued. A newspaper later noted 'a more dreadful scene is not on record' and recounted that 'two of the poor women on a portion of the ship were seen struggling together in the height of passion' as they vied for a position clinging to floating parts of the wreck. It was in this 'dreadful state with each other's hands tearing the hair of the other' that they were both washed off the wreckage and drowned. The convicts, passengers and crew were all pitched into the water, and only fifteen survived. Among them were less than ten women and no children. All other lives on board – more than 200 – were lost. Amongst those drowned were the old, and young, the guilty and the innocent. Women like nineteen-year-old Jane Gordon from Lisburn, who ultimately paid with her life for the theft of a pair of scissors, a gown, and some other articles.

Ellen Galvin, Mary Slatterly, Ann Cullen, Rose Ann Hyland, Rose Dunn and Margaret Drury were the only convicts to survive the wreck, and were taken to Van Diemen's Land after rescue, to carry out their sentences. Their involvement in the wreck had no bearing on their treatment in the convict establishment, and no allowances were made for the emotional and psychological trauma they may have sustained. Rose Hyland, who had been sentenced to seven years at the Antrim Sessions for the theft of £10 and a gold watch in June 1834, made troubled progress through the convict system. Her record was peppered with instances of absconding from assignment, drunkenness, insolence and unexplained absences, and breach of the conditions of her licence, for which she was punished with solitary confinement and a punishment diet of bread and water at the female factory. Rose's pattern of disruptive behaviour continued up until, and after, she received her Certificate of Freedom in 1841. Rose may have proved herself a difficult convict even without her experiences on the *Neva*. Yet Rose was not the only one of the survivors to find life in Australia after the wreck difficult to navigate. Ellen Galvin of Limerick was also frequently punished for being absent without leave, for using obscene and abusive language, insolence, drunkenness, and breaking her curfew. Ellen's behaviour on arrival in Van Diemen's Land was deemed so bad that her existing sentence of seven years was extended, and her freedom not granted until 1842. So too did Rose Dunn, a vagrant and thief sentenced for seven years at Cavan in 1832, but whose drunkenness, disorderly conduct, and frequent absences without leave earned her a six-month extension on her sentence. Rose continued to drink and work as a prostitute after her release. Ann Cullen, transported for life from Kildare, spent more than a decade in the convict establishment after the wreck, being punished frequently for obscene language and insolence, improper conduct on work assignments (from which she was several times removed), for being absent without leave, and for disorderly behaviour. Margaret Drury, sentenced to seven years at Cavan in 1833, was granted her Certificate of Freedom on time in 1840, but also had incidence of drunkenness recorded against her, and on one occasion the 'indecent exposure of her person'. Margaret was further confined for an extra six months in the house of correction, having attempted to hide herself on an island in the Bass Strait when a rescue party arrived after the wreck. Of all the convict women to survive the sinking of the *Neva*, only Mary Slatterly seems to have settled into the convict system without issue.

The wreck of the *Neva* is the most fatal convict disaster in Australian history, and the second most fatal of all Australian maritime disasters. Responses to the wreck were considerably different to those from the *Amphitrite*. The disaster was reported widely in Australia, initially with sympathy, but comparatively little was made of it in the British and Irish press. Once convicts departed from British waters, they were truly out of sight and out of mind, and anything that occurred to them thereafter was of little concern to those back home. In later reportage there were tales of the convict women becoming drunk on rum as the ship was sinking (the *Neva* carried with it more than 300 litres of rum). The veracity of this claim is hard to test, but provided a convenient narrative for the death of so many women, shifting responsibility for drowning onto the convict women and away from the captain and vessel, which sailed with no lifeboats and no protocol in the case of the wreck. Around one in three of the crew survived, but fewer than one in twenty of the convict women. Allegations of drunkenness and incapacity stopped further questions as to why there was such a disparity.

The early 1830s were arguably the worst years for convict shipwrecks, with the three largest wrecks occurring within a two year period. Little over a fortnight before the *Neva* set sail from Ireland on her own doomed journey, the convict ship *George III* pulled out of Woolwich bound for Van Diemen's Land on 14 December 1834. On board there were approximately 220 male convicts and 88 crew members and their families. The voyage experienced its fair share of difficulties, including a fire that was reported to have broken out on account of poorly stored alcohol, a few weeks after departure, and which destroyed some of the ship's stores. Rations were reduced, causing an outbreak of scurvy amongst the prisoners and the deaths of fourteen men. The ship had reached the coast of Van Diemen's Land by March 1835 when strong winds prevented the ship from landing. As the ship changed course, it struck a submerged rock and began to take on water and break apart. A small boat was sent to raise the alarm and fetch help from nearby land, and the free women and children were evacuated. The convicts were kept locked below decks whilst guards with guns kept order. As the convicts attempted to break out of the hold, the guards fired on them, although it is not clear if anyone was injured. The guards were given further instructions that if the prisoners managed to break their way onto the boat deck, the guards should open fire to prevent them escaping. While some did eventually escape, a number of convicts, particularly the sick, were drowned below decks. Eventually 134 lives were lost when the *George III* sank, 128 of them convicts.

The sinking of convict ships was exceedingly rare, and there was never again one so deadly as the *Neva*, *George III* or *Amphitrite*, in which almost all convict lives were lost. But wrecks, more so than death from disease (which claimed far more lives), are a stark reminder of the danger faced by convicts at every stage of their journey. This was not only because of the conditions and challenges of long months at sea, but also because of their very status as convicts, which meant that when crisis struck, their needs and safety could be ignored. The voyage to Australia was not simply a swift trip between two states of incarceration, it was a perilous and dangerous crossing in which every storm, every patch of rough sea or fault with a ship could lead to an untimely and terrifying end.

Conclusions

The voyage to Australia itself often plays a minor role in the recounting of convict stories. The crimes that sent men and women to the colonies, and what they experienced once they arrived, dominate histories of transportation. Yet the journey to Australia was not a simple footnote in a greater tale. A convict voyage was rife with danger, from the threat of insurrection on board a ship, to the terrifying prospect of riding a wooden boat through thousands of miles of open ocean dependent on the wind. For those unable to swim and manacled in heavy irons, death by drowning must have been a daily fear. More than anything else, the squalid conditions in which convicts were forced to sail and the prevalence of disease must have made those months below decks in each vessel unbearable. Although the earliest convicts undoubtedly fared worst in ships controlled by men who cared more for profit than their lives, even those who came later had to contest with cramped conditions, no sanitation, sea-sick comrades, and a lack of fresh food and water. Such was the nature of the nineteenth century sea voyage. With so few convicts leaving a record of their time on board a convict ship, it will be difficult to ever fully know if and how convicts carried the trauma of the voyage with them for the rest of their lives, or if it contributed to the large number of convicts who never attempted a return journey at the end of their sentence. For those who survived the many dangers and degradations of a transport voyage long enough to make land in Australia, the view of their new home must have been a sight for sore eyes indeed.

Chapter 3

Bound for Botany Bay:
New South Wales 1787–1850

The Dutch are thought to have been the first Europeans to land in Australia, more than 150 years before Captain James Cook and his team arrived in 1770. Between the first Dutch landing, and British settlement, a number of explorers visited the country throughout the seventeenth century. They mapped but never settled or extensively explored the land, which they referred to as 'New Holland'. Although they sailed extensively along the west coast, and up to the north of the country, it is unclear if they understood quite how extensive a territory Australia was.

When Cook arrived on the uncharted east coast more than a century later, he mapped the land more thoroughly than his predecessors, and reported home the potential he believed Australia held for the Empire, claiming the territory of New South Wales for Britain. It was not until almost two decades later, when domestic and international events conspired to leave the British in need of new land for their unwanted subjects, that the very first British settlers arrived to establish a colony. Just three weeks into the new year of 1788, eleven ships, carrying more than onethousand people, sighted land on the horizon. They had been travelling for more than eight months, and had not made port in more than three. The relief of finally arriving at their destination, at any destination, must have been significant (Image 6).

The three fastest ships in the fleet, carrying most of the male convicts, had been sent ahead of the rest with instructions to find clear ground and fresh water ready for the fleet to settle. As events transpired, all of the ships arrived within a day or so of each other at a curved bay on the north-east of Australia. Botany Bay had earlier been reported as a place of great bounty, abundant in fish and native plants. Thus, almost twenty years later, when the British were ready to colonise Australia, the bay was their first port of call. We can only imagine what the sight looked like to the Aboriginal Australians who had inhabited the land for thousands of years. People who, in remarkably short order, were about to find their way of life irrevocably changed, their culture under threat, and their very existence endangered.

Botany Bay remains synonymous with convicts and transportation to Australia, and appeared in songs, novels, and prints shaping how many contemporaries felt about transportation. Botany Bay captured both contemporary and historical imagination, and became part of the common lexicon of transportation. There remains something inescapably adventurous about the notion of being 'Bound for Botany Bay', and generations of convicts after the First Fleet continued to reference the site. However, the bay lacked adequate access to fresh water and had limited food supplies. The land was covered in boggy swampland and was assessed as unsuitable for permanent settlement within days of arrival. The fleet sailed north to Port Jackson, dropping anchor at Sydney Cove (now just a stone's throw away from the world-famous Sydney Harbour and Opera House). Sydney became the primary place of convict settlement, and, in time, the largest urban settlement in the colony. The European domination of Australia had begun. By the end of the first month, Philip Gidley King, along with seven free men and fifteen convicts, had made a secondary settlement on Norfolk Island, the tiny spit of land east of Sydney that would become a penal colony within a penal colony, playing home to some of the colony's most infamous offenders.

Within two years more ships and more provisions had arrived, and within twenty years Sydney was estimated to have more than 6,000 inhabitants, both convict and free settlers. As time-expired convicts became liberated settlers in the colony, the population grew at a considerable rate. In 1836, the population of Sydney was estimated to be more than 20,000, and continued to grow until the suspension of convict transportation to New South Wales in 1840. The first Australian penal colony was more than just Sydney and Norfolk Island, of course. The Blue Mountains to the north-west hampered some expansion, but the British had made substantial settlements at Parramatta, Hawkesbury and Newcastle too, and within decades boasted smaller free-settler and expiree communities living throughout the state of New South Wales.

This chapter takes a look at the stories of a handful of convicts that found themselves washed up on Sydney's shore. It tries to capture the fascinating diversity of the first European men and women to settle Australia, from the youngest convicts, to the more elderly arrivals, from the earliest settlers voyaging into the unknown with the First Fleet, to celebrity convicts of later decades. We'll hear from famed escapees, and those that served their sentences in relative obscurity, staying to face the challenges and rewards of building a new life miles from home. Several of the stories in this chapter are known to be exceptional, but, even in these fantastical tales, there are glimmers of the everyday reality of life in early convict Australia. Each of the stories has something to teach us about convict life in New South Wales. Their stories, some left behind for us in the words of their own letters and memoirs, show us the terror of early settlement in a strange new land, and the opportunities available to convicts and their families as New South Wales moved towards its post-convict future.

The first few decades of transportation that followed the First Fleet shaped ideas about convicts and transportation to Australia for the rest of the transportation period, and long afterwards. For those waiting anxiously to be shipped to Australia, and family and friends back home awaiting news of convict loved ones, even to the present day, the word transportation has the power to conjure up images of ragged convicts, toiling in irons under the fierce Australian sun. In total, approximately 80,000 men, women, and children, were sent by the British government to New South Wales as convicts between the voyage of the First Fleet and the abolition of transportation in 1850 (although no new convicts from Britain had arrived in the last decade). But what was life like for those early settlers on the other side of the world, and what on earth did ordinary men and women make of life in such a strange new land?

'For I must say this is the wickedest place I ever was in all my life'

In early New South Wales, with the Australian convict system so new to all those involved, the hard labour and restrictions of freedom were not the only hardship convicts had to contend with. Survival in the colony itself – a harsh and unfamiliar land with so many dangers – was a daily struggle. While the difficulties of life in the penal settlement were documented in the journals and letters of government officials, we have very few first-hand accounts of life in the colony from the perspective of convicts. This is not only due to the destruction of many early convict records (making life in New South Wales one of the harder convict histories to trace), but also due to the low literacy rates of the overwhelmingly working-class population. Exceptional memoirs (like those left by James Vaux and Mark Jeffrey) give us some insight, but always through the lenses of a fantastical personal story set out for an audience which pays more attention to the individual than to their day-to-day life or surroundings. Much more candid accounts can be found in the rare correspondence early convicts sent back to Britain, describing the fearsome new world in which they found themselves.

Margaret Catchpole was born in Suffolk in 1762, the daughter of Elizabeth Catchpole, and a local farm labourer (Image 7). Although her parents were not married, Margaret grew up with both of them on the various plots of land which her father worked. From her early teens, Margaret worked in various domestic situations, until settling with the Cobbold family, of Ipswich, with whom she lived for a number of years acting as cook and nursemaid to the family. Margaret was evidently well liked by the Cobbold family who taught her to both read and write, skills that would see Margaret make history. The mutual affection between master and servant was evident as Margaret and the family kept in touch until the end of Margaret's life in 1819, despite her leaving their employment in 1795. More surprising still given that in 1797, after two years of illness and unemployment, Margaret stole one of John Cobbold's coach horses.

Margaret, apparently dressed in men's clothing, stole the horse and rode it in a single night over seventy miles to London, where she intended to sell it. She was quickly apprehended and placed on trial for the theft. Although it was only Margaret's first offence, the value of the horse made her guilty of grand larceny, and she was sentenced to death. She was soon granted a pardon, on the condition that she be transported to Australia for seven years. Unusually for a female convict, Margaret spent almost three years inside Ipswich prison, waiting to be shipped to Australia. After a failed escape attempt for which she was again sentenced to death, before having it commuted to transportation for life, Margaret was placed on board the *Nile* and sailed for Australia in June 1801, arriving in December that year.

Just a few weeks after her arrival, Margaret began writing home, to her uncle and aunt, and to her former employer, Mrs Cobbold (Image 8), letters which have been miraculously preserved into the twenty-first century, and which formed the basis for the fame Margaret obtained long after her death. Margaret is heralded in the Australian Dictionary of Biography as 'One of the few true convict chroniclers with an excellent memory and a gift for recording events.' Margaret's life was immortalised by the popular play *Margaret Catchpole, Horse Stealer*, and recounted in great detail by the Reverend Richard Cobbold, son of her former employer, who fictionalised her life in *The History of Margaret Catchpole, a Suffolk girl* decades after her death. However, it is Margaret's own writings that give us the most remarkable glimpse into her experiences, and to life in New South Wales.

Margaret was an eighteenth century woman, and although she had a remarkable education and level of literacy for a woman of her time and class, she wrote in an age without standardised spelling, where the words she wrote appear as she might have pronounced them in her broad accent from rural Suffolk. This, of course, makes her account no less valuable to us; it does however, make her narratives harder to read. The following quotes taken from a series of letters written by Margaret during her time as a convict in New South Wales have been edited to include modern spelling, punctuation and grammar for ease of reading. The content of Margaret's writing has in no way been changed. However, for those who would like to read some of Margaret's account in her own terms, a full transcript of her first letter from Australia can be found at the back of this book.

In January 1802, Margaret wrote her first letter from Sydney, back to Mrs Cobbold, describing her surroundings and her initial impressions of the place she would call home for the rest of her life. Margaret must have been told many horrors about the penal colony for which she was bound, so on arrival, seeing the lush greenery of New South Wales, a land full of colour and sunlight, her surprise and pleasure was obvious. Margaret wrote:

It is a great deal more like England than ever I did expect to have been. For here is garden stuff of all kinds, except gooseberries, currents, and apples. The gardens are very beautiful indeed, all planted with geraniums and they run up seven or eight foot high …

It is a very woody country, for if I go out any distance here is going through woods for miles – but they are very beautiful – and very pretty birds. I only wish my good lady I could send you one of these parrots, for they are very beautiful, but I see so many die on board it makes me so very unwilling to send you one …

The crops of wheat are very good in this country for it produces forty bushels per acre – it is a very bountiful place indeed for I understand them that never had a child in all their lives have some when they come here.

Over the next two years as her letters continued, Margaret would learn that Australia was not only rich in flora, but in fauna too. Snakes, spiders, strange mammals, sharks and jellyfish were but a few of the deadly creatures that lay in wait for unsuspecting settlers:

The black snakes are very bad for they will fly at you like a dog and if they bite us we die at sun down – here are some twelve feet long and as big as your thigh and many very dangerous things.

Even the weather was more of a challenge than convicts and free settlers alike had bargained for. Margaret observed one December:

> This is a very hot country – the ground burns our feet in the summer part – which is at this time – and the winter is very cold, but no snow – just very white frosts – it is a great deal colder than it used to be for it was a very woody place, but now it only is in some places – it will be a very [populated] place in time – it is a great deal better than it was when I first came here …
>
> I took a very long walk of thirty miles and overheated myself. I came out with blisters on my back as if I had been burnt by smore coals of fire and swelled so bad I thought I would be dead very soon – but bless me God, I did recover.

One of the first and most essential jobs for the convicts, as well as the free settlers who arrived in New South Wales, was to cut back the dense bush and make the land fit for building and cultivation. The early 'starvation' years experienced by the First Fleet meant that the ability to produce food to feed the settlers was of the utmost importance. Even fifteen or twenty years after the First Fleet arrived, building infrastructure and growing crops were still amongst the most important roles of newly arrived convicts and free settlers alike. In 1804 Margaret reported:

> The free people are the farmers, they have one hundred acres given to them when they come here, but it is all like a wood so they have to cut down the trees and burn them away before there can be any corn grown.

Good harvest could make the difference between life and death in early New South Wales. Crops, livestock and the convict population were all connected. A weak point in one could lead to catastrophe for the rest. Just as the sick convicts from the Second Fleet meant a burden to the colony and a lack of healthy men to engage in agriculture – which threatened everyone in the settlement— a failed crop could likewise spell disaster. On one occasion Margaret wrote 'a very bad crop of wheat this season, times will go very hard with us next winter I am afraid.'

Those farming in New South Wales had to get used to new soil types, and for the first few years, trial and error were required to ascertain what would grow in the climate and what would not. Of those who left written accounts of life in New South Wales, many mentioned the extreme weather with which colonists had to contend:

> Everything is very forward in the country – but very uncertain – we may have a good crop of grain on the ground today and all cut off by the next in places by a hail storm or a blight or a flood. On Monday last … a hail storm went over in places and cut down the wheat just as it was in bloom – the hail stones were as big as pigeons' eggs.

In 1809 Margaret was witness to the devastating floods in Hawkesbury which claimed many lives and ruined crops, plunging convicts and settlers into disaster:

> There has been a flood in the month of May which distressed us very much – the next flood – on the last day of July and the first day of August – the highest that was ever known by the white men – went over the tops of the houses and many poor creatures crying out for mercy, crying out for boats, firing off guns in distress, it was shocking to hear … many a one was drowned and at the time the flood was at the height we all were in great fear we should be starved when the wheat stacks – barns and houses went – many thousand bushels of indey corn were washed away – we make bread of that instead of wheat – most parts of the wheat that was in the ground was killed by the flood.

It was not only in navigating hostile, unfamiliar, terrain and living within the confines of a restrictive government regime that convicts like Margaret struggled with. Convict settlers were part of a colonising population, appropriating land and resources from an indigenous society that had lived in Australia for thousands of years. Although the convicts had been bought to New South Wales unwillingly, to the indigenous peoples every white settler was part of the same problem – the ransacking and seizure of communal lands and the destruction of Aboriginal cultures. In 1802, shortly after her arrival, Margaret wrote of her initial impressions of the Aboriginal Australians that she had observed:

> The blacks, the natives of this [place] – they are very savage for they always carry with them spears and tomahawks so when they can meet with a man they will rob them and spear them. I for my part

do not like them – I do not know how to look at them – they are such poor naked creatures – they behave themselves well enough when they come in to my house for if not we would get them punished. They very often have a grand fight with themselves, twenty and thirty all together – and we pray to be spared. Some of them are killed – there is nothing said to them for killing one another.

Of course, most of all, Margaret's reflections on the 'savage' nature of the indigenous population tell us far more about the perspective of an eighteenth century European, than they do about indigenous cultures. However, despite indigenous customs and cultures being alien to Margaret, her initial account seems to broadly corroborate other accounts of the relationship between the two groups. Aboriginal Australians would interact peacefully with settlers in the lands that settlers inhabited. Violent clashes between the two groups occurred mostly as a result of European expansionism, and settler society encroaching further and further into lands in the bush. After writing the first section of her letter, Margaret added a sudden update, after a shocking incident between settlers and the local people:

> The black natives of this place killed and wounded eight men, women and children – one man they cut off his arm halfway up and broke the bones that they left on very much and cut [his] legs up to [his] knees and the poor man was carried in to the hospital alive – but the Governor has sent men out after them to shoot everyone they find – so I hope I shall give you a better account next letter.

Terrifying attacks on settlers like these undoubtedly fuelled the fears of convicts living in the colonies, and intensified the fearsome reputation of transportation in Britain. Yet violence and antagonism between the local population and the white settlers was an ongoing factor of life in the colonies (indeed, the difficult relations between white Australians and indigenous peoples was a factor in every colony, continued well after the end of transportation, and continues to be a source of social, economic, and cultural tension in the present day). Clashes between the two groups were sporadic and episodic in nature, becoming less concerning to white settlers the more acclimatised they became to the presence of local inhabitants.

Less than three years after her arrival, Margaret wrote in a letter to her aunt and uncle, 'This is a very dangerous country to live in for the natives they are black men and women – they go naked – they used to kill the white people very much but they are better – but bad enough – now' suggesting that there had been some change in the relationship between the two groups. In reality little had substantially changed, either in the approach of colonialists to the native population, nor in the experiences of indigenous inhabitants. Margaret's sense of progress in relations was likely due to a reduction in her own anxiety (produced by her growing familiarity with Aboriginal peoples) and perhaps a period of relative peace.

The convict system itself was also a considerable source of anxiety for convicts like Margaret, who had to balance navigating life in the beautiful and deadly natural world and interactions with hostile local people, with the strict rules and routine of life under sentence. It was, perhaps, life under the convict system that Margaret disliked most of all. She expressed particular sympathy for her convict peers sent to sites of secondary punishment, like the penal settlements in Newcastle and Norfolk Island. She wrote to Mrs Cobbold:

> If I should continue long in this country I certainly will send you something out of this wicked country – FOR I MUST SAY THIS IS THE WICKEDEST PLACE I EVER WAS IN ALL MY LIFE ... Not that I am in such great trouble at present, but God only knows how it may be for here is many one that has been here for many years and that have their poor head shaved and sent up to the Coal River, there [they] carry coals from daylight in the morning until dark at night, and half starved, but I hear that is going to put by and so it had need for it is very cruel indeed ... Norfolk Island is a bad place enough to send any poor creature with a steel collar on their poor necks, but I will take good care of myself from that.
>
> I am pretty well off present for I was taken off the stores two days after I landed so I have no government work to do, nor they have anything to do with me – only when here be a general muster, then I must appear to let them know I am here, and if I have a mind I go up to Parramatta, twenty miles, or to town Gabbey, thirty miles, or to Ocberrey, forty miles. I have to get a pass or else I should be taken up and put in prison – for a very little will do that here ... for I cannot say that I like this country – no, nor never shall.

Margaret, like the majority of her convict peers, was never sent to Norfolk Island, or set to work in a chain gang, or imprisoned for some minor infractions of colony rules. While all of these fates were a possibility for those that failed to obey colony law, their primary purpose (like public floggings and executions) was as a deterrent to wrong doing. As Margaret's writings show, the very sight of men labouring in neck chains, or the stories of awful conditions on the dreaded Norfolk Island, were enough to keep most prisoners in line.

After her arrival in the colony, Margaret continued to socialise with the women she had been confined in Ipswich prison with, and who had accompanied her aboard the *Nile*. Her recounting of her peers indicates that the assignment system was not in full operation. Whilst some were put to work, 'Sarah Barker has to spin for government and she is up on the stores, but she can get her work done by twelve or one o'clock if she works hard at it,' others like Margaret were left largely to their own devices until work could be found for them. Margaret informed her correspondents: 'Elizabeth Kellett lives very near to me and does very well and she is off the stores and so we are not driven about after work for the government like horses, we are free from all hard work.'

Margaret was one of the lucky few not to be assigned government work on her arrival in New South Wales, giving her time to acclimatise to her strange surroundings and the convict system in which she had to operate. There was, admittedly, less government work for women than for male convicts who were engaged in creating roads and buildings, logging and mining, but there were still plenty of uses for convict women, the predominant one being the provision of service to free settlers. After her initial few weeks with no work, Margaret was assigned as a servant. By 1804, she was living and working with a number of other convicts in the house of John Palmers. Margaret served as cook and 'darrey servant'. She was later transferred to another free settler. There Margaret acted as housekeeper to an unnamed man who 'had the misfortune to lose a good wife' and who was left with two small children.

Asides from her writings, which have made her worthy of attention from historians, Margaret was a largely unremarkable convict. She lived an ordinary, stable, and apparently happy, life, especially after she received her freedom in 1814. After she was pardoned, Margaret undertook a range of employments, from keeping a shop (this was likely to be a much more informal trading venture run from her home than the commercial enterprises we think of today), and nursing. At the age of fifty, Margaret was still unmarried, and wrote that she had no intention of becoming so. It was still her wish to return to England, and see her home once more, though how likely she believed the chance is unclear. Margaret does seem to have been happy enough in her life in Australia, writing:

> Thank God I can do so well as I do. I rent a little farm about fifteen acres, about half of it standing timber and the cleared ground. I hire men to put in my corn and I work a good deal myself. I have got thirty sheep and forty goats and thirty pigs and two dogs. They take care of me for I live all alone, no one in the house, there is a house within twenty two [unclear] of me. I have a good many friends that I go to see when I think proper such as I have nursed when they have lay in. They cannot do without me.

Margaret was very fortunate not to have been forgotten by friends and relatives back in England, especially her affluent former employers who from time to time sent her clothing, writing materials, and supplies. The majority of ordinary convicts could not have relied upon such luxuries from generous acquaintances. Even those like Margaret in regular contact with friends and family back home could never be sure of when the next letter or package would arrive. Margaret notes in some of her correspondence that some packages arrived with her more than two years after they were sent from England. Even the most well connected convicts ultimately found themselves alone in the colony.

As far as records allow us to know, Margaret never married and she had no children. She died in New South Wales in 1819, after just five years of freedom. Margaret maintained the hopes of receiving a Free Pardon and returning to England until she died. Through her writings, Margaret's story became the stuff of plays and poems and novels far more exciting than her real existence in New South Wales is likely to have been. Nevertheless, it is writings like hers that help us to go beyond the records of punishment, assignment, and freedom in the penal colonies, and to imagine the setting in which thousands of convict men and women succeeded against the odds, failed to thrive, carved out lives, families and homes, or plotted their escapes. A bright and colourful land, where the climate, surroundings, and weather could be as dangerous and hostile as the local peoples the convicts displaced.

Perhaps because of accounts like Margaret's, which charted Europeans settling in a beautiful and deadly paradise, it is New South Wales more than any other colony that brings to mind the most exotic and jarring images of convict transportation. Ragged thieves and swindlers from the lowest strata of British society facing starvation, exposure, and the lash at the hands of British justice – on white sandy beaches surrounded by palm trees. Desperate men and women making for the bush, or dying in the sun. While stories of such convicts and such fates can easily be found amongst the tens of thousands of convict stories waiting to be told, there are other stories too. Of survival, of defiance, and even of success. The backgrounds and experiences of early convicts could be wonderfully diverse. This diversity is perhaps best captured not through the writings of individual convicts, but in the stories of three women who shared many things. All of these women were transported to New South Wales from Britain. They all experienced the colony in the early 1790s. They even shared the same name: Mary. Three women whose journeys to, through, and even from, the penal system in New South Wales show just how varied the convict experience could be.

Mary Bryant's escape from Botany Bay

Almost from the first reports that trickled back to Britain of the new penal settlement across the world, New South Wales was a place of contradictions to the men and women destined to be among its first colonisers. As Margaret Catchpole illustrated a decade later, to the first settlers, Australia was a land of bright birds, strange animals and extreme climate, abundant with plants and trees, sights, smells, and sounds that Europeans had never experienced. Australia's was a hostile landscape that made settlement a far more challenging prospect than it had been in America centuries before. While many of the officers and crew that sailed with the First Fleet kept journals of the voyage and fledgling days of the colony, there are virtually no first hand accounts to tell us how the men and women dragged to Sydney in chains found this extraordinary adventure. What we do know is that the first years in the colony were hard and dangerous, and remained so into the nineteenth century.

The situation for early convicts and colonials could be desperate. As the first European settlers, the men and women of the First Fleet had to cope with the dangers and deprivations of an inhospitable land, in which snakes and spiders could kill and finding food and water was a daily struggle. As we've seen, convicts and free colonists clashed violently with the local population, whose land they were colonising. There were also inherent tensions that existed between the convict population, and the military personnel that were simultaneously their gaolers, protectors, and peers. It is little wonder that many dreamed of escape. However, absconding from the penal settlement carried a punishment of whipping, or even death. With such small numbers at their disposal to conquer a vast country, the colonial authorities could not afford to lose a single man or woman.

The harsh punishments meted out to convicts dragged back from the bush were used as a deterrent to their fellows. There are no records to show how many absconders who never returned from the depths of the New South Wales outback survived. With the lack of food and fresh water, limited means for shelter, and dangers posed by Aboriginal Australians, lives out in the bush were rarely likely to be long ones. Even if an absconder survived for years, such a form of freedom was not really freedom at all. They might be free from the lash of the whip and the hard labour of the penal settlement, but the privations of life in the bush of Australia were arguably worse, and the distance from home just as great. The only true way for early settlers to escape their torment was by sea, navigating back across the vast ocean to some kind of familiar civilisation.

Within half a century of the First Fleet's landing, Sydney Harbour would become a thriving metropolis with ships arriving and departing daily from all over the world. Later convicts looking to escape the colony had only to find a suitable hiding place upon a vessel (or bribe a captain for their passage) in order to be free of Australia. For those on the First Fleet though, the isolation of their life in Australia was almost total. It would not be until 1790 that the Second Fleet carrying new convicts and supplies arrived, and the majority of vessels that landed in January 1788 had sailed for home or elsewhere in the world within a few months of arrival. There were no passenger ships on which to seek refuge. If escaping convicts wished to brave the ocean, they had to go alone.

Though many dreamed of escape, the thousands of miles of open ocean that surrounded the colony was thought by many to be impassable. There was only one well-documented successful escape of convicts from the First Fleet. Mary Bryant was amongst a group of eight convicts whose bid for freedom remains one of the most famous in Australia's history.

Mary Bryant (maiden name Broad, but also recorded as Brian, Briant, and Braund) was a Cornishwoman living in Plymouth, convicted at Exeter Assize in 1786 for highway robbery. Alongside two other female accomplices, Mary was sentenced to death. Her sentence was later commuted on the condition of transportation for seven years. William Bryant, a local of St Ives, was convicted in 1784 and given death, which was also commuted to transportation. James Martin and James Cox were also amongst the more than 100 men and women loaded on board the *Charlotte* convict ship which

1. *Black-eyed Sue and Sweet Poll of Plymouth take leave of their lovers who are going to Botany Bay.* Unknown artist (1792). National Library of Australia.

2. Abel Magwitch depicted in Charles Dickens' *Great Expectations (1862).*

3. The *Warrior* hulk at Woolwich with the *Sulphur* washing ship in the background. From Mayhew and Binney's *Criminal Prisons of London* (1862).

4. Four convicts wearing the broad arrow (late nineteenth century). Wellcome Images, courtesy of the Wellcome Trust.

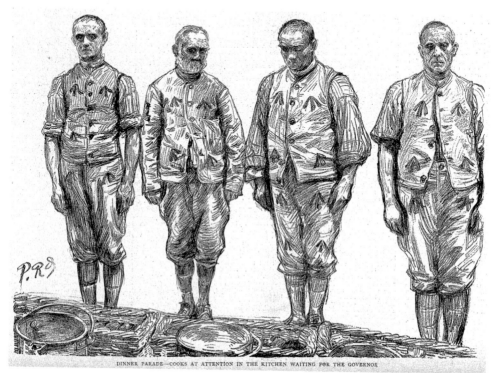

DINNER PARADE—COOKS AT ATTENTION IN THE KITCHEN WAITING FOR THE GOVERNOR

Melancholy and Dreadful Loss of the
AMPHITRITE.

Bound from Woolwich to Botany Bay, with 108 Female Convicts and 12 Children, together
with a Crew of 16, being in the whole 136 souls: of which 133 perished in the dreadful Gale
of Saturday, the 31st of August 1833, off Boulogne.

COME list you gallant Englishmen, who ramble at
your ease,
While I untold concerning of the dangers of the seas:
It's of the ship, the Amphitrite, with 108 females,
With children, crew, and cargo, boys, bound down to
New South Wales.

Twas August on the 25th we sailed from Woolwich
shore,
(ed sore,
Leaving our friends behind us, whose hearts were griev-
Along the shore away we bore, till friends were out of
sight,
(of the Amphitrite.
Crying, fare you well, each bright young girl, on board

We sailed away without delay & arrived 3 off Dunger-
ness,
(tress,
When we arrived at port Bologne it fill'd us with dis-
On Friday morning the 4th day it was a dreadful sight,
Surrounded by a dreadful gale was the dreadful Amphitrite.

Our Captain found she was near aground, her anchor
did let go,
(fate you'll know !
Crying, set your main and topsails, boys, or soon your
The raging sea ran mountains high, the tempest did u-
nite,
(Amphitrite.
Poor souls in vain did shriek with pain, on board of the

At 3 o'clock in the afternoon we were put to a stand,
Our fatal ship she ran aground upon a bank of sand :
Poor children round their parents hung, who tore their
hair with fright,
(Amphitrite.
To think that they should end their days on board of the

Our moments they were ending fast, and all prepared
to die,
(cry ;
Down on our bended knees did fall, and loud for mercy
Our ship she gave a dreadful roll, and soon went out of
sight,
(of the Amphitrite.
Their shrieks and cries must reach the skies f o n aboard

Great praise belongs unto the French who tried us all to
save ;
Our Captain he was obstinate to brave the stormy wave,
But he went down among the rest to swim the briny sea,
The rocks beneath the briny deep his pillow for to be.

Poor souls were toss'd, and all were lost, but two poor
lads and me,
(ging sea ;
For on a spar we reached the shore and cleared the ra-
But one exhausted by the wave he died that very night,
So only two's saved from the crew of the fatal Amphitrite.

So now the Amphitrite is gone, her passengers & crew,
So think upon the sailor bold that wea.. y the jacket blue;
God gave relief to end the grief of those distracted quite,
Lamenting sore for those no more on board of the Amph-
itrite.

J. Catnach, Printer, 2, & 3, Monmouth-court,
7 Dials.

5. *The Melancholy and Dreadful Loss of the Amphitrite* (1833). The
National Library of Australia obj1822464-1.

6. *Landing of Convicts at Botany Bay*. Unknown artist (1789).

THE LANDING of the CONVICTS at BOTANY BAY

7. Sketch of Margaret Catchpole.
Unknown artist (c.1800). Dixon
Library, State Library of New
South Wales

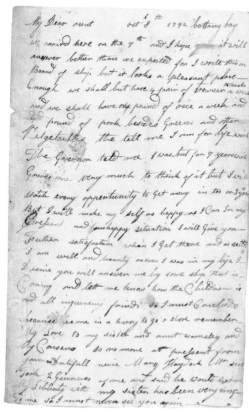

8. Letter from Margaret Catchpole to Mrs Cobbold (1802). State Library of New South Wales, Call Number: A1508; Safe 1/272 Ref: 423940.

10. Letter from Mary Reibey to Penelope Hope (1792). State Library of New South Wales, Call Number: A142002; Safe 1/155.

9. Portrait of Mary Reibey, watercolour on ivory miniature. Unknown artist (c.1835). Mitchell Library, State Library of New South Wales. Call Number: MIN76 File Number FL1048692.

11. Portrait of James Hardy Vaux. Originally published in Knapp and Baldwin's *New Newgate Calendar* (1825).

12. Hyde Park Convict Barracks and courtyard.

13. The bunk room at Hyde Park Barracks.

14. Ruins of the penitentiary at Port Arthur.

15. Portrait of Mark Jeffrey (date unknown).

16. Portrait of George Langley at Port Arthur (1874). National Library of Australia obj-142920761-1.

17. Portrait of Julia Rigby. Courtesy of the Female Convict Research Centre.

18. Cascades Female Factory complex. Tasmanian Archives and Heritage Office ref: TAHO_NS1013145.

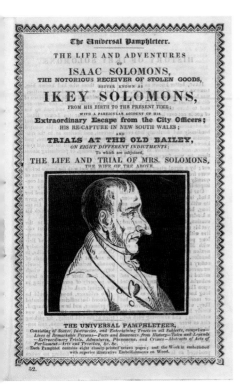

20. Fremantle Prison.

19. The Life and Adventures of Isaac Solomons (1830). The National Library of Australia obj-248498847.

21. Rows of cells at Fremantle Prison.

25. Photograph of Samuel Speed published in *The Mirror* (Perth) 27 August 1938.

23. Joseph Bolitho Johns, otherwise known as 'Moondyne Joe'. Taken by Alfred Chopin (late nineteenth century).

22. Convict era cell at Fremantle Prison.

24. 1899 Prison Register entry for Edward Carlton. State Records Office Western Australia.

sailed for New South Wales in 1787 as part of the First Fleet. Mary was already pregnant as the ship set sail (details of the child's father were never listed, but he may well have been one of her gaolers). She gave birth to a little girl during the voyage, who she named Charlotte, after the ship on which they sailed. A month after arrival in New South Wales, Mary married William Bryant, whom she had met on the *Charlotte*, or perhaps even on the *Dunkirk* hulk on which they were held at Plymouth. The Bryants, along with the rest of the fleet, were assigned to the task of building a new settlement.

Life in the colonies was hard, and many dreamed of returning home even after they were granted freedom. Although William Bryant's sentence had practically expired by the time they made their escape, the reality of life for free men and women in the colony was little different from that of convicts. Labour was just as hard, rations just as scarce, and the fight for survival just as precarious. After the birth of a second child, a son, Emanuel, Mary, William, the children, and seven others decided that their best hope of survival was escaping from the colony.

In March of 1791, a week after two colonial ships capable of capturing small boats left the harbour for supplies, the convicts made the escape which would see them become some of the most famed in the colony's history. The voyage of these intrepid convicts who 'travelled upwards of 3,000 miles by sea in an open boat, exposed to tempestuous weather' has become tantamount to a legend. Yet theirs was a real voyage in which ordinary men and women risked life and limb in hope of seeing England again. In 1792, while waiting to hear of his fate for his role in the escape, James Martin, one of the men who sailed with Bryant, recorded memoirs of the escape, and in doing so became the author, not only of a fantastical escape narrative, but one of the earliest verified accounts of an Australian convict. Far from escaping on a whim, the group had spent more than a year accruing supplies, planning their route, and waiting for the right moment to strike out. Martin wrote:

On the 28 day of March made my escape in company with 7 men more & with one woman & two children in an open six oar boat – having provisions on board one hundred weight of flower & one hundred weight of rice, 14lbs of pork and about eight gallons of water, having a compass quadrant and chart.

They sailed around the coast of Sydney for two days before landing at a creek which, due to its bounty, James claimed they termed 'fortunate creek'.

They found fish to eat and cabbage leaves too. They continued sailing north from Sydney, pulling inland to find fresh water and supplies wherever they could, and to make repairs to their boat which was already beginning to leak. In some spots, they traded peacefully with the local people, in others they were driven away with violence:

> We attempted to land when we found a place convenient for to repair our boat when accordingly we put some of our things part being ashore there came the natives in vast numbers with spears and shields &c we formed in parts one party of us made towards them the better by signs to pacify them but they not taking the least notice accordingly we fired a musket thinking to affright them, but they took not they least notice thereof – on perceiving them rush more forward we were forced to take our boat and to get out of their reach as fast as we could.

The party continued to sail along the shore, stopping wherever they could to take on food and water and materials to mend their already severely leaking boat. With only a small number of them, and no real means of defending themselves, they were often at the mercy of the local population, who, given their experience of white settlers, more often than not prevented them landing. They made out properly to sea once they reached the top of north Australia, surviving on turtle meat, shellfish, and fresh water that they found on small islands along the way. After four and a half days of continuous rowing, the party made it to shore across to the side of the gulf, and from there, sailed to the Dutch settlement of West Timor. Posing as survivors of a shipwreck, the group were initially well treated:

> We went on shore to the governor's house where he behaved extremely well to us, filled our bellies and clothed [us] double . . . we remained very happy at our work for two months until William Bryant had words with his wife, went and informed against himself, wife and children and all of us which we was immediately taken prisoners and put into the castle.

When the British Captain Edwards arrived on Timor, during his course searching for pirates and mutineers from the HMS *Bounty*, Martin, Bryant and the rest of the group became his prisoners and were put in irons on board a Dutch guard ship. Conditions on the ship were considerably worse than at the settlement, and Mary's infant son, Emanuel, contracted a fever and died. Less than a week later, her husband William followed. Soon afterwards Mary, her daughter, and the seven surviving members of the group set sail for the Cape of Good Hope, though William Morton, the group's navigator, and Samuel Bird, died on the voyage. Another of their number, James Cox, went overboard whilst chained in irons and is suspected to have drowned. The survivors were transferred to a British ship and taken back to England. On the last part of the voyage home, Mary's three-year-old daughter, Charlotte, died. When they arrived back in London, only Mary Bryant, James Martin, William Allen, John Broom, and Nathaniel Lilly – just half of the original party – were confined to Newgate.

Martin, Bryant and the rest of the surviving absconders could have been subjected to a number of punishments for their escape. They could have been executed, faced a flogging, or been sent on the next ship back to New South Wales. Even though, technically, it had not been their choice to return to England they could have each been charged with a new felony – returning from transportation – which might require them to be re-transported for life, or at least held in prison for another two to seven years. However, the awful cost in human life that the voyage had taken, and widespread sympathy for the group, and for Mary in particular, who had lost her husband and both of her children in the escape, saw them simply confined in prison for the rest of their original seven-year sentences. In Mary's case, six years had already passed. Within the following year all of the escapees were released, disappearing back into obscurity and the lives they had before their incredible voyage to and from Botany Bay.

Mary Wade: mother of a nation

Mary Wade was just ten years old when she and her friend, Jane Whiting, were convicted of highway robbery at London's Old Bailey. The name of this crime might stir up images of carriage robberies at gunpoint, or an unwitting member of the public being relieved of their purse or watch in a dark alley at knife point – Mary Wade was not that kind of offender. Nor was their victim a wealthy merchant, a finely dressed lady, or even a careless adult in a busy crowd.

In October of 1788, seven-year-old Mary Phillips was sent out of her house in Westminster on an errand to fetch water. On her way, the girl met Mary Wade and Jane Whiting, who forcefully made her remove her clothing before making away with it. This crime of 'child-stripping' was not uncommon. Young children made easy victims, even for those not much older themselves. The garments could be sold on or pawned for a quick and easy profit. For robbing the little girl, Mary and Jane were reported to have made eighteen pence.

Several witnesses saw the girls with the items, and they made no denial of the crime. Mary Wade, it was rumoured, had committed a similar crime earlier that year, 'stripping a child, and chucking her into a ditch', but being so young, she had not been prosecuted.

No violence was used by the girls, in what might have, in other circumstances, been considered little more than bullying, even though the event was undoubtedly very distressing for the young victim. However, laws of the time made no distinction between adult and child perpetrator, and both girls were found guilty of robbery and sentenced to death for the crime. Mercy was quickly forthcoming, and both were granted a pardon on the condition that they be transported for a term of life.

Little over half a year later, Mary bid goodbye to her mother and siblings forever as she was loaded onto the *Lady Juliana*, which sailed with more than 200 female convicts aboard and arrived in Sydney in June 1790. Less than a year before Mary Bryant would make her escape from the colony, and just weeks before the ill-fated Second Fleet arrived. Fortunately for Mary, the conditions of the *Lady Juliana* were vastly superior to the *Surprize*, *Neptune*, and *Scarborough*. Having been sentenced to transportation for life, Mary, around twelve years old on arrival, was taken from Sydney to Norfolk Island.

Transportation and life in a penal settlement must have been truly disorientating for Mary, who had so little experience of normal life. There are few records of what Mary did on Norfolk Island, but she was likely to have been assigned as a domestic servant to free settlers on the island. Even if allowances were made for her young age, she would still have had to contend with the hard work and poor rations (Norfolk Island was heavily dependent on Sydney for supplies). Whilst living on the island, Mary gave birth to two children. Her daughter was born in 1793, when Mary was fourteen or fifteen, and her son in 1795. Mary was unmarried, and the paternity of her children unverified. Mary's children may have been the product of a consensual relationship with the man she later lived with. However, as a teenage convict, Mary would also have been vulnerable to the sexual exploitation and abuse of fellow convicts and the free settlers for whom she worked.

By the turn of the nineteenth century, Mary, now in her early twenties, had returned to Sydney. In the following decade, Mary had more children.

A son was born to her and a fellow convict called Harrington in 1803, with whom she maintained a relationship until 1806. Mary eventually settled with freed convict John Brooker at the settlement of Hawkesbury by the end of the decade. Mary received her Certificate of Freedom in 1812, more than two decades after her conviction. Brooker and Mary Wade acquired land and settled in Airds, a settlement to the north-west of Sydney. Life was seemingly stable for the family, but by no means easy. Land grants gave Mary and Brooker a plot to farm, but clearing the ground and cultivating crops, as well as building a dwelling, was left to them. Droughts, bushfires, and failed crops were all possibilities as convicts subsisted on the edge of destitution. They could not guarantee help from colonial officials if their endeavours failed. Mary died in New South Wales in 1859, having lived to witness the final convicts arriving in the colony almost two decades before. Mary was approximately eighty years of age at the time of her death and is recorded to have given birth to twenty-one surviving children.

Mary Wade was a child offender and convict. Her crimes were not remarkable, nor was her time in the convict system, which surviving records suggest was passed with little disruption. Mary did not gain fame or notoriety during her time as a convict, nor afterwards. Like thousands of Sydney's convicts, she settled, and struggled, and persevered to make the most stable and prosperous life she could in a challenging land. It was the very ordinary nature of Mary's story, and her family, that saw her gain posthumous fame as one of the country's founding matriarchs. Mary's twenty-one children went on to have their own families, and her descendents now number in the tens of thousands, including a former Australian Prime minister. Her story has become, to some, proof of the benefits convict settlement had for Australia. The childhood infraction for which she paid so heavily is but a small part of a story in which Mary has been recast as a tenacious survivor of a brutal British system, a pioneer in the harsh lands of early colonial Australia who helped to build a prosperous country, and as a mother and founder of a proud nation.

Mary Reibey: a success story of early Sydney

The life of convicts in Australia under sentence, and indeed their fate upon release, was as diverse as the offences that saw them arrive in the colonies. Not all dreamed of escape, or toiled in the hostile bush of rural settlements. After the first few decades in which early convicts faced their biggest fight for survival, some have contended, during the convict period and since, that life in Australia offered convicts better chances post-release, than life back in Britain.

At home the stigma surrounding crime meant that the convict 'stain' was often indelible, and saw ex-prisoners live a life of diminishing returns which eventually led back to the courtroom. In Australia, with the right timing and luck, there was no limit to how high an ordinary convict might rise. Mary Reibey (born Mary Haydock) was one of the more remarkable success stories from New South Wales (Image 9). Mary, an orphan living with her grandmother, was convicted just a year after Mary Wade, and was just a few years older at thirteen. She was convicted at the Staffordshire Sessions for horse stealing in 1790. Mary, tenacious, even as a teen, had dressed as a boy and used the name James Burrows to commit her offence. Mary was sentenced to be transported for a term of seven years. She arrived in Sydney aboard the *Royal Admiral* in October 1792.

Mary had come from rural Lancashire. Unlike some of her convict peers, Mary was not displeased with what she saw when she arrived in Australia. Mary's initial view of life in the colony was captured in a letter to her aunt (Image 10) written the day after they made port, before she had even been able to leave the ship:

> My Dear Aunt,
> We arrived here on the 7th and I hope it will answer better than we expected for I write this on board of ship, but it looks a pleasant place enough. We shall but have 4 pairs of trousers to make a week and we shall have one pound of rice a week and a pound of pork besides greens and other vegetables.

Mary's sentence was only for seven years. On gaining her freedom she would still have been a young woman. Yet Mary seems to have had little conviction that she would ever return to England. She wanted to be freed from sentence, and saw the opportunity to build a successful life in Australia, even from these earliest days:

> They tell me I am for life which the governor told me I was but for seven years which grieves me very much to think of it, but I will watch every opportunity to get away in two or three years. But I will make myself as happy as I can in my present and unhappy situation. I will give you further satisfaction when I get there and am settled. I am well and hearty as ever I was in my life.

> I desire you will answer me by some ship that is coming, and let me know how the children are ... I must conclude because everyone is in a hurry to go to shore; remember my love to my sisters and aunt Wamsley and my cousins so no more at present from your dutiful niece Mary Haydock.

Once unloaded from the ship, Mary was quickly assigned to work as a nursemaid in the service of Major Francis Grose, and no complaints were made of her service. Two years after arrival, Mary was granted permission to marry. Her husband was free settler Thomas Reibey, a sailor in the service of the East India Company. The pair had met on the initial transport out. They became reacquainted when he returned to New South Wales as a free settler. Mary, still under sentence, was assigned to her husband's service and the pair moved to the Hawkesbury river area of Sydney where Thomas Reibey purchased property and established a trading business. Mary was fast approaching her own freedom but, content with life in New South Wales, made no plans to return to Britain.

Mary's husband ran a successful business which kept Mary and their seven children comfortably, though saw Thomas frequently taken from home for months at a time. Thomas died in 1811, leaving Mary in sole charge of his business affairs. Mary was no stranger to hard work. She had been running a hotel in Sydney for several years whilst her husband worked away, and had managed her husband's affairs whenever he was absent from the colony. Under Mary's control, her husband's business flourished and expanded. Mary was an astute and formidable business woman, dealing with debtors and creditors, pushing for profit, and enjoying an association with the great and the good of the colony, even Governor Macquarie himself. By 1820 she was worth an estimated £20,000 and held 1,000 acres of land. By this time, still only in her early forties, Mary had sold extensive property. She had considerable means and had received her freedom long ago. Her sons were established in business, and even the story of her own convict origins were fading.

Mary did return to England, but not to stay. In 1820 she took her daughters, Celia and Eliza, to visit the place of her childhood. Reports of her visit suggest she was much admired, and caused much interest in rural Lancashire, informing others about life in Australia. Mary was a walking and talking advertisement for the prosperity of the colonies. She and her daughters returned to Sydney the following year, where business continued to be good. Mary was even responsible for the erection of 'many elegant and substantial buildings in Macquarie Place near the King's Wharf, and in the centre of George Street'. The Reibeys were amongst the greatest families in the city of Sydney. As she aged, Mary took an active interest in charitable pursuits, donating generously to the church and schools of the colony. Mary died, wealthy and much respected, in Sydney in 1855, just a few years before her contemporary of more humble circumstances, Mary Wade.

Having reached such a peak of wealth and influence in the first half of the nineteenth century, future generations of the Reibey family settled down into less remarkable lives, though there could be little doubt that the descendents of a teenage convict from Lancashire enjoyed a comfortable middle-class existence for many generations. Her sons moved to Tasmania and continued to flourish there, engaging in shipping, trading, and banking. The Reibeys remain one of the most successful convict families in Australian history. In fact, so inspirational was the story of Mary's rise from common child horse thief to pillar of Australian society, and so long-lasting her legacy, that her story became emblematic of the benefits of the convict system, the hard work of convict settlers, and the opportunities open to all in Australia's society. More than a century after her death, Mary was one of the Australians honoured by having her likeness printed on the $10 note, where it remains to this day.

How convicts fared in New South Wales was dependent on so many factors. The ship on which a convict travelled and the date at which they arrived governed not only their own state of health upon arrival, and the labour to which they could be assigned, but the state of the colony. Earlier convicts faced harder conditions than those who came half a century later when good infrastructure was in place, and the colony was no longer facing starvation. But a fledgling colony, however hard, also offered some the opportunity to rise above their previous station and their convict background. Builders, traders and farmers could all find routes to success and prosperity as the colony developed, although such remarkable journeys were harder for later convicts, and those in later colonies, who might find themselves thrust into fully fledged societies with some of the same disadvantages as life in Britain. Those living in parts of New South Wales during the early nineteenth century had to contend with natural disasters too, such as devastating floods and raging fires which could destroy the new lives they had built for themselves. Being caught in events like these was pure luck, but, in the later years of transportation to New South Wales, better infrastructure and a larger population meant help came more easily to hand.

Not only timing and environmental factors determined a convict's experience. Personal circumstances could make all the difference to the fortune or failure of a convict, both in the penal system and afterwards. The length of a sentence obviously had a large impact on how and when an individual could begin building a post-conviction future life; so too could recreating the family and friendship networks many had been ripped from when sent to Australia. Transportation to New South Wales more often than not separated a convict from all they knew and loved. Across such a vast, and to many, seemingly insurmountable distance marriages dissolved, children were bereaved of their parents, and men and women were torn from friends, family, and all they held dear. Finding a partner, having children, or simply surrounding themselves with the familiar faces of good friends and neighbours could make all the difference to convicts beginning their lives anew. Convicts marrying free settlers may have found a rise in station much easier to achieve than those who married fellow convicts, or married no-one at all. In a society where a large proportion of the population arrived with no friends or family to depend upon, those who found new support could thrive, while those who never replaced such relationships might find it substantially harder to do so.

Of course, not all convicts were alone when they arrived in Australia. As was the case for Mary Bryant, some had children with them. Likewise, both male and female convicts in New South Wales might arrange to have their families sail out to join them as soon as permitted. There were also those convicts who found themselves transported alongside their nearest kin and closest friends; men and women who had stood in the dock with them. Being transported with friends and family from Britain was not necessarily of benefit when it came to building a new life in the colony. Ties to an old life might mean ties to old problems and old habits or complications when it came to integrating into the convict system. Even those who shared the journey with their closest relatives might find themselves unable to come to terms with the trauma of transportation.

Two sisters, two convicts

In January 1823, two teenage girls, sisters Hannah and Elizabeth Ford, stood in the dock at the Old Bailey. They were charged with stealing twenty-one silver forks and thirteen silver spoons, the property of Joseph May, from his house in Marylebone. The theft was a significant one, with the cutlery amounting to around £20 in value. Hannah and Elizabeth found a servant's entrance open and had let themselves in to the servants' floor (below stairs) of May's house in Lower Montague Street. Inside, the sisters went straight to the plate cupboard where they began stowing as much cutlery as they could about themselves. The theft was brazen and risky. If they were quick and unapprehended, they would have made a profitable theft in a few minutes, worth more money than their family could have made in a year. However, the pair were quickly discovered by an under-footman, who, despite their ruse that they were selling laces, detained them until a watchman arrived to take them into custody. In court Elizabeth, at nineteen the elder sister to sixteen-year-old Hannah, tried to take the blame for the crime entirely on her own shoulders. Elizabeth claimed that the pair really had been in May's house to sell lace to the staff, and that Hannah was trying to find the cook when Elizabeth found herself unable to resist temptation and stole the items. Elizabeth's gallantry was to no end. Both sisters were convicted and sentenced to death, commuted later to transportation for life.

Such a severe sentence for two young women seems unusual. At the sessions Elizabeth and Hannah were two of just twelve convicts sentenced to death (and two of just four women). When we look back through court records, it becomes clear that their punishment may have been related to not only the 1823 cutlery theft, but a way of arresting a burgeoning pair of criminal careers. The sisters had been in court before. Just six months previously both sisters, using the last name of Miller, had stood in the same dock, in the same court, charged with a similar offence. Hannah and Elizabeth had walked into the house of Lady Mountnorris, in the affluent Grosvenor Square in London, shortly after breakfast. While the servants busied themselves clearing away after the morning's meal, Elizabeth and Hannah collected up two silver spoons and a tablecloth. Elizabeth took the items and made her way out onto the streets, while Hannah loitered below stairs in the housekeeper's rooms, presumably looking for more items to take. When discovered, Hannah feigned that she had entered the house in order to see if any of the staff were interested in buying purses, or cotton goods. The missing spoons and table cloth were noted by the butler, and both sisters arrested. While there was not enough evidence to convict Elizabeth, who walked free, fifteen-year-old Hannah was given three months in prison.

Elizabeth was fortunate indeed not to have been convicted, as even this offence was not her first. She had been in court before in 1820, charged with stealing trousers. Although she had also been found not guilty in 1820, sometimes just a history of previous appearances in court – regardless of the outcome – was enough to call a defendant's good character into question. As it transpired, Elizabeth's good character had long been in question. She was first brought up to the Old Bailey in 1817, at the age of just thirteen. Ten-year-old Hannah was evidently too young for this first criminal outing of Elizabeth's, and instead, she was placed on trial with her friend, eleven-year-old Ann Burton. Together, Elizabeth and Ann stole a gown, three yards of calico, one apron, a handkerchief, and two towels by walking into the servant's quarters of a house and taking them. This was almost certainly Elizabeth's first conviction, but we have no way of knowing whether it was her first offence.

The Ford girls were not particularly remarkable (other than the unusually long punishment they received; it was more usual for women in this period to be given seven or fourteen years of transportation), either in their crimes or their circumstances. Hannah and Elizabeth, born at the turn of the nineteenth century, came from a poor family in Soho. Their crimes were undoubtedly a product of poverty which saw the girls lodge from an early age with extended family as their parents worked as travelling peddlers. After her 1817 conviction, Elizabeth was even sent to a home for destitute children, where she received training as a servant, an employment in which she later found a position. Nineteenth century society may have had some sympathy for impoverished children, but it had little for young adults fighting a life-long battle with chronic want, or for the impossible choices young women were often forced to make. Although Elizabeth's life found a kind of stability after her release from the home for destitute children and finding work in service, Elizabeth had been plunged back into difficulty in 1820, when she gave birth to an illegitimate daughter. Elizabeth had lost her place in service in a chain of events that in all likelihood set her, and her younger sister Hannah, on their path to the Old Bailey and, ultimately, to Australia.

It's difficult to know exactly how women like Elizabeth and Hannah felt about their transportation. A reprieve from death may have been warmly welcomed, but a life of banishment must have been a prospect greeted with mixed feelings. They would be removed from the dire poverty and the cycle of offending in which they had been stuck since childhood, and they would even be together, but they would leave everything else they knew behind. The Ford sisters were fortunate in that their transportation journey kept them together, of which there was no guarantee (by 1823, both New South Wales and Van Diemen's Land were accepting convicts, and it was infinitely possible in joint convictions for two defendants to serve sentences in different colonies). In June of 1823, six months after their conviction, Hannah and Elizabeth sailed for Sydney on board the convict ship *Mary*. Elizabeth's daughter, who shared the name of the ship, sailed with them.

On arrival at Sydney, in October 1823, Elizabeth and Hannah were sent to the north of the colony, to Parramatta, where a new 'female factory' had opened in 1821. This institution was built for the purpose of processing female convicts. Female factories were effectively receiving prisons for female convicts where they would be processed into the colony, assigned to initial labour and assessed, and after a probationary period, pending good behaviour, assigned out as servants to colonial officials and free settlers (for more information see Chapter four). Mary Ford was permitted to accompany her mother to the female factory, where convict women could care for their children until they reached four years of age.

Elizabeth's conduct was good, and she was soon given assignments in service around the rural suburbs of Sydney. Hannah too was assigned to service in the colony, but her work proved less satisfactory than her sister's, and by 1827, she had been returned to the female factory due to her poor conduct and drinking. Back at the factory Hannah was placed in third class labour (the lowest level of labour for the most disorderly convicts). Here the labour women carried out would not have been dissimilar to the laundry, sewing, knitting, and production that would come to define the female convict system in England decades later. Hannah would have been one of the women present in the factory when inmates staged a riot over poor rations and conditions in 1827.

As was typical under the convict system, both Hannah and Elizabeth were granted permission to marry whilst under sentence. Both women married fellow convicts. Elizabeth married Bryan McGrouder in 1825, who had arrived in the colony on a seven year sentence for the theft of livestock in 1819. Hannah married Thomas Matthews in 1826, a Welshman transported for life for the theft of a horse in 1825. Although both Elizabeth and Hannah managed to reform, and had no further convictions during their time in New South Wales, both sisters married men who were reconvicted, causing crises for their respective families.

Bryan McGrouder was convicted just once, a few months after his marriage to Elizabeth, and just a few months away from the expiration of his original sentence. As a convict committing an offence whilst under sentence his penalty was harsher than it would have otherwise been. For animal theft, he was sentenced not, as a free settler might have been, to months or a year in a local prison, but to three years hard labour at the penal settlement of

Port Macquarie (not to be confused with Van Diemen's Land's Macquarie Harbour). Elizabeth remained in the main colony without her husband, but with him gone she was liable to be reassigned to another settler. She was soon sent to a position on the outskirts of Sydney, to which she could not take her daughter, Mary.

Elizabeth and Mary had been fortunate enough to stay together in Parramatta until Mary was eight years old. Yet when her step-father was sent to Port Macquarie, and her mother to a new assignment, Mary was placed in the female orphan school. At the school, Mary would have received a basic education (enabling her to read and write, unlike her mother and aunt) and have been trained to undertake work as a servant, just as her mother before her in the home for destitute children in London. The parting was hard for Elizabeth, who after two months was returned to the female factory for drunkenness. She may have turned to alcohol in grief after the loss of her husband, or her daughter, or perhaps as many convicts did to break up the monotony and loneliness of their labour assignments. It would be another seven years before Mary left the orphan school and became reacquainted with her mother, step-father, and new half-siblings. The family moved north of Sydney, towards the Blue Mountains where Bryan became a farmer. Elizabeth's life seems to have been relatively calm for the next twenty years, as she and her family settled to a quiet rural existence. The family never truly escaped the poverty from which Elizabeth and Mary had come. Mary married a local ex-convict and shepherd and remained living close to her family until her death at the age of forty-three. After the death of her daughter, and her husband, after forty years in the colony, Elizabeth committed suicide at Billabong in 1863.

Elizabeth's younger sister seems to have had a similarly tragic life. Hannah Ford made a bad start in the colonies, and was unable to find stability in Australia for almost twenty years afterwards. No records indicate that Hannah reached out for the support of her sister during this time. Both Hannah and Thomas, as convicts under a life sentence, found their lives frequently disrupted by the requirements and regulations of the convict system. While Hannah was assigned out to private service miles away from her husband (in between frequent returns to the female factory for bad behaviour), Thomas laboured on the hulks at Sydney Harbour and, after absconding, in a chain gang elsewhere in the colony. Despite her marriage, and the birth of multiple children between 1829 and 1833, juggling the conditions of her freedom and family life proved impossible for Hannah, even after her Ticket-of-Leave was granted in the 1830s. In 1839 Hannah was found to be absent from the district stipulated in her Ticket-of-Leave and it was cancelled. She was returned to Parramatta away from Thomas and her children. Hannah was several times in trouble for the misuse of alcohol, and was plagued by ill health. She died in January 1841 'in consequence of the busting of certain ulcers on the leg, by means of which she had bled to death'. She was just thirty-five years old. That same year, Thomas was sent to Norfolk Island for ten years for animal theft, and died from the results of alcohol abuse a year after returning to Sydney in 1852. No records as to the fate of their two sons, aged eight and ten on Hannah's death, can be found.

Transportation was often heralded as not just a punishment, but a life alteration. Transportation uprooted convicts from the lives, associations, and circumstances that saw them offend, but it was not by default a solution to the personal and social problems that pulled men and women into crime in the first place. As the case of the Ford sisters sadly shows, a new life did not always mean a better one. Especially for those who found the practicalities of living so frequently at odds with the rules of the convict system. Transportation did provide convicts with opportunities they may never have found in England. Particularly those from large towns and cities, who might experience for the first time, fresh air, space, the chance to acquire land of their own or begin a business. Yet, transportation did little to cure the poverty and personal trauma that caused men and women to become trapped in dysfunctional lives, whatever side of the world they were on.

Just as the deprivations and chaos caused by poverty could follow convicts as they attempted to reconstruct their shattered lives in Australia, so could privilege. Although in colonising Australia the British had the opportunity to start society anew across the world, the familiar problems caused by class, ingrained privilege, and prejudice were transported alongside the convicts. For the majority of offenders this meant that they would still find little understanding for their problems and disadvantages from convict establishment staff and colonial magistrates. For a select few, however, all the benefits of class, education, and status from home could be reproduced in the colony. At least the firsttime around. The small number of well-to-do offenders who made the voyage to Australia found ways to bend the system to their favour.

A swindler, a pickpocket, a gentleman

Just as with their famed contemporaries facing tough justice at home on Britain's gallows, tales of the transported captured the imagination of the

British public. In its early years, transportation to Australia was perceived as so extreme, and so unknown, that the voyages of otherwise ordinary convicts became suddenly extraordinary, and every bit as good as fiction. Rumours of 'savages', starvation, and the unyielding bush gave Australia's convicts a noticeably more dramatic backdrop than those that had gone to America before them. The lives of some of Britain's earliest Australian transportees provided easy fodder for a curious public, and proved every bit as fantastical as something Dickens or Defoe created.

James Hardy Vaux (Image 11) was born in Surrey in 1782, a year after his parents, Hardy and Sophia, married. Although Vaux contended that his mother's family were of notable social standing, both of his parents were somewhere between the upper-working-class and lower-middle-class of the time. From the age of three, Vaux lived with his maternal grandparents in Shropshire. While living with his grandparents, Vaux attended both a preparatory school and then a seminary, where he received both a general and religious education. By his own account, Vaux lived a happy and largely unremarkable childhood in the care of his grandparents. At nine, Vaux and his grandparents moved to London to live with his parents (with whom Vaux had experienced very little contact) who were running their own hosiery business. Shortly after arrival, Vaux was placed in a boarding school in Surrey. At age fourteen, Vaux came to the end of his formal education and, with little money left for his upkeep, was apprenticed to Swan and Parker, drapers (cloth merchants) of Liverpool.

Apprenticeships were a common way for young men to learn a trade or profession. A typical apprenticeship would last for a term of seven years in which an apprentice would live and serve his master in return for bed and board and a small yearly sum paid to his family. Life as an apprentice could be hard. Apprentices would work long hours at menial, unpleasant, or difficult tasks, and often found themselves subjected to strict discipline. After only a few weeks as an apprentice, Vaux struck up a friendship with an older boy by the name of King, already several years into his own apprenticeship with the drapers. Along with King and his associates, Vaux began breaching the terms of his apprenticeship, staying out beyond his curfew, gambling at cockfighting, drinking, and visiting brothels. He began to steal small sums of money from his employers in order to fund his gambling. The thefts were soon noticed, and after just five months in his apprenticeship, Vaux was dismissed.

The teenage Vaux moved alone to London, and through his grandfather's connections secured work as a copying-clerk. His wage was small and his mode of life soon far outstripped his income. After a few months, Vaux was dismissed from his work as a clerk for poor conduct and found better paying work with a stationers. However, he continued to accumulate debts. Vaux moved lodgings frequently and purchased clothing and other goods on credit, knowing that as a minor he would not be arrested. He continued to gamble and associate with questionable company.

Vaux contested in his memoirs that before his first conviction, he was involved in several illegal activities in a bid to raise funds to support his profligate lifestyle. On several occasions Vaux claimed to have had great success at fraudulently acquiring charitable donations in Portsmouth, where he stayed for a time. Whatever money Vaux had managed to raise through his family, short spells of clerical work, and the charitable donations of strangers was quickly squandered. He left Portsmouth for London once again, leaving a trail of debts in his wake and using his respectable name and high level of education to obtain employment.

Vaux worked for a short period as a midshipman on board the naval ship *Astraea*, but found himself a better sailor in theory than in practice. After a few months at sea, finding himself incompatible with the tasks of a midshipman and the biting cold of winter, Vaux deserted his post and returned to London. Leaving his most valuable possessions behind on his ship, unable to send for them at the risk of apprehension, Vaux began raising money by pawning his remaining belongings, until there was nothing left on which to live. To support himself, Vaux contends that he became a billiards sharp alongside a group of other young men, setting up false matches between themselves where it appeared they were wealthy but somewhat hapless players, in order to entice in less experienced gamblers hoping for an easy win. Finding such gambling insufficient to support his lifestyle, Vaux turned to various forms of property crime – obtaining goods by false pretences, theft, and feloniously pawning.

By his late teens, Vaux even claimed to be part of a gang carrying out 'buzzing' (picking pockets), 'sneaking' (robbing carts or carriages), 'hoisting'(entering a dwelling or commercial property unobserved and stealing whatever was most readily available), 'pinching' (shoplifting), 'jumping' (uttering counterfeit coin or banknotes), 'spanking' (breaking a shop window and stealing the contents of the display), 'the order racket', (defrauding errand boys and porters by false pretences), and even 'the snuff racket' (throwing snuff into the face of a shopkeeper and making away with whatever cash or goods were within reach). All in all, Vaux spent almost four years moving in and out of the capital and the home counties, perpetrating various frauds and offences and working in administrative jobs for a few weeks at a time to raise funds. Despite recalling several brushes with the law, and apprehension for these crimes in his later accounts, Vaux was never prosecuted for any of these early offences.

If his memoirs faithfully recall his criminal exploits, there is a strong class dynamic to his experiences. As an educated young man from a respectable and relatively affluent family, Vaux would have been treated as a gentleman, even by constables and those he defrauded. Social customs in the eighteenth century were far more predisposed to give sympathy and the benefit of the doubt to a 'respectable' felon than a common working-class street thief. There is also the suggestion, both in Vaux's autobiography and in subsequent trial reports, that victims were less willing to prosecute those who robbed or defrauded them knowing that a conviction might lead to a capital sentence.

It wasn't until 1800, at the age of around eighteen, that Vaux's luck ran out and a case was brought against him in court. Remarkably, given the high value and audacious scams and thefts that Vaux claimed to have been perpetrating since the age of fifteen, the offence that brought him to court was the theft of a single handkerchief. His victim, William Dewell, testified that while he was standing in a crowd in Cheapside, both Vaux and his associate Alexander Bromley put their hands into his pocket and pulled out a handkerchief, a statement corroborated by witnesses. Within a few moments, Dewell noticed the missing item, and Vaux and Bromley were apprehended.

Vaux fervently denied the charge, stating in his account that he knew nothing of the robbery until he was apprehended. Vaux declared himself innocent and claimed he made no attempt to flee when bystanders called for him to be detained. Vaux hired counsel to defend him at trial, a luxury few defendants could afford. His co-defendant produced four witnesses to come and testify to his good character, and Vaux even managed to find two. Unfortunately, both men were found guilty of stealing goods worth just eleven pence and sentenced to be transported for seven years.

There were several witnesses who could attest to the crime, and despite his denials it seems likely that Vaux did take part in the offence. Vaux's staunch denial, almost two decades later in his memoirs, seems strange, given the number of crimes he boasts of having committed before conviction. His unwillingness to confess to the theft of the handkerchief may well have been a product of the crime not suiting the narrative of exceptional swindles and glamorous thievery on which his reputation had been based. Picking pockets in a crowd was, after all, the resort of 'common' criminals, of which Vaux did not consider himself to be one.

Through the intervention of his family, Vaux was held in Newgate, rather than the dreaded hulks, until the time of his departure. While his co-defendant Alexander Bromley languished for years in the hulks, Vaux was placed on board the convict ship *Nile*, ready for voyage to Australia. Vaux made himself useful on the voyage and secured extra privileges by offering his clerking services to keep the captain's log, journal, and accounts. Privilege could be found at every step of the convict journey for those with the skills and right background. The ship set sail in early June, and at the end of August the boat arrived at Rio de Janeiro to take on fresh supplies, before finally arriving at Sydney in December 1801.

While the majority of prisoners arriving on the *Nile* were sent 'up the country' to carry out hard physical labour outside of Sydney, Vaux was sent to the town of Hawkesbury to act as clerk to a storekeeper there. The settlement at Sydney was more than a decade old when Vaux arrived but other sites in the colony, as well as travel to and from them, could still prove dangerous. Large swathes of the bush were still unconquered in 1800, and tensions continued to run high between colonialists and the Aboriginal population. Vaux noted:

> I joined a party of travellers, accompanied by a cart in which I had deposited my luggage; these persons formed a sort of caravan, and were all well-armed, the natives being at this time in a state of warfare, and the roads thereby rendered dangerous.

Vaux passed three years of his sentence in service to Mr Baker at Hawkesbury, and when not at work was permitted to live in his own lodgings and socialise freely. Vaux was fortunate to serve almost half of his seven-year sentence in this way. Had he continued for another year, he may well have become eligible for a Ticket-of-Leave and been able to establish himself in business in the colony. However, after three years he was recalled to Sydney to take up a role as a clerk in the secretary's office of Government House. A prestigious post. On his return to the capital, Vaux found it to be 'a vortex of dissipation, folly, and wickedness ... compared to my late place of abode' and soon fell in to bad habits with other clerks in the office, drinking in the daytime, frittering money (which he was privileged to earn as a convict) and once again gathering mounting debts. Astonishingly, even this bad behaviour was not enough to lose him his position in government offices. This didn't happen until Vaux was discovered to have been embezzling funds from the office, a crime which he confessed under threat of twenty-five lashes of the whip.

Punishing convicts like Vaux, already under sentence, was a difficult balancing act for the early Australian authorities. Making a regime so punitive it was deemed to be unjust risked plunging the thriving colony back into the misery and disorder of its early years. However, too much lenience risked the loss of control over a large population of convicts – among them violent and dangerous criminals only too ready to take advantage of a weakness in authority. As such, whilst capital punishment and re-transportation to sites of secondary punishment (like Port Macquarie and Norfolk Island) were used to punish the very worst crimes of convicts under sentence, they could not be used in all cases. Vaux's status as a 'gentleman' felon undoubtedly saved him from the worst outcomes. He was, however, in punishment for his crime, placed in irons and set to hard labour in a 'chain gang', one of the lowest classes of labour for convicts in New South Wales. Gangs of chained convicts were forced to labour on public works, especially road building, and incarcerated in a prison each night when not working. Not only was this a severe loss of the liberty that Vaux had enjoyed under sentence for three years, but gang work was also hard, heavy, and long, and would have come as a shock to the bookish Vaux. He recalled:

> As I had never before used a heavier tool than a goose-quill I found this penance to bear hard upon me, and repented me of the evil which had brought me to this woeful condition.

Vaux was stationed in the suburb of Castle Hill, north of Sydney, to carry out his hard labour. When not at work his liberty was strictly curtailed. Unable to obtain a pass to travel to Parramatta (where he had acquaintances from his years as a clerk), Vaux took the risk of un-sanctioned travel, which was classed as absconding by the authorities. Lists of convicts deserting their posts was circulated amongst constables throughout New South Wales, and Vaux contends that on several occasions on his weekly visits to Parramatta, he was apprehended and punished with flogging. After ten months of hard labour, a position as a clerk became available at Castle Hill, and Vaux, being the most literate and experienced of his fellow convicts, was appointed. This relieved him of the back breaking work of the chain gang. Vaux's new role put him, although a convict, in a position of considerable authority. He was not only responsible for apportioning the land to be worked by convict gangs daily, and measuring their progress (individual convicts and entire gangs could be punished for failure to complete work), but he was also responsible for the Monday convict muster (checking all convicts were accounted for and ready for duty) and issuing weekend passes so that convicts were at liberty to travel elsewhere in the colony.

In 1806, with only a year left of his sentence, Vaux's work as a clerk at Castle Hill had gained him favourable attentions elsewhere in the colony. The chief magistrate of Parramatta, Reverend Marsden, contracted Vaux to help in the production of a muster for the entire colony. In quick succession, Vaux was appointed clerk to Reverend Marsden, and given an office and comfortable lodgings in the court house at Parramatta. He was also, astonishingly, provided with a government servant (assistant) and a housekeeper of his own. In addition Vaux was paid not only a small weekly sum for his employment, but was also able to collect fees from his various public duties, allowing him a comfortable living – all still while under sentence. Vaux, a convict himself, played an important role in the administration of colonial justice and weekly court sittings. Vaux's work was deemed by Marsden to be of such high quality that Marsden arranged for the remaining months of his sentence to be remitted, and offered him a post in his service that would allow him to travel back to England with the Marsden family later that year. Vaux, eager to return home but, like many ex-convicts, unlikely to ever raise the money for his own passage, jumped at the chance.

In February of 1807, Vaux boarded the passenger ship *Buffalo* as a free man, along with Reverend Marsden and Philip King, the governor of New South Wales. Vaux found the journey home to be equally as arduous as his initial transportation, as the entire crew and passenger population suffered from a lack of provisions, saw their daily rations reduced as food ran out or was lost to spoilage through rats and cockroaches. After a brief stop in South America, Vaux and the others landed back in England at Falmouth in early November 1807, just over seven years from the day of his conviction. While other passengers were allowed to disembark and make for home, Vaux had been enticed to join the navy by Governor King, and was required to journey on to Portsmouth.

Within a few days of arrival at Portsmouth, Vaux had deserted the navy and made for London, where he was able to reunite with his mother and sisters. Vaux was able to obtain employment as a legal clerk at Crown Offices in London, for which he received a generous wage of two guineas a week. Many ex-convicts who managed to return to England did so with the intention of living law abiding lives. However, ex-convicts often found on their return that the economic circumstances and social circles that had contributed to their previous convictions remained. For many, much less fortunate than Vaux, beginning a new life free of crime post-transportation was much more complex than it seemed. Not only could poverty be just as acute as before, but the convict 'stain' on their reputations could intensify previous hardships. Vaux was one of a fortunate few who had a stable family and a good living on his return to London. Yet even he was not immune from falling back into old habits when reunited with acquaintances from his former life.

In 1808, Vaux met by chance Alexander Bromley, with whom he had been convicted in 1800, and was soon induced back into petty thievery. He met a local prostitute, Mary Ann Thomas, soon after and married her in July of 1808, in St Paul's church, Covent Garden. Mary was already pregnant at the time, and gave birth to their son later that year, who died just a few days later. In November of 1808, Vaux had a narrow escape from the law when he was placed on trial once again at the Old Bailey (using the name of James Hardy to avoid identification with his previous conviction) for stealing a silver snuff box. He was acquitted due to lack of evidence. Vaux himself noted:

> I was fortunately not known by any of the turnkeys or officers of the court, who never fail, when an old face appears, to give private intimation to the judge, if (which is very rare) he should not recognise the party.

Vaux later lamented his acquittal from this offence, given that the penalty for his guilt may have only been seven years. Instead, a newly free Vaux embroiled himself in a much more serious crime. Having made the acquaintance of two young jewel thieves while awaiting trial in Newgate, upon release Vaux was almost immediately put in touch with their contacts on the outside, and convinced to engage in jewellery robbery. A week to the day from his appearance at the Old Bailey, Vaux walked into the shop of a jeweller, Mr Bilger, and requested to see a number of diamond set articles. While Bilger was distracted serving another customer, Vaux pocketed three diamond rings, a brooch, and a lady's clasp, which he sold a short time later to a pawnbroker. Despite Vaux's initial pleasure at the success of the venture, almost two months later, the pawnbroker to whom Vaux had sold the articles betrayed him to the authorities. He was detained in Tothillfields prison, until his trial on 15 February 1809, using the name James Lowe (his grandfather's surname). Both Bilger and the pawnbroker testified to the offence, and Vaux was unable to find anyone to testify to his good character, having survived almost entirely on the proceeds of crime since his return from Australia. A further witness stated:

> My lord, I think it my duty to inform the court what I know of the prisoner at the bar. I have been given to understand that he is a very old offender and that he has been but a few months returned from Botany Bay!

The value of the crime was so high, and the knowledge of Vaux's criminal record so damning, that when found guilty, Vaux was sentenced to death. When asked his age, Vaux, twenty-seven at the time, stated that he was nineteen, knowing that mercy was more likely to be granted to a youth than an older habitual criminal. With help, a week or so after his conviction Vaux petitioned for mercy and after eleven weeks in the condemned cells with other capital convicts, he was finally granted a reprieve of his death sentence, on the condition that he be transported back to Australia for the term of his natural life. Vaux would have the chance to earn a Conditional Pardon in the colony, and to live again as a free man. Yet, a sentence of life rendered it highly unlikely that Vaux would ever be permitted to return to England again.

Vaux accepted his fate and was keen to board a vessel for sail as swiftly as possible as he:

> was not in circumstances to subsist for any length of time in a prison; and wished if possible to avoid going to the hulks, as I had been fortunate enough to do on my first transportation.

Only those with the financial means were able to obtain preferential accommodation and treatment in Newgate, otherwise being left at the mercy of the fetid conditions, meagre rations, and whims of the gaolers. Unlike his last confinement, Vaux no longer had relatives willing to bribe a clerk to put him directly on a convict ship's list, and so he found himself for the first time at the mercy of the convict system.

His wife Mary, Vaux recalled, was keen to accompany her husband into exile. While arrangements could be made for the wives and children of male convicts to travel to Australia as free passengers on board ships, Mary Vaux was not deemed to warrant sufficient kindness. Being a young woman with no children, her application to join Vaux was denied, the authorities no doubt expecting that she would have the ability to support herself after his departure. With no money or influence, Vaux was also unsuccessful in having himself transferred to the convict ship *Ann*, which left England in August 1809. Instead, Vaux was transferred to the *Retribution* hulk moored at Woolwich.

Vaux was not the only convict on board facing his second stint of transportation. He noted:

> I soon met with many of my old Botany Bay acquaintances, who were all eager to offer me their friendship and services; that is, with a view to rob me of what little I had … [in such a place] all former friendships are dissolved.

The brutal reality of the hulks saw otherwise ordinary men driven to extremes as they fought for resources, space, and survival (see Chapter one). Each morning, Vaux would be shipped ashore to labour on public works, much like the gang labour he had despised back in Sydney. His labour would conclude at sunset, at which time he would be secured below decks for the night. Mary managed to obtain permission to visit her husband approximately once a month during this time. Vaux passed a year on the *Retribution*, suffering poor food and dangerous company, before he was taken aboard the *Indian* in June 1810. On board he joined 200 fellow convicts from England and Scotland, including some soldiers under sentence after court martial. The majority of prisoners, like Vaux, were facing a life sentence. In July of 1810, the *Indian* set sail for New South Wales. Vaux had been unable to see his wife before departure, and the two would never meet again.

Once sailing for Australia, circumstances improved notably for Vaux. His experience and education was again brought to the attention of the captain, and he was released from irons and appointed to assist the ship's steward in issuing and logging provisions, and to assist the captain in keeping his logs. His role earned him special favour, and Vaux enjoyed a more comfortable voyage than the majority of his fellow convicts. The voyage took them via Madeira and Rio de Janeiro for supplies, before arriving in Sydney in December of 1810, less than four years after his departure from the same spot as a free man.

Even in his few years away, Vaux found the regime at Sydney changed. The new governor had replaced most colonial government staff, leaving Vaux with few acquaintances he could call upon for favour. Moreover, as a returning convict, his character was doubly damaged, allowing him less benefit of the doubt than those fresh off the boat. Instead of being assigned a privileged clerical post, as he had been lucky to receive on his first arrival, Vaux was taken straight to Parramatta with other convicts, and assigned to service with a free settler – John Benn. Free settlers who paid the government of New South Wales to have a convict assigned to them were allowed to put such a prisoner to any work they saw fit, and had only to provide them with bed and board in return. Much to his outrage, Vaux was put to hard labour on Benn's farm, breaking sun-baked ground with a hoe. Convicts who refused to carry out their master's instructions could be punished by local authorities, and when Vaux voiced his objection to hard labour, he was threatened with a flogging. Vaux was ordered to serve Benn for a period of three years, at which point he became eligible for re-assignment, or for a Ticket-of-Leave.

However, after only five weeks of 'laborious work in the field or some drudgery about the house, from morning till evening and sleeping in a barn over-run with vermin at night', Vaux feigned illness in order to have himself sent to the general hospital back in Sydney. Vaux spent a month in the hospital, during which time Benn obtained another convict for his service, effectively releasing Vaux who was assigned to a work-gang labouring in Sydney for a few weeks before he was promoted to overseer of the gang. As overseer, Vaux did not have to reside nightly in the barracks (Image 12 & 13) with the other convicts, and was at liberty to socialise with other convicts in service to government officials in Sydney. In doing so he almost immediately became embroiled in a case of theft – some money and a watch – from a colonial official, and was sent back to labour in a chain gang on public works for a term of twelve months. After only three weeks, with no explanation, Vaux was placed in double irons on board a ship, and sent down the river to Newcastle, a much feared penal settlement 100 miles north of Sydney. Newcastle had a reputation as the fate of the most unruly, dangerous, or habitually offending convicts who were sent there to carry out hard labour in coal mines, or cutting timber. It was the place of which Margaret Catchpole had written with much trepidation.

Places like Newcastle were intended to be harsher environments than the main penal settlement in Sydney. Here, in Newcastle, armed guards kept constant watch over prisoners, labour was hard and long and rations were tightly controlled. Unlike regular convicts, those at sites of secondary punishments did not have the opportunity to socialise with the free population (and thus trade for supplies and provisions) nor to indulge in leisure when not at work. Sites like Newcastle were remote and surrounded by inhospitable bush, making desertion too difficult and dangerous for most convicts to attempt, although some might try.

On arrival at Newcastle, Vaux was set to carting coal out of the mines. Aside from the hard physical demands of such a task, work in the mines carried significant health risks, from coal dust which damaged the eyes, skin, and lungs, to the dangers of injury from runaway carts, and cave-ins. Serving a life-term, Vaux was lucky to only spend two years labouring in the coal mines – he could have been required to do so for five or ten years, or even indefinitely if his behaviour was judged to be poor enough. After two years, Vaux returned to Sydney, and unable to find any colonial official willing to give him a position as a clerk, he attempted to abscond from the colony on board a ship bound for Bombay. He was found, along with more than twenty other stowaway convicts, and given fifty lashes of the whip as punishment. Most of the captured convicts were sent back to their regular employment, but Vaux, a known trouble maker, was transported back to the Newcastle settlement for another year. There, by remarkable luck, the storekeeper was in need of a clerk, and Vaux was appointed to the post. Vaux stayed as clerk in Newcastle for four years, where he hoped his continued good conduct would allow him, if he ever returned to Sydney, to obtain a more preferable situation.

All records indicate that Vaux's conduct at Newcastle after his return was exemplary, apart from a bigamous marriage to Frances Sharkey in 1818. Vaux was still married to Mary when he wed Frances. His new wife was a convict from Dublin, granted a Certificate of Freedom in 1814, the year Vaux arrived in Newcastle. Fortunately for him, Vaux's bigamy, like that of many others who began new lives in Australia, was never discovered. He even struck up a friendship with Thomas Thompson, commandant of Newcastle penal settlement, and Justice of the Peace for that area. It was Thompson who persuaded Vaux to write his memoirs, which he completed in 1817. Vaux dedicated his memoirs to Thompson:

> The humble tribute of my thanks, for the many favours I have received at your hands; for the indulgent treatment I have generally experienced; and more particularly for the distinguished honour you have conferred on so unworthy an object as myself.

It was doubtless thanks to the recommendations of Thomas Thompson that Vaux was given a Conditional Pardon in 1820, having served ten years of his life sentence. The pardon effectively enabled Vaux to live as a free settler in the colony, providing he committed no further offences. Because Vaux was transported for life, he was not permitted to leave the colony, as his sentence would never truly expire. Any further conviction would come not only with its own punishment, but would also result in the reinstatement of his life sentence too.

Vaux and his new wife returned to Sydney and within a year he was employed as a clerk in the Colonial Secretary's Office. For six years, Vaux lived as a respectable member of Sydney society. He owned land, had a comfortable income of around £166 per annum, and even subscribed to various charitable and religious funds. Vaux developed a reputation as a reliable, amiable, man with many surprised that such an educated and professional man could be a pardoned convict. He was even described in *The Sydney Monitor* as 'a quiet civil man: no blackguard'. Vaux had finally settled into the law–abiding life that had eluded him in Britain. It was not to last.

Vaux was suddenly sacked from his government position in December 1826, with no reason given other than it had come to Governor Macquarie's attention that he was a former convict who had been transported twice. As such, he could be dismissed with no cause other than his bad character. Vaux rallied against the injustice in the papers, but received little sympathy. He found work for three years with an ironmonger, Mr Iredale, and married for a third time, to Eleanor Bateman in Parramatta in 1827, before making the risky decision to flee to Ireland. No account was ever given for why Vaux escaped the colony, but perhaps he sensed that life in New South Wales was unlikely to afford many lucrative opportunities after his fall from grace. Vaux's journey to Ireland was an illegal act. He was returning from transportation: a felony.

In less than a year, Vaux was back to his old trick of forging banknotes, which were soon discovered. He was placed on trial in Ireland and pleaded guilty. He was sentenced to return to New South Wales for seven years. He was transported on the *Waterloo*, his third voyage in just over twenty years. As an escaped convict, Vaux was not eligible to return to the main penal colony. Having absconded on his Conditional Pardon from a life sentence, on return to New South Wales his previous sentence was reinstated and to make matters worse he would be required to serve it at Port Macquarie, another site of secondary punishment.

Even in the early nineteenth century, life rarely meant life and he was again conditionally pardoned after six years – a year short of serving his full third sentence. Vaux was granted his Ticket-of-Leave in 1836, although a story was circulated that the ticket was fraudulent, and that he was to be immediately apprehended if seen, and brought to Hyde Park Barracks. This mix up, *The Australian* newspaper reported, may have been due to some offence he gave to the colonial secretary after his dismissal from post ten years previously. The Ticket-of-Leave was eventually found to be genuine, and Vaux returned to Sydney under a Conditional Pardon in 1837. He soon found work as a clerk to Mr Wood, a wine merchant.

Less than two years after arriving back in Sydney, Vaux was on trial at the Supreme Court, charged with committing an indecent assault on eight-year-old Ann Arundel. Despite his denials, and testimony of several witnesses to his good character, Vaux's attempts to offer a cash sum to Arundel's father to let the matter drop was taken as proof of his guilt. Vaux was sentenced to two years' imprisonment. The assault on Ann Arundel was not in keeping with Vaux's previous criminal career, nor his propensity to plead guilty to offences. The victim in such cases is to be believed in the face of contradictory evidence, and so we must assume his guilt. However, Vaux's offer of payment may have been as much about avoiding a trial, in which he doubted he would receive a fair hearing, as an admission of guilt.

On his first transportation, Vaux had found Sydney a tolerant place and the system easy to navigate. Somewhere a convict might easily serve his time and move on to a new life. Yet after several reconvictions, and two more terms of transportation, it became clear that the convict stain could be hard to remove. Even for a convict with as privileged a background as his. Vaux found that convict history could be used to defame a defendant even decades later. Vaux's convict history was far richer than most.

Vaux would have been released in 1841, but no further records of his life in Australia are available. He was not convicted again, nor did he play a role in public life as he had previously. Vaux may have died, being around sixty years of age, although as a 'celebrity' convict it is surprising that this was never reported. He may have returned to Britain and lived again under a false name as he had in 1830, though as discovery may well have led to him spending the rest of his life in a site of secondary punishment, at the age of sixty, it is questionable how likely he would have been to take this course of action. What is most likely is that Vaux, on release from prison after a conviction for child abuse, made a quiet life for himself elsewhere in the colony of New South Wales, possibly adopting a new name, giving friends, neighbours, and employers no hint of the famed celebrity convict who lived in their midst, and who had once been so proud to share his story with the world.

One door closes as another one opens

From just the few examples we have seen here, the convicts who arrived in New South Wales were every bit as tough and resilient as their surroundings.

More so than in either of the later colonies, the convicts who arrived in New South Wales truly faced the unknown, and survived some of the toughest journeys to get there. What's more, after arriving in a strange and hostile land, convicts still found the resources to build lives for themselves, to excel, find stability, or even to plot escape. The experience of transportation to New South Wales was also more variable than it was in later colonies. The tents on the beaches that housed the first arrivals would have been unrecognisable to the last convicts who arrived in Sydney in 1840 and found a thriving city full of grand buildings and prosperous businesses.

The story of New South Wales was, broadly speaking, a journey from obscurity to prosperity. One that was mirrored by some of the convicts that found themselves there. Of course, not all prospered. There were those who managed to survive the convict regime, and carve out a hard life of agricultural work as free men and women, and those who went onto lead lives similar to those they would have back in Britain – lives of petty crime, of drunkenness and clashing with authority. Many men and women were unable to overcome the psychological impact of their dislocation, or the experiences of hardship they had in the colony.

There could however, be benefits to life in New South Wales. When crops prospered and rations were forthcoming, convicts had an abundant supply of fresh fruit and vegetables. There was space, sunshine, and fresh air, things lacking from the lives of those brought up in London's slums or the industrial heartlands of Britain. Governor Hunter once proudly proclaimed 'there is not a more healthy country in the world than that [Australia], nor a more beautiful one'. Life in Australia could hardly fail to be an improvement from the hell of the hulks and prisons left behind at home.

Certainly, by the 1820s, the worst deprivations of early settlement were over, and Sydney was already looking forward to a post-convict era. The reputation of transportation in New South Wales markedly improved as the nineteenth century progressed. At least, that was, in comparison to the second of Australia's three great penal settlements, just two decades old, which had cultivated its own fearsome reputation. Compared to the reports coming from Van Diemen's Land of starvation, exhausting labour, isolation, harsh discipline and even cannibalism, Sydney must have looked from a distance more than ever like a sunny paradise.

Chapter 4

Sent Down South: Van Diemen's Land 1803–1856

lmost twenty years after the settlement of New South Wales the British established their first military outpost on a ragged little island off the south-eastern coast of mainland Australia. The settlement of a small military detachment and a handful of convicts arrived in 1803. Their arrival was, in no small part, an attempt to prevent colonisation by foreign powers. Both the French and Spanish had been sailing around the island and charting the Bass Straight (the body of land separating the north coast of Tasmania from mainland Australia). For two decades, Van Diemen's Land was not a separate administrative colony; its central governance was directed from New South Wales.

The year after its initial settlement, a few hundred convicts from a failed attempt to create a new penal settlement in Port Philip (Victoria) joined the military settlement. In the years after that, more convicts came from Sydney and from Norfolk Island. Van Diemen's Land, as it transpired, was a useful overspill facility for the excess of convicts on the mainland in New South Wales. The first ships bringing convicts direct from Britain to the island did not arrive for more than a decade after the first prisoners, but as the Napoleonic war came to a close, ships from Britain and Ireland began depositing convicts on Van Diemen's Land's shores.

For five decades, until the colony suspended transportation in 1853, Van Diemen's Land was one of Britain's primary penal colonies, receiving around 75,000 convicts. After the suspension of convict transportation to New South Wales in 1840, Van Diemen's Land spent a decade as Australia's main penal colony (having separated into its own administrative colony in 1825).

The British may have had almost twenty years of experience in running an Australian penal colony by the time they began a new settlement in Van Diemen's Land, but the early years on the island were just as hard as those faced by the First Fleet. The initial settlement at Risdon Cove proved inadequate to sustain its convict community, and a new site was selected on the west of the Derwent River as Sullivan's Cove. The settlement became known as Hobart Town, and remains the capital of present-day Tasmania.

Early British settlers found the land harsh and hard to clear. Ships bearing provisions came only seldom from the mainland, which meant that rations were poor, and had to be subsidised with what little flora and fauna the island had to offer. On arrival, convicts were immediately put to the task of clearing ground, and ploughing and sewing what little agricultural land they could salvage. Convicts grew crops if they could, and raised livestock, and hunted for meat on the island. The unluckiest and most poorly behaved convicts were set to work in chain gangs clearing ground, constructing roads and bridges and buildings essential to the colony's survival. During the creation of the colony on Van Diemen's Land, almost all of the indigenous peoples on the island were forcibly removed or killed.

The main penal settlement at Hobart was not felt sufficiently equipped to deal with the colony's worst and most habitual offenders. In 1822 Macquarie Harbour, a penal settlement for secondary punishment, was established on the island, followed the next decade by Port Arthur, a small peninsula to the south-east of Hobart. These places became notorious sites of misery, degradation and death. Their harsh regimes and psychological and physical torment were intended to inspire such horror that convicts in the main colony would be dissuaded from committing further offences, and that resident offenders would be ground into submission to the law. Those sent to Macquarie Harbour (predominantly men, with only a few female convicts to carry out duties in hospital, laundry, and domestic positions) were engaged in logging and shipbuilding, often kept in irons, and could be subjected to brutal floggings for any law breaking or regulatory infractions. Macquarie Harbour was difficult to access by sea, and had no road access to other parts of the colony inland, and so starvation and disease could be rife amongst prisoners.

It is unsurprising that many convicts at the settlement dreamed of escape, but with no way of leaving the island by sea, and nowhere to go inland, convicts had little option but to resort to ranging in the hostile bush, hunting kangaroos, and doing whatever they could to survive. Alexander Pearce was one of the Harbour's most famed escapees. Alexander was convicted as a shoe thief at the Sessions in County Armagh, Ireland, in 1819 and sentenced to be transported for seven years. He sailed aboard the ship *Castle Forbes*. A 'pock-pitted' man who stood just five feet three inches tall, Pearce did not take to life in Van Diemen's Land. In 1822, having committed various misdemeanours whilst under sentence, he absconded from the colony. When he was apprehended just two months later, he was sent to Macquarie Harbour as punishment. Shortly after arriving, Pearce and seven others escaped from the settlement whilst on work assignment. The men wandered in the wilderness for two weeks, with no food and only sporadic access to fresh water.

Nearing starvation, the men drew lots and selected one of their number to be killed in order to feed the rest. After this, three of the men attempted to make their way back to the penal station to hand themselves in. Suffering under the lash for their escape would be far less brutal than killing, or being killed, to feed their fellows. Pearce and the rest continued into the bush. They killed another member of their party for food, which left three of the men remaining. Another died of a snakebite soon after and provided food for Pearce, and his only remaining compatriot, Robert Greenhill. There was just one axe between the two starving men, and ultimately, Pearce survived by killing Greenhill and eating him. Somehow, Pearce survived in the bush, raiding Aboriginal camps for food until he came upon British settlers. Joining two other convicts on the run, Pearce was at large for almost four months.

He was apprehended and returned to Macquarie Harbour, the authorities at first refusing to believe his story of cannibalism. Evidently, his fellow convicts were sceptical of the tale too. In 1824, Pearce made another escape from the Harbour, this time with fellow convict Thomas Cox. Both men were heavily ironed, and had nothing with them but the axes they had been put to work with. According to *Hobart Town Gazette*, when the prisoners got to the King River and Pearce discovered that Cox could not swim, he attacked him with an axe, eventually killing him. With his former comrade dead on the ground in front of him, the paper reported:

> He then cut a piece off one thigh which he roasted and ate; and, after putting another piece in his pocket, he swam across the river, with an intent to reach Port Dalrymple.

Apparently wracked with remorse, Pearce soon turned back and surrendered himself, and the grizzly fate of Cox came to light. Pearce had not merely cut flesh from the thigh, he had butchered the man. Witnesses found Cox's mutilated body with much of the flesh and organs removed; the head and hands had also been removed from the body. When asked how he could have done such a thing, Pearce was reported to have answered simply, 'No person can tell what he will do when driven to hunger.' From escape to surrender, Pearce had been gone just one week. He had murdered Cox within a few days of leaving the settlement. Pearce was hanged for his crime, and his exploits commemorated in songs, a novel, and even in the twentieth century, a film. He was by no means the only man to commit such atrocities living outside of the law on the tiny island. Just two years later, Thomas Jeffries, a Scottish convict, was hanged after weeks on the run from Launceston Gaol which had involved murder, rape, robbery, and cannibalism.

Macquarie Harbour, and another site of secondary punishment, Maria Island, were both closed by 1833, and their convict populations transferred to a new, and much longer-lasting penal station at Port Arthur. Port Arthur was another logging station on the opposite side of the island to Macquarie Harbour, where convicts in work gangs carried out the backbreaking work of cutting and moving timber. Port Arthur was larger than previous sites of secondary punishment, and within just a few years of opening had more than 1,000 'incorrigible' offenders were stationed there. The early regime at Port Arthur was as punitive and draconian as its predecessors, with many reported floggings for minor infractions. After the first decade or so of operation, the system at Port Arthur shifted to more closely mirror the penal estate back in Britain in which psychological methods, like solitary confinement and silent association, were favoured over physical correction. Convicts were put to work building their own penal estate. They constructed a chapel and penitentiary (Image 14).

Like those that had gone before, Port Arthur was thought near impossible to abscond from, surrounded by (supposedly shark infested) water, with the perimeter manned by guards and dogs. Escape was not impossible, but rare. The majority of those sent to Port Arthur were convicts who had been convicted of crimes after arriving in the colony. These men (again, only a skeletal number of convict women were taken to Port Arthur to carry out domestic duties) for the most part served their time in order and solitude, hoping to survive the brutal regime and earn their freedom. More than one offender, though, would return time and again to the site, finding their criminal careers outlived even this most feared of penal stations.

A burglar's life

Mark Jeffrey was a big man, with a big appetite and a temper to match. Mark spent the majority of his life living in a penal settlement, and was one of the most famous prisoners ever to arrive in Van Diemen's Land (Image 15). His fame was in part due to his uncontrollable temper and constant appearances in court, and in his later years for the autobiography he produced titled *A Burglar's Life*. Mark's account, one of the few from a convict, prided itself not only on recounting the 'facts' of his life, but also giving a rare insight into 'the dark days of convictism in Australia' in the words – or purportedly so – of a convict himself.

Mark was born in Cambridgeshire in 1825, one of six children. His father was a gardener and agricultural labourer, a trade his son would one day turn to his own advantage. In later life, by Mark's account, his father was also a destitute drunkard. At the age of fifteen Mark left home with his younger brother Luke to find agricultural work elsewhere in the county. Life was hard for Mark and his brother. The young boys were effectively living as adults, moving around the country as work demanded. During this period, they became acquainted with an older man, known to them as 'Wicksty', who convinced them to join him in travelling the country and hawking personal wares like razors, belts, knives, and stockings.

After a few months of work, finding their new associate to be of 'intemperate habits', the Jeffrey brothers parted company with Wicksty, and continued their trade alone. In the following years, Mark moved around Lincolnshire, Lancashire, and Yorkshire. He returned home to Cambridgeshire in 1845 and found that his parents had separated. Their mother was living with a new man, another abusive drunk, and their family had disbanded. With nothing to keep them at home, Mark and Luke resumed their work as travelling 'cheap jacks' across England for the next few years. By this time, Mark had grown in both size and temper from his fifteen-year-old self. By the mid-1840s Mark was five feet eleven inches tall (remarkable for a time when men were regularly only five and a half feet tall) and more than fifteen stone in weight. As he moved around London and the home counties, Mark became a keen boxer, and a drinker. Mark took great pride in his physical prowess and his autobiography is filled with accounts of the various men he beat in fights as he travelled about the country. In 1848, when travelling back through Cambridge, Mark and Luke met with an old acquaintance, Thomas Hart, with whom the brothers conspired to make fast money by committing a burglary.

It may have been that Mark and Luke Jeffrey had been treading the line between legal and illegal activity for some time before the burglaries. It was not unknown for hawkers and street sellers to make a good profit in trading in stolen goods. However, until this time, the pair had never before been in trouble with the law. According to Mark, an initial spate of burglaries against farmers and land owners in Cambridgeshire, Bedfordshire, and Norfolk went well and the men avoided detection, but the profits of their raids were quickly squandered on drink, gambling, and prostitutes. Despite efforts to conjure up images of glamour and valour in the recounting of his early life,

Mark, Luke, and their accomplices committed dangerous and violent crimes. Their luck at avoiding detection did not last long. Mark and Luke Jeffrey were convicted, alongside Thomas Hart and his brother John, of burglary with violence against Henry Mitchell at Haddenham in Buckinghamshire. Henry Mitchell was threatened by Mark Jeffrey at gunpoint, and tied up alongside his wife and young child. Mark himself admitted, 'I ordered him to be quiet instantly, threatening to blow his brains out if he made any trouble for us.' Mitchell did as he was bid, and escaped the terrifying ordeal without further harm. The group made away with sixty pounds in cash, and other items. The gang separated, with Mark and the Hart brothers going their separate ways, intending to meet up at a later date.

Mark managed to avoid apprehension for some time, travelling through Cambridgeshire, staying at a variety of pubs and lodging houses. However, as with any joint enterprise, Mark's own discretion was not enough to ensure his safety. On the road, he began to hear reports of two men incriminating themselves in a robbery, having retained jewellery and other trinkets from the crime. Fearing their capture would lead to his own, Mark kept moving nightly from pub to pub, but ultimately in vain. The police had been pursuing Mark and the other suspects since the robbery was reported, and he was finally apprehended in Bedfordshire around a week later. Mark was taken to a magistrate at Ely, just a few miles from where the robbery had occurred, where he was reunited with Luke and the Hart brothers.

Mark was confined whilst awaiting trial, which he claims saw him become 'for a time totally deranged.' Mark was not a man who enjoyed imprisonment. He noted:

> I was tortured by my confinement – at being deprived of the sweets of liberty and enjoyment – and the rough, unsubstantial fare, after my former good living irritated me beyond measure.

This is perhaps the most telling of all Mark's musings about captivity. It was not the last time he would claim to be driven to distraction by lack of adequate food. Hunger would prove to be one of the most destructive forces in his life. When Mark was hungry he claimed:

> My rage and hatred towards my gaolers became ungovernable, and I bore a stronger resemblance, in my impotent wrath, to a caged beast than to a human being.

Mark quickly made a name for himself inside the prison, arguing with and even assaulting his gaolers over the lack of food. He was placed in solitary confinement on several occasions. In solitary confinement Mark was violent and caused serious damage to prison property. He was placed in restraints for twenty-four hours at a time, and had his diet even further reduced to nothing but bread and water. For the entirety of his remand as he awaited trial Mark was caught in a cycle of destructive behaviour, a pattern that would repeat itself over the course of his life. To try and contain his violent behaviour, Mark's mother began visiting the gaol and bringing him extra food at her own expense.

Mark and his brother were some of the few defendants lucky enough to be able to engage the services of a defence lawyer when they came to trial. Yet even his lawyer was hard pressed to provide a defence for not one, but fifteen burglaries committed by Mark, after his co-offender John Hart had turned evidence against the rest of the gang in hope of a more favourable sentence. Mark and the others were found guilty, and were lucky to escape the penalty of death, given the violent nature of their crimes. The judge, taking into account the youth of the defendants, sentenced them all to be transported. Mark remembered:

> Fifteen years' transportation appeared to me equal to being consigned to a living grave. What a vista of utter misery and torture stretched before me. Surely death itself would be thrice welcome before the enforcement of such a life.

Mark and the others were then transferred to Milbank Prison, the reception prison for men awaiting transportation, where he laboured for nine months before he was transferred to the *Warrior* hulk moored at Woolwich. John Hart died in Milbank, and Thomas Hart and Luke were transferred to Portland Prison, and later on to Western Australia (See Chapter five).

Mark had been comparatively happy at Millbank, with light labour, plenty of food, and the opportunity for education and religious life. Existence on the hulks was considerably worse, not least when it came to Mark's primary preoccupation – food. Although Mark's writing had a flair for both the dramatic and self-pity, his observations about the corruption of the hulk system were echoed by more than a few prisoners who found themselves in this unhappy place. From a poor family and with no friends on the outside to advocate on his behalf, Mark found himself at the bottom of the convict heap.

Mark's complaints to the hulk attendants and anyone else who would listen fell on deaf ears. Although, we might assume in part to keep him quiet, Mark was assigned labour in the cook house of the hulk. A position in such close proximity to the food he craved led Mark into disagreements with other cooks when it came to the watering down of gruel. His fractious conduct in the cook house resulted in punishments, and more time spent in solitary confinement on a bread and water diet. When not undergoing punishment, Mark was reassigned away from the kitchens to labour in the dockyards at Woolwich. He recalled, 'I was cold and hungry and despairing.'

Mark's situation came to a head in May of 1849, less than a year after his trial. Returning from a morning's labour in the dockyard, Mark was shipped back to the hulk for dinner. After eating, Mark attempted to transfer himself into another labouring group after hearing a rumour that they were to receive a portion of beer. He was found out, and sent back to his own group to return to the dockyard. When he arrived there, he refused to pick up tools and work. Second Mate Joseph Allen, in charge of Mark's work party, informed him that if he failed to do as he was told, he would be placed back in solitary confinement. As Allen turned his back on Mark, who was standing a few yards away, he testified to feeling 'a tremendous blow on the back of the head'. Allen was knocked to the ground, stunned. As his senses came back, he watched Mark strike out at Henry Masterman – the overseer of the hulk – with a plank of wood. Masterman pulled his head out of the way just in time, sustaining a hit to the arm as he raised it in defence. Mark was only disarmed at the end of a bayonet, where he expressed satisfaction with the attack on Joseph Allen, who lay bleeding on the floor. He was placed in irons and taken to a cell.

The following month he was taken to the Old Bailey to answer charges of wounding and intent to maim and disable. Mark admitted to the crime, but contested he should not be convicted on the grounds of his ill treatment on the hulks, testifying, 'I did not get sufficient food to support my human nature', and further complaining that all of his objections to his treatment had been ignored. Officers of the hulk and the ship's surgeon all testified that Mark's treatment and rations were no worse than that of any other prisoner, and that they considered rations to be sufficient enough to maintain prisoners at hard labour. Mark was found to be guilty of the offence, and his existing sentence of transportation for fourteen years was upgraded. Mark was set to be transported for life. Given the opportunity to address the court, Mark protested his sentence. He asked not to be freed, but rather to be sentenced to hang instead of returned to the hulks. Mark recalled making the following petition directly to the judge:

> Life in gaol is worse than torture to me, and I long for hanging, so as to be removed from such a cowardly, tyrannical mass of humanity as that in authority over the helpless prisoner. I call upon your honour to carry out the law to its fullest extent. It is your duty to do so, and if I had the means I would shoot you at the present moment and so make sure of what I most desire – the gallows.

Mark was returned to imprisonment and in the following weeks repeated this desire to die in several petitions. There was little doubt now, to the officers of the hulk, that Mark was not only a troublesome prisoner, but a dangerous one. A man who longed to be hanged had little to fear from committing further crimes. The easiest solution to prisoners like Mark was to send them to Australia with as much haste as could be arranged. Just six months after his second trial, Mark was loaded on board the convict ship *Eliza* and bound for Van Diemen's Land. However, due to the nature of his crime (a double conviction, and a history of violence against convict establishment staff), Mark was not unloaded in Hobart with the rest of the convicts, and was instead transported to Norfolk Island.

Arriving in the colony's autumn months, the 'savage grandure' of Van Diemen's Land that Mark had spotted whilst anchored off shore, with its 'sylvan glades' and 'health giving breezes', had been a 'bitter disappointment' to him. When he arrived at Norfolk Island, despite the knowledge that the regime at this penal settlement was harsher than that to be expected in Hobart, Mark found himself delighted:

> The tropical isle shone out in the rays of the sun like earthly paradise. The sumptuous colours and glow of the rich foliage of the tropics dazzled the eye, and the colours of fragrant blossoms were delightful.

Mark had been given a record of good conduct by the ship's doctor that delivered him to the island, and after a few nights in the convict barracks, he was assigned to the house of a colonial clerk to work as a gardener. This was a favourable assignment of those available to the doubly convicted men and hardened recidivists that made up the island's prisoner population. For many, days at Norfolk Island were spent wearing heavy irons and labouring in a quarry gang.

Regulations at the settlement were strict, and infractions punished harshly with floggings and punitive labour assignments. Mark managed to navigate the first few months there without trouble. Food was abundant, and his work easy enough. Although, from almost his arrival, Mark suffered from regular bouts of dysentery (common in the heat and insanitary conditions of the convict establishment) which would plague his time on Norfolk Island. Mark was told that it his good conduct continued he would be recommended for a Ticket-of-Leave in just two years. When his master's cook was replaced with a new man, however, a familiar obstacle appeared on his path to a successful life in the colonies. The new cook provided neither the quantity nor quality of food that Mark required to satisfy his enormous appetite.

One evening, in a row over dinner, Mark struck the cook and knocked him to the ground. When the man refused to get up, Mark proceeded to beat him almost to death. Remarkably, Mark only had to serve a few months labour in light irons for the infraction, but at the same time his chances of quickly acquiring a Ticket-of-Leave disappeared. He even managed, some months after the punishment was served, to find himself promoted to 'sub-constable' in the colony, and put to work supervising other convicts in a lumber yard. His newfound powers did not last. When he was found asleep on duty, Mark was dismissed from the police and placed in solitary confinement on punishment rations.

In the months that followed, Mark imagined himself frequently at odds with fellow convicts, and men in positions of authority all over the colony. By his own account, he escaped serious trouble several times, either by his own cleverly conceived schemes, or by thwarting various enemies who attempted to have him convicted of various crimes without cause. The truth of many of Mark's dealings in the colony are lost to history. He did however, move assignments several times, carrying out labouring roles and a number of service jobs with different masters, until he was transferred, due to his misconduct, to the dreaded quarry gang. Here, Mark spent every day in irons, transporting heavy stones. He quarrelled frequently with the overseer of the gang, and was placed in and out of solitary confinement. Mark claims on one occasion to have been sentenced to fifty lashes of the whip, and placed in 'heavy' irons, weighing fifty-six pounds which he wore day in and day out for seven weeks, fed only on starvation rations. After almost two months, Mark's irons were removed and he was taken to the hospital where he stayed for three months to recover.

Mark remained at Norfolk Island until the settlement was abandoned in 1853, as transportation to Van Diemen's Land from Britain was suspended. The convicts from the island, almost all serving long sentences for serious offences, were not freed, but transferred instead to Port Arthur. At Port Arthur, Mark was first assigned to farm labour and then, given his experience, assigned to be gardener for the resident chaplain, avoiding the hard labour undertaken by some at the settlement. Mark was tasked with tending the chaplain's potato crop and, as an incentive for a job well done, was told he could take ten per cent of the profits from selling the produce he grew. With crops selling well to those out in the Victorian goldfields, Mark had the opportunity to acquire a good income – the first he had made since leaving England.

In 1854, Mark had almost served the mandatory six years required of a life-sentence prisoner to obtain a Ticket-of-Leave (recently reduced from twelve years as Van Diemen's Land eagerly raced towards its post-convict era). Mark travelled from Port Arthur to Hobart Town gaol for a few days and then on to finish his probation on a work assignment. He was released from the gaol and sent to a settler twelve miles outside of Hobart Town, where he was once again put to farming. Despite having a number of quarrels with his master, after his first harvest season on the farm, he was given his Ticket-of-Leave.

Mark returned to Hobart. He used the money he had earned in his last assignment to buy clothing and provisions, the first things he had owned in the colony. Obtaining his Ticket-of-Leave did not remove Mark totally from the convict system, but did confer on him a level of freedom far and above that he had experienced at Port Arthur and Norfolk Island. Mark was entitled to be paid for his labour, and could socialise and barter with others in the colony as long as he committed no further crimes or regulatory infractions, and providing that he stayed in the colony and met a curfew each evening.

However, quite predictably, Mark's Ticket was revoked in 1856 when, after a night of drinking, he found himself in an altercation with a police magistrate, slapping the man across the face. With his Ticket revoked, Mark's original convict status was re-instated, and he was returned to labour at Port Arthur for another eighteen months. Mark wrote:

> Opportunities had offered themselves to redeem the ignominious name I bore – to elevate my standpoint in the battle of life – but these advantages I had thoughtlessly spurned, and I was thrust deeper than ever into the dangerous complications surrounding on every side a protracted term of enforced imprisonment in the companionship of other hardened criminals.

Back at Port Arthur, Mark was put to hard labour. He remembered:

> I was placed in one of the hardest-worked gangs of the settlement –
> that known as the wood gang – where the prisoners were employed
> to fell trees, cut them into two feet lengths, split them into billets,
> and stack the wood in divisions...

If Mark or one of the other convicts failed to complete the required wood
cutting quota each day, they would be punished with solitary confinement.
After four months, Mark was appointed as a delegate in the cook house of
the settlement. His job was to assist the cook, and ensure that rations were
shared equally amongst the men. Almost immediately on reporting to the
kitchen, Mark quarrelled with the cook and was reported for refusing to
work. Mark's conduct earned him an extension of six months on his sentence
during which he was sent to the new prison (modelled on the regime of the
convict institutions in Britain) to serve. Mark was confined to a separate cell,
and communication with the other prisoners was prohibited. At exercise,
Mark recalled how he and the other convict men were required to wear masks
to obscure their identities to prevent friendships forming between convicts.

On appealing to the governor of the settlement, his additional sentence
was cancelled and he was sent to a remote location away from Port Arthur
to undertake more woodcutting work. However, a short time later after a
fight with a Ticket-of-Leave holder named Moreton, Mark was taken back
to the settlement to serve a month of solitary confinement on bread and
water. Mark was granted a second Ticket-of-Leave and returned to Hobart
in 1857. Mark undertook various jobs around the colony. Other than a six
month stay in hospital after developing ulcers on his leg, which would pain
him intermittently for the rest of his life, Mark stayed out of trouble for
almost five years.

Mark's autobiography notes only that between 1861 and 1871 he 'made
several journeys between Port Arthur and Hobart Town with the object of
improving my condition in life, but I was at last compelled to relinquish
that attempt'. Other records indicate that he spent a decade in a cycle of
perpetual offending. Renewed trouble began for Mark in 1862, when one
August evening he was seen by a passerby to be 'hauling a female about
... molesting the female against her will'. When the passer-by intervened,
Mark struck him down, and was sentenced to three months hard labour
for the offence. It later transpired that when apprehended for striking the
passer by, Mark had turned his violence on the arresting constable. For this,

he was given additional time at hard labour. The following year he received two weeks in the house of correction for disturbing the peace and using bad language in public. Two years later he was sent to prison for a month for the same offence, and given another two months for assaulting the constable that tried to apprehend him for it. In 1867, Mark attacked a man named George Davies who lived in the same lodging house as him, knocking him to the ground and beating him with a fire poker. Mark was sent to prison for another two months. Soon after release he was sent back to prison for another three months for disturbing the peace. The following year Mark was imprisoned again for the same term after being found fighting in the street. In February 1869, he received two months for breaking five panes of glass in a pub window when drunk, and another month for assaulting the constable who arrested him. At the end of that same year, he was sent to prison for three more months for disturbing the peace.

Mark was considered by the authorities of Hobart to be a dangerous man and a perpetual nuisance. The above are just a few of the petty public–order crimes for which he was apprehended and imprisoned. Small infractions soon led to a serious crime in 1871, more than twenty years and a dozen convictions after his arrival in the colony. Mark had been drinking in a pub with a man by the name of James Hunt, when Hunt insulted Mark by calling him a 'Port Arthur Flagellator'. A a dispute between the two ensued. Mark knocked Hunt to the ground, and kicked his body repeatedly. Hunt died a little over a week later at Hobart Infirmary from a ruptured bladder and other injuries. In early 1872, Mark was put on trial for murder, found guilty of manslaughter, and sentenced to be returned to Port Arthur, for life.

Mark was almost fifty when he arrived back at Port Arthur under his second life-sentence. His ulcerated leg was in such poor condition that he was taken straight to the hospital where he remained for three months until it was somewhat recovered. Mark spent a year back in the penitentiary in a separate cell. When discharged, he was put to hard labour, but the ulcers on his leg returned, and he was taken back to the solitary cells of the prison. Even in his incapacitated state, Mark continued to prove a troublesome prisoner. He was eventually sent to the 'Island of the Dead', a small plot of land where dead convicts and prison guards were buried. On this small island, Mark occupied a solitary hut and when his health permitted, dug graves and maintained the grounds. His years on the Island of the Dead were some of the most orderly in his entire life. He committed few infractions and had little opportunity for quarrelling with prison staff or other convicts. Mark achieved amongst the dead what he had struggled to find amongst the living, peace and stability. Mark recalled his days tending the island as some of his happiest.

Mark was only removed from the Island of the Dead in 1877 when Port Arthur was closed, more than two decades after the end of the convict system to which it belonged. Mark and many other prisoners were transferred to Hobart Penitentiary. Mark's health had declined to the point where he was essentially bedridden, and he was admitted to the hospital wing. Mark petitioned constantly for freedom, but his record spoke against him. He eventually was granted a Ticket-of-Leave in 1890, but was fit only to be transferred to the Launceston Invalid Depot. It was here that he penned his autobiography, writing of the depot:

> Here I still remain in a degree of comfort and contentment, living in the fond hope that the freedom my heart had long yearned for will be returned to me.

Mark's autobiography was published in 1893, after which his health sharply declined. In the final year of his life, he was said to have favoured the phrase 'I have given my life; read it and see how I have suffered.' It is undeniable that Mark's life was one of suffering. He did not flourish in the penal colony, settle into freedom, or manage, until ill health prevented his offending, to reform. He died at the age of almost seventy at the Launceston Invalid Depot in 1894. His was a sad end to a rather sad life. Mark was not a typical convict, nor was his life, in and out of Van Diemen's Land's penal system, representative of most experiences. It is because of its very remarkable nature that we have the opportunity, more than a century later, to read in such depth about his life. Mark undoubtedly suffered at the hands of British justice, and in the punitive regime of the Australian penal penal colonies. However, much of his misery and suffering was borne as much from his own temper and poor decision making as it was by the draconian regime of Norfolk Island, Port Arthur, and Hobart's penal institutions.

Second chances and second sentences

Transportation was a steep price to pay for many of the relatively minor crimes for which convicts were sentenced. However, life in Australia could open up a world of new opportunities for convict men and women. After the expiration of their sentence, convicts in Van Diemen's Land would have the chance to find paying work; some were given land grants, and many would eventually integrate into free settler society. Some might manage to build stable lives that lasted for years or decades after the expiration of their sentence. Unfortunately, convicts beyond the seas faced many of the same issues that hampered offenders' reform back in Britain. Not least was a complicated and destabilising association with a large network of other offenders. Once on the slippery slope of reoffending, former convicts (already at a disadvantage when it came to securing work and housing) fell further down the social scale, and might end up perpetrating crimes much more serious than those for which they were transported.

George Langley was little more than a boy when his journey began. Langley was just thirteen the first time he found himself in trouble with the law. He was the son of a tailor, living with his parents and four younger sisters in St Pancras, London. At the beginning of December 1841, George had found work as an errand boy for Mr Pouchee, a stationer who ran a business off of Tottenham Court Road, just a mile away from the family's lodgings. As well as general fetching and carrying for his master, George was entrusted with collecting accounts for his employer. He would be sent with a bill to a customer who owed money and was expected to bring the payments he received back. George was in post for just one week, and in that short time, he collected over thirty-eight shillings in payments. However, he failed to return any of the money to Mr Pouchee.

George was from a working-class family who would have been considered respectable, but by no means affluent. His wages – had he kept the job long enough to receive any – would have been small and in all likelihood co-opted quickly into the family coffers. Thirty-eight shillings would be more than a boy like George could expect to see for an entire year of work. It is easy to understand that a young boy with access to so much money found temptation hard to resist. When George failed to deliver the collected debts to his employer, Mr Pouchee was immediately suspicious and went to the Langley home. Along with George's father he searched the boy's room. In the foot of a sock Mr Pouchee and Mr Langley discovered a five shilling piece, and a half sovereign.

Initially George tried to explain that he had lost some of the collection money and was intending to save up the missing amount until he could pay Mr Pouchee back. When he saw his audience was unconvinced, he next tried to explain that he had met a distressed boy in the street and given him some of the money out of charity. Noting that George had a new great-coat, no doubt purchased with the illicit funds, Mr Pouchee called for a constable and had the boy taken into custody. Despite being only thirteen George was sent for a full criminal trial at the Old Bailey. The trial was short and the evidence against him conclusive. George pleaded for mercy, stating 'If you will forgive me this once, I will never come before you again.' George was not forgiven, but he was recommended to mercy, most likely on account of his youth and previous good character. As such he was sentenced to two months of confinement and a whipping.

George would have served his time in an adult prison, mixing with a range of more experienced offenders. If his whipping was carried out, he would have experienced perhaps ten, twelve or twenty lashes before being turned out onto the streets. The punishment would have been a brutalising experience for a fully grown man, let alone an adolescent boy. On release, George would have found it difficult to find further work on account of his tarnished character. After these experiences it is perhaps unsurprising that four months later George was again back at the Old Bailey. This time he was charged with stealing nine forks and a pair of sugar tongs with a combined value of £8. George was still an inexperienced offender and after a fairly unsophisticated deception, he had been quickly apprehended and taken to the police station. Although he denied ever being in the house from which the goods were stolen, he candidly asked the arresting constable 'Do you think I shall be transported?' He also asked the constable not to mention his former conviction, promising to turn himself over to the Marine Society (an organisation that gave poor boys naval training) when he went free. In court, George had no such luck. Evidence of his current offence and his former crime were submitted to the court and he was found guilty. At fourteen years of age, George was sentenced to be transported for ten years. George spent almost two weeks waiting in Newgate before he was transferred to the *Euryalus* hulk at Chatham. He waited on the hulk for five months before transfer to the convict ship *John Renwick*. He set sail for Van Diemen's Land in November 1842. The ship travelled via South Africa, arriving in Australia in April of 1843.

George settled into the convict routine with minimal disruption, though he was found to be a little disobedient and on one occasion was punished for misconduct with seven days' solitary confinement. Otherwise, he passed his time quietly and was approved for a Ticket-of-Leave halfway through his sentence, in 1847. The Ticket-of-Leave allowed him to live outside the convict establishment, and to find paying work, which he did. His Conditional Pardon was granted in 1850 – meaning if he remained out of trouble he could live as a free man. In 1853 his sentence expired and twenty-four-year-old

George was unconditionally free. It was around this time that Langley met Maria Miller, another expired convict, and the pair began cohabiting. Although never formally married, Maria became Langley's wife in all but legal document.

George had served his time and was still a young man. The potential of a new life free from the past awaited him. Unfortunately, George was one of a not insignificant number of convicts who found the transition from convict life difficult to manage. It is hard to say with any certainty why some offenders found it difficult to reform. It may be that their lives and offences would have continued in much the same way even if they had faced prison in Britain rather than transportation in Australia. In other cases, however, it was the emotional trauma of transportation that set their later lives on a disrupted path. Whilst some flourished in the colonies – away from old homes, old temptations, and old habits – others found being dislocated from support networks of friends and family, and everything familiar, difficult to navigate. The overuse of alcohol, vagrancy, and further offending were not uncommon amongst released convicts. George, who had spent his adolescence under the strict control of the convict system, may have found it harder than most to adjust to life as a free man.

Whilst under his original sentence, George had begun working as a sawyer for timber merchant Mr Wilson. By all reports, George was a good and reliable worker. He worked in the same position for seven years. In 1855, two years after his sentence expired, however, George was charged with stealing timber from his employer. It may have been financial pressures, or personal issues that caused George to take the timber, or simply an opportunity too good to resist. The presiding judge seemed as shocked by the crime as Mr Wilson and his son, who stated in court that throughout their association with George Langley they 'never knew anything dishonest of him'. George protested his innocence but was found guilty. In sentencing him, the judge noted that George had only had a few minor brushes with the law during his decade in Australia, and that he sympathised with George's wishes to provide for his wife and children. However, even with a passable character, the judge felt he had little choice but to sentence George to hard labour in Hobart Prison for eighteen months. George was only two months into his sentence when he absconded from the prison barracks while working in a labour gang at a nearby orphan school. He was recaptured after a few days and the episode served only to make his sentence longer.

After eventual release, George's life entered a period of stability. He continued living with Maria, and avoided any further convictions. The couple moved from Hobart to begin afresh in a settlement in rural Tasmania. They relocated to a logging community in Oyster Cove. Here, George began to associate with a number of other former convicts, and fell into old routines. In February 1865, in the company of a Maurice Fitzgerald, George was fined for disturbing the peace, and the following month, with Fitzgerald again, he was convicted of stealing a chain from Alfred Fowler. A short time after these relatively minor convictions, the company George kept took a more sinister turn.

In August of 1867 George acted as witness for the prosecution in a murder trial. He and Maria had been at the home of a fellow ex-convict and timber worker, John Dunn. George testified that he and Maria had visited the Dunns for dinner and while they remained sober, both John Dunn and his wife Jane were drunk. John Dunn had been sleeping on the floor, and when he woke in a disorientated state, he picked up a nearby hammer and threw it in a random direction – unwittingly hitting his wife on the forehead. Jane apparently cried out 'oh dear' before falling insensible and dying twelve hours later. Although George testified that he had witnessed no violence or quarrelling between the Dunns on the day of Jane's death, his testimony hinted at the fact that the Dunns had a volatile relationship. Dunn was convicted of his wife's manslaughter and given eight years penal servitude. George and Maria remained living in Oyster Cove. Six years later, however, history was to repeat itself when George himself stood in court accused of a murder. In an almost unbelievable turn of events, the victim was George's wife, Maria.

On 31 May 1873 Maria had spent the night drinking at a local pub, and George had arrived some time in that evening to bring her home. Maria had a history of drinking to excess, and the night she and George left the pub was no exception. Witnesses noted that she was 'the worse for liquor'. The pair quarrelled as George tried to force her home and Maria resisted. Later that night Maria was seen lying on the side of the main road halfway between the pub and the Langley's hut. Maria was heard by a witness to call out in the dark 'Oh George, don't kick me.' While his wife was crying out, George went to a nearby house and asked those inside for assistance for his wife, who he claimed, 'was feeble and unable to get along'. The men followed him to Maria's location, but on arriving discovered that she was dead. George Langley was said to be in a state of disbelief and distress at the sight, weeping bitterly and telling witnesses that Maria wandered away from him when he went in search of light for their journey. However, a post-mortem carried out on Maria two days later concluded that she had died from a number of violent blows to the abdomen. Langley was immediately taken into custody.

At trial, George did not contest that, in a fit of anger, he had repeatedly kicked Maria, and that he was responsible for her death. His only defence was that he had not intended to kill her. George explained that Maria had been a drunken woman for most of their twenty-year relationship. Despite their troubled circumstances George claimed to always have treated Maria well, and remained adamant that he would never have intended to kill her. Sympathy for George or, more likely, a lack of sympathy for Maria (at this time it would be difficult for a known drunken and 'troublesome' ex-convict woman to illicit much sympathy from a court) saw the jury take just forty minutes to return a verdict of manslaughter against him. George had been in Australia thirty years. He had spent ten as a convict, and twenty as a free man. The scales were rebalanced as he was sent to Port Arthur for a further ten years of imprisonment (Image 16).

George's sentence was remitted in 1877 when Port Arthur closed, and he was released that year, having served less than half of his time. Nothing more is known about George after his release. Reoffending and return to incarceration was a constant spectre in the lives of those released on a Ticket-of-Leave, and even after their original sentences expired. Convict men and women could, and did, carry the stain of how they arrived in Australia with them for all of their lives. Yet petty thefts and public nuisance was a far more common pathway to a secondary sentence than serious or violent crimes. Many of these crimes were not planned, but simply part of disrupted existence in which ex-convicts might find that work was sporadic, support networks loose, and drink freely available. In such circumstances, especially for those with a shadow already cast over their reputations, trouble was easy to find.

The surprising journey of Julia Rigby

As we've already seen, life for convicts after transportation could be a time of optimism and opportunity, as well as trouble. Early convicts in New South Wales were already rising to great esteem, carving out their place as founders of the nation by the time the first convicts arrived in Van Diemen's Land. The convict era of Van Diemen's Land might be more famous for its torturous sites of secondary punishment, and the fearsome outlaws who escaped their chains and lived wild in the bush, than its success stories. But there were many nonetheless. Convict success should not only be measured in the contribution former prisoners made to the colonies after their sentences expired, nor the fame or wealth accrued in later life. For some convicts, success came in the form of living happy, stable lives free from reconviction and in building families and businesses and a stake in their community. In changing their start in life, and ending their journeys in far better circumstances than they began.

Julia Rigby (Image 17) grew up in Lambeth, South London, but had actually been born at sea in 1829. Julia would next step foot on a boat twenty years later when, once again, a new life would begin. Little is known about Julia's early years. She was likely from a poor family, and while her mother, Ellen, and brothers, William, James, and Edward, are all listed as her next of kin on official records, there is no mention of Julia's father. There is no record of Julia's employment, only of the living she made by picking pockets, or stealing from shops. Julia was only a young woman when she pleaded guilty to stealing a watch from the person of Frederick Armytage at the Old Bailey in August of 1850.

Both the victim himself and a police constable had seen her pick Armytage's pocket while clinging to him, asking if he wanted to buy her a drink (a common tactic of both prostitutes and thieves, looking for easy prey in the evenings). With key eye witnesses, a verdict of not-guilty was unlikely should she go to trial. Although Julia was only twenty-one, she had reason to be fearful of facing a severe punishment. There were other convictions known by the court against her. Cumulatively, Julia had served several years in prison. She spent ten days in prison for her first offence as a teenager after stealing gingham (fabric). Then she served fifteen months for stealing a watch and chain, another two years for stealing another watch, and three months with hard labour in Brixton prison in 1848 for the theft of twenty shillings' worth of flannel. Prior to her latest offence, Julia had been convicted just months before, in March 1850, for receiving stolen goods, for which she served another three months.

Julia's criminal career stretched back to her mid-teens and she had only been out of prison two months when indicted for the theft from Fred Armytage. To the court there would have been little doubt as to her 'bad' character, and she could probably have expected to be punished with the full force the law would allow. Julia chose not to go to trial and pleaded guilty to the offence. Saving the court the time and money of a trial in this way often meant an offender could expect a more favourable sentence. Julia may have been hoping for this. There is also evidence to suggest that she pleaded guilty in an attempt to save her lover, William, who was accused alongside her.

By pleading guilty and avoiding a trial, Julia took responsibility for the theft and was dealt with swiftly. She was sentenced to be transported for seven years. William Jones, with whom she lived 'as man and wife', had been with her that evening, likely picking out victims for her to target and receiving the stolen items when she was done. William opted to plead not guilty to the charge and went to trial. In court he denied all knowledge of the crime, and even that he had been with Julia. He was found guilty in taking part in the robbery, but given just twelve months imprisonment for his role. The two would never see each other again.

Four months later, Julia sailed for Van Diemen's Land aboard the *Emma Eugenia*. By the time she arrived in the colony in March 1851, her accomplice had less than six months of his sentence left to serve. On arrival in Australia, Julia claimed to be a housemaid, although this was unlikely to be true, due to her repeated spells in prison throughout her working-age life. She was five feet tall, fresh faced, with dark brown eyes, and a string of letters and numbers tattooed on her left forearm, commemorating the initials of loved ones, and her criminal history. The most recent were two characters '7 Y' denoting the journey she had just begun. The tattoo was most likely done while in prison awaiting the ship, or on the voyage itself.

After bad behaviour throughout the journey, Julia was taken to Cascades Female Factory, where she spent three months under supervision. She was assigned labour in the summer of 1851, but returned to the factory to undertake three months of hard labour later that year for insolence. After being re-assigned following her punishment, Julia was relatively well behaved during her time in the convict system. She was returned to hard labour for a month on just one occasion, in 1852, after being found to have money concealed on her person.

While on work assignment, Julia met Joseph Lodge, a fellow convict, and the pair were granted permission to marry in 1853. Joseph, a Yorkshireman, had been transported to the colony in 1842 aboard the *Marquis of Hastings* for a term of fifteen years. He had been found guilty of murder (a case of the victim's mistaken identity and a quarrel over a missing hat). Joseph had a wife and children back in Yorkshire, whose fate at the time he married Julia is not known. Julia was granted her Ticket-of-Leave in 1854, three years before the expiration of her sentence. Her Conditional Pardon followed in 1856 (Joseph had received his in 1851). The pair went on to have seven children in the next fourteen years, and eventually settled on land they were granted in Tunbridge, roughly sixty miles each way between the major settlements of Hobart and Launceston.

Julia's record read like that of a convict who would easily slip back into reoffending after the expiration of her sentence. She had a significant record of offending before transportation, had exhibited troublesome behaviour under sentence and had married a fellow convict, a murderer and a bigamist. Yet despite their criminal pasts, Julia and Joseph, a pickpocket and a murderer, built good lives together. Tunbridge was a busy coaching town, providing accommodation and supplies for those travelling between two major settlements. The Lodges were a testament to the penal ideals of transportation; that by displacing convicts from their former lives, rather than just disciplining them and turning them loose at home, they were given the chance for a new start. An opportunity to build new, law-abiding lives.

It certainly seems that Julia and Joseph seized this chance. They were by all accounts respected members of their community. Joseph's testimony on the drunk misconduct of a local police officer was key in his removal from post, Julia acted as witness in a case for theft, and Joseph was well known in the district as a fair employer and a reliable workman. They created lives simply out of reach of many British convicts rebuilding their lives on home soil.

Julia only ever came to the attention of the authorities again once, in 1870, when she visited an old friend from her convict days, Ann Reed, back in Hobart. Reed, like Julia, was now an innkeeper. After a couple of drinks together at Reed's establishment, the Tasmania Arms, a fight took place between the two women in a dispute over money, which Julia said that Ann Reed and her husband had stolen. The case dragged on in court for over a week, with Reed prosecuting Julia for assault, and Julia bringing a counter-suit. The case was quickly and mysteriously settled when Reed agreed to pay Julia compensation to the sum of sixteen pounds. Julia returned to Tunbridge, her business, her family, and her law-abiding life.

Julia lived the last years of her life in peace and obscurity. She died at the age of forty-seven at her inn in Tunbridge in 1878, after a short illness. She was respectably buried in Tunbridge and mourned by family and friends. Julia's life was a story of two halves, each beginning at sea. She had been a thief and pickpocket, a fallen woman living with a man outside the bonds of marriage, and would have undoubtedly been seen as part of the feared 'criminal class' at home in England. Julia would have seemed like a prime candidate for recidivism and a disorderly life in the colonies. Yet after her transportation Julia formed a family, became a property holder, a businesswoman, and pillar of her community. Julia's journey beyond the seas was remarkable, but not in its length or hardship nor particularly its impact on history. Her journey was remarkable because she travelled from poverty to prosperity, and from ruin to lasting respectability – much more than many of the girls raised in London's slums could ever have expected, let alone a convict.

Female factories

Records of the convict system in Van Diemen's Land survived far better than those of its predecessor. Modern-day Tasmania boasts a rich and well documented convict history, revealing stories from the lives of its convicts both while they were under sentence and afterward. Yet despite the abundance of evidence available, histories of Van Diemen's Land's female convicts, like Julia, have received scant attention when compared to its male population. Despite there being a dedicated Female Convict Research Centre (more details can be found at the back of this book) in Tasmania bringing the experience of convict women to light, their history is still largely dependent on the research and enthusiasm of volunteers and convict descendants.

The scarcity of female convict narratives from Van Diemen's Land is made all the more astonishing given that it was the final British penal settlement for women, and one with an extensive carceral network developed specifically for them. 'Female factories' were the local name for a series of houses of correction throughout Van Diemen's Land that housed female convicts for a variety of reasons. There were female factories in the colony's capital Hobart and nearby Cascades, as well as sites in depots at George Town, Launceston, and Ross. Altogether, these institutions were in operation from the 1820s until the end of penal transportation in 1856 when the colony began self-government under the name of Tasmania.

The factories had three primary functions. They housed convict women newly arrived in the colonies until they could be assigned a work placement (a significant change to the idleness and wandering experienced by unassigned women, like Margaret Catchpole, in the early days of New South Wales). In this respect, the factories were processing centres, acclimatising women to their new convict lives and putting them to immediate use. The factories also served as a home to pregnant women waiting to give birth, and those nursing young children. The final group of convict women sent to the factories were those under secondary punishment. Female convicts who had misbehaved in their work placements, absconded, or committed another offence were sent to the factories for punishment. The factories did not have the same fearsome reputation as the sites used for male punishment, and the flogging of women was not common practice. However, women sent to the factories could be punished in a number of ways, particularly in solitary confinement and restriction of diet.

Each factory was different, and depending on its years of operation and location, so would be the experience of its inmates. The earliest female factory in Hobart was little more than a holding place for refractory convicts. It was a crowded and disorderly prison, with no way of instituting a practical system of work. Hobart Female Factory was replaced by the nearby Cascades Factory in 1828, which remained one of the primary institutions for convict women until the end of transportation (Image 18). Cascades had five separate yards and a range of accommodation, so that women could be segregated and put to different work depending on their 'class'. George Town Factory and Launceston (which replaced George Town in 1834) operated to the north of the colony, while Ross Female Factory operated as a staging post for convicts in transit between settlements, and a lying-in hospital for pregnant convicts.

In theory, although not always in practice due to overcrowding, women housed at a female factory were expected to undertake daily labour within its walls (a system replicated in both local and convict prisons in England after the end of transportation). The work women carried out was subject to the same class system that permeated nearly every aspect of the convict journey, from the hulks to eventually obtaining a Ticket-of-Leave. The first class of convict women included all those newly arrived from Britain and Ireland by default unless they had misbehaved badly on the voyage. Those with the best behaviour would be given positions of responsibility within the establishment. This might mean work in the kitchens (any labour with access to food gave inmates considerable status amongst their peers, and indicated a level of trust from prison staff), or attendant roles in the ward or hospital. First class women were also the only group who were considered for work assignments outside of the factory when they became available. Second class convicts were those women who had committed minor infractions while on assignment, like stealing or shoplifting, or who had originally entered in the penal class, but who showed improved behaviour. Second class women would undertake primarily domestic tasks at the factories, sewing, making, or mending clothes, or doing the laundry. Those in the third penal class were the most unruly and disobedient of convicts. Women who had been transported for the second time, or who had committed misconduct on the voyage, would be placed in the penal class, but if their conduct improved they could progress to the second or first classes. Those who had been convicted of serious crimes in the colony or committed crimes inside the factory itself were also placed in the penal class, but would never be allowed in the first class or positions of authority. Third class convict women could be put to a range of manual labour like spinning, wool work, picking oakum or horse hair, or cleaning.

Just like fledgling convict prisons in England, the factories were subject to strict regulation and hard discipline. 'Cleanliness–quietness–regularity–submission–and industry' were reported to be the watchwords of these establishments, and the women were expected to reflect these values in all that they did. At Cascades Female Factory from the day of their arrival, the lives and movements of female convicts were strictly controlled. New arrivals were stripped, washed and examined by a surgeon. Those sent to the factory as a result of an offence in the colony also had their hair cropped. If their clothes were decent, these and any other belongings would be kept for them to receive on discharge. However, many clothes were ragged, soiled, and infested with vermin after the voyage to Australia, fit only to be burned. All convicts were placed in the factory uniform: a dress, petticoat, jacket, and apron made of 'cheap coarse materials' and a straw bonnet. Convicts would wear visual identifiers to show their class. Each week the women would receive clean clothes, and each day inmates would carry out the same draconian regime.

Between 5.30am and 7am (depending on the season) they would assemble to hear a muster called, and begin labour until breakfast at 8am. Breakfast was invariably a quarter pound of bread and a pint of gruel. After half an hour for breakfast, they would attend prayers, and return to labour until lunch at 12 noon, where they would receive a half pound of bread and a pint of soup. Labour would then continue until sunset, followed by the evening meal of a quarter pound of bread and a pint of soup, prayers, and bed. In ideal conditions, though evidently not in Hobart or George Town, women slept twelve to a room in hammocks, with one of the woman appointed 'overseer' and responsible for the behaviour of the other eleven. Any infraction of the rules, bad behaviour, or wanton failure to stick to the factory routine could be punished.

After transportation to Van Diemen's Land was suspended in 1853, and the burden of financing the penal estate fell on the colony rather than the British government, the need for factories, and the justification for their expense, ceased. Of the three remaining factories, from that period, Ross was closed (no more convicts meant no more need for a staging post for travelling between convict depots or an assignment station), while the factories at Cascades and Launceston became houses of correction.

Fleeing the factories

Whatever they were called, the female factories were prisons. They had high walls, manned internal gates, and cells to keep convicts under lock and key. With many inmates in a small area, watched constantly by staff, escape was not easy. Escape usually meant going over, or through a wall, which was no mean feat for diminutive women on meagre rations. Desperation could lead to recklessness, and recklessness to harm. When Ann Livingstone attempted to escape from Hobart Factory in February 1827, the jump from the perimeter wall caused a compound fracture to her leg. It would be five years later, recuperated and sent out on assignment, that Ann would be able to successfully abscond, halfway through her fourteen year sentence.

After the failures of overcrowding and poor discipline at early factories in Hobart and George Town, the Cascades and Launceston female factories offered convicts even less chance of escape. The towns of Hobart and Launceston were both small, and surrounded by little more than rural backwaters with the occasional convict station. Van Diemen's Land was a small remote island. Even when female convicts did manage to escape the factories, they had high chances of being recognised, and little option of somewhere to go unless they managed to board a boat and leave the colony. A tall order for women with little more than a convict uniform to their name. As with their male counterparts, the poor odds of success did not deter desperate women from attempting to escape – it only necessitated using desperate measures to do so.

In August of 1839, Catherine Hendries and Mary Lindsay, 'two women notorious for their roving propensities', made their escape from Launceston Female Factory by making their way into the drainage system underneath the building. The pair escaped into the sewers from factory grounds as muster was being taken one afternoon. As their names were called, Hendries and Lindsay were immediately missed, and the route of their escape soon discovered. Watchmen were stationed at the outlet where the sewer emptied into the river. Despite soon realising that their route to freedom was blocked by watchmen, the women could not be drawn out, preferring to stay in the sewer in unimaginable conditions until the following afternoon rather than resign themselves to returning to the factory. When a man was sent into the sewer to finally fetch them out, they were taken to gaol, and both were given twelve months of imprisonment and transferred to Cascades Factory for their trouble. Mary Lindsay had been apprehended less than a month before, after escaping from the factory by breaking through a brick wall. Mary had been caught then, too, but her accomplice fared better, and months later had still not been recovered.

Escape was not the only way in which women could make their displeasure with the factory system known. Individual women would make daily shows of defiance and insubordination. They might refuse to labour, offer insults to staff or other inmates, make complaints of the regime, and engage in violent or obscene conduct. Punishment for such infractions would be a few days of solitary confinement, demotion to a lower convict class, and in the worst cases of violence, an extension of their sentence. Individual acts were easy to deal with, and complaints easy to ignore. It was only when women acted together that a real threat to the system was posed. Riots were rare and repercussions for the women involved were serious. Yet, riots posed such a threat to public order, and the safety of all involved, that they had the capacity to call attention to the failings of the system.

In 1844, two riots occurred at the Launceston Factory in little more than a week. The previous year another had occurred in which:

> The ladies had taken up arms, alias spindles, to secure redress for some imaginary grievance, and proceeded to such extremities as to threaten the entire subversion of all discipline.

One riot may have been possible to dismiss, but three in the space of a year called into question not the women causing disorder, but the regime encouraging them to do so. While reports called for better discipline of inmates, they also decried the lack of efficient control exhibited by those running the establishment. The *Cornwall Chronicle* noted:

> We cannot in common justice, and in the absence of all proof to that effect, take it for granted that the whole entire blame rests with the fair belligerents ... It becomes therefore the principal business of those trusted with their management, carefully to watch for the first indications of the unhappy propensity.

The riots created space in which journalists questioned the prison regime, the *Chronicle* stating:

> We consider nearly the whole system of prison discipline (as far as it affects the female prisoner) to be essentially and radically wrong.

Though every woman involved in the Launceston riots was punished, criticisms of the punitive regime and inappropriate labour forced on prisoners (stone breaking) led to the resignations of the superintendent and matron of the factory the following month.

The stuff of stage and screen

Van Diemen's Land may have been physically a much smaller penal settlement than New South Wales, but in its fifty years of operation it received almost the same number of convicts. Rates of transportation to Van Diemen's Land were particularly high in the 1820s, 1830s and 1840s, as the cultural impact of transportation was taking hold at home in Britain and Ireland. Like the highwaymen and the hanged who had become minor celebrities in the previous century, the stories of some transportees not only captivated contemporary audiences when told, but have remained some of the most famed characters in our own time. The colony inspired just as many songs and stories as New South Wales had before it. Reports of Van Diemen's Land's brutal punishments, inhospitable shores and bush, and the hard labour convicts were put to, shaped the fearsome reputation of transportation for new nineteenth century generations. Whilst many of the real-life convicts who found enduring fame had been sent to Sydney, transportation to Van Diemen's Land was the fate of those who gave inspiration to some of fiction's most notorious criminals.

When Jack Dawkins, the Artful Dodger of Dickens' celebrated *Oliver Twist*, was finally 'lagged' for stealing a snuff box, he was sentenced to be transported for life. The novel reaches its end without the reader ever knowing if Jack survived the hulks, and if and when he departed for Van Diemen's Land, which at the time would have been his most likely port of call. The Dodger could have been based on any one of the hundreds of juvenile offenders, like George Langley, that ended up in the colony. Yet it was another transportee, a grown man and notorious 'kidsman' who is widely believed to have inspired the book's most famous character: Fagin.

The fine life of Australia's Fagin

Fagin, the trainer of child thieves and hoarder of stolen goods, met his fate at the end of a hangman's rope. But by the time readers joined him, half mad with fear, waiting in the condemned cell, the man who inspired him had already earned his Ticket-of-Leave on the other side of the world.

Ikey Solomon captured the public imagination more than a decade before Dickens published *Oliver Twist*. It is not difficult to see why Dickens found such inspiration in the case. Ikey's tale was even more fantastical than that of his fictional counterpart.

Isaac Solomon was born into a Jewish family living in London's East End in the late 1780s, one of nine children. He was popularly known by the name of Ikey. An impoverished working-class family, it is likely that the Solomons lived, as many families did, on the edge of the law. While much of their income may have come from legitimate employments, Ikey's family also obtained money from theft, selling stolen goods, and a cut from receiving the same. Towards the end of his life Ikey's father, Henry Solomon, stated:

> I am upwards of seventy years old, and have worked hard to support my family. I never got a penny dishonestly in all my days – I have worked for every factory in London. I hate the very thought of a thief and a receiver.

He was, however, at that time on trial for grand larceny, having been apprehended amongst a veritable Aladdin's Cave of other people's belongings, including twenty-seven watches, seven pairs of earrings, twenty-eight rings, fourteen watch-keys and five watch straps, and even two glass eyes. Ikey was probably involved in his father's criminal business from an early age, possibly as a pickpocket, or a go-between for thieves and his father. Narratives of his life, published after he gained notoriety in England, state that he assisted his father from the age of nine. There is no record of his earliest offences, but he was well practiced in obtaining and selling stolen goods by the time he was first arrested. In 1807, when Ikey was around the age of twenty, he married Ann Julian, the daughter of a local coachman. The pair would go on to have a large family together, and challenge the law on both sides of the world.

The first record of Ikey's trouble with the law was in 1810, when his first major trial took place at London's Old Bailey. Ikey was already known to the authorities by this time, but no records of how or when he first came to their attention survive. Ikey, along with an accomplice, Joel Joseph, was prosecuted for picking the pocket of Thomas Dodd, stealing his wallet, forty pounds' worth of bank notes, and a payment warrant worth more than fifty pounds. Ikey and Joel were the consummate thieves – Dodds neither saw them nor noticed the loss of his belongings until after they had made away with his goods. However, both men were known to on duty Bow-Street constables John Preston and John Vinney as 'noted characters' and when spotted in a crowd, the constables followed them on a hunch. As the constables approached, Joel Joseph attempted to eat the bank notes he was carrying while Ikey dropped the wallet. Both Ikey and Joel were searched and not only Dodd's property, but numerous bank notes, dollars, and stolen items were found secreted all over their persons.

Theirs was a substantial theft, and could have warranted the death sentence. Yet both defendants were young. Ikey was recorded as only twenty-one. When they were found guilty, both men were sentenced to be transported for life. Joel Joseph was sent to New South Wales the following year, while Ikey was one of the many men who escaped transportation.

Although this was unusual for someone under a life sentence, Ikey may have successfully petitioned to have his sentence reduced to a term of seven years (as a first felony offence). If so, he would have been eligible for release around four or five years into his sentence, which records indicate he was. Ikey survived the hulks, obtaining favourable conditions due to the constant petitions and attentions of his friends and family. After release, he returned to London and established a shop reported to be a pawnbrokers, and a place which dealt in 'all kinds of goods'.

Ikey's initial business may have been legitimate, but just a few years after establishment, he began to use the business as a venue for receiving and disposing of stolen goods. Ikey's practice was, by some accounts, common knowledge. Through a large network of informants, and it was suggested, bribes to local police officers, he managed for more than a decade to escape arrest. One chronicler wrote:

> In the course of a few years he amassed great wealth, always contriving, by means that are thought not overly creditable to the police, to evade the vigilance of that immaculate fraternity.

Ikey worked with many different kinds of thieves, but was noted to be a 'kidsman', an offender who trained young children in the art of theft and profited handsomely from their endeavours.

Ikey's luck eventually ran out, and in 1827 he was arrested for receiving a large quantity of stolen goods, all found at his house in Petticoat Lane. Ikey was taken to Lambeth Street Police Court to be charged, and then confined in Newgate to face trial. In May 1827, the *London Courier* reported that Ikey made an application to the King's Bench for bail. He was taken to court for the hearing, at which bail was denied. Yet the application had only ever been a ruse for what came next. On leaving the court, Ikey was loaded into a carriage to be returned to prison, accompanied by his wife and father-in-law as carriage driver. Ikey asked that the carriage take a short diversion to allow his wife to be dropped off, to which the gaoler consented. The coach was diverted much further than originally agreed, and pulled up in Petticoat Lane, where 'a party of Jews, who were in waiting' assisted Ikey's escape, while keeping the gaolers confined in the coach. Within minutes, Ikey had disappeared into the streets of London. The police questioned locals and Ikey's family and in-laws repeatedly, but all refused to give him up.

Ikey wasted no time quitting England for America. His case became national news, and the subject of several sensationalised accounts (Image 19). Ikey's growing notoriety proved humiliating for the English authorities, who were quick to seek retribution with the rest of the Solomon family. Both Ikey's father and his wife, Ann, were placed on trial later in 1827. Henry Solomon was found guilty of the crime of grand larceny, but had his sentence respited due to his advanced age. Ann, however, was not so lucky. She faced three separate indictments in September 1827 for receiving stolen goods. She was found guilty of receiving a single watch, valued at £6, into the family shop. The owner of the watch, Joseph Ridley, testified that it had been stolen from him less than a fortnight before. Ann, who had no known criminal record, was sentenced to be transported for fourteen years. Less than six months later she sailed to Van Diemen's Land on board the *Mermaid*, accompanied by the youngest of her children. Her adult sons, John and Moses, later sailed out to Hobart to join her. Her husband Ikey remained in hiding.

On hearing his wife had been transported, Ikey travelled to Van Diemen's Land to reunite with her. Some sources suggest that he made the trip in part to escape prosecution for 'a system of forgery on one of the American banks', which he left three co-defendants to stand trial for. With so many criminal associates now residing in Van Diemen's Land, Ikey was easily recognised, but could not be apprehended as he had broken no laws in the colony. While Governor Arthur wrote to London for a warrant to arrest him, Ikey set up a tobacconist shop in the centre of Hobart, and petitioned to have his convict wife assigned to his service. Ann was eventually assigned to Ikey, after serving additional time for fighting in the female factory. Just months later, however, a warrant for Ikey's arrest arrived. He was apprehended and deported to England to face trial.

On 8 July 1830, three years after his escape, Ikey stood trial at the Old Bailey on eight separate indictments. The offences ranged from burglary and simple larceny to receiving stolen goods. Ikey was found not guilty on several of the charges, but ultimately found guilty and sentenced to be transported for fourteen years. As a high-profile prisoner who had not only escaped justice for three years, but had previously been released from a term of transportation having never left England, the authorities wasted little time in ensuring Ikey served his proper sentence. In May 1831, Ikey was loaded on board the *William Glen Anderson* and transported back to Van Diemen's Land as a convict.

Ikey arrived in the colony in November of 1831, and was processed into the convict system. He worked for a time as a member of the field police, but was removed due to ill health and later appointed as a convict constable. Despite being put in a position of authority as a 'javelin man', Ikey's conduct was far from exemplary. He was punished for the use of abusive language, and disorderly conduct, and found to have made 'false and malicious' charges against fellow convicts. Ann's conduct in the system was similarly bad.

The Solomon's marriage never recovered from Ikey's betrayal which had seen him flee the country, leaving Ann to face punishment in his stead. The pair tried to reunite after both of them were released on Tickets-of-Leave in 1835. However, the relationship deteriorated into verbal disputes and physical violence. On several occasions, these disturbances saw Ann or Ikey back in court. Ann was fined five shillings in 1834 for an assault on Ikey, and in 1835 he was noted to have exhibited 'drunkenness and violent conduct towards his family'. In 1840, the Solomons both received Conditional Pardons, and in that same year, Ann took Ikey to court for assault. The case was dismissed as the magistrate found that the event in question 'originated in a great measure from her violent temper'. Three months later, the Solomons were back in court again, and this time, Ikey was found guilty of 'ill-usage' towards his wife, fined, and bound to keep the peace for six months.

Ikey received his Certificate of Freedom in 1844, leaving him free to return to England, where Dickens' Fagin had become a household name. However, by this time Ann and Ikey had separated. He remained estranged from Ann, and by all reports, from his children, for the rest of his life. His father was presumably dead and Ikey had been absent from London, other than for his trial, for more than fifteen years. There was nothing for him to go back to and no one to go back with. Ikey died in Hobart six years later in 1850, estranged from his family and impoverished. Despite speculation that he had accumulated thousands of pounds' worth of property during his criminal endeavours, and his running a number of successful businesses, his estate was worth less than £100.

As one of the few famed convicts not to capitalise on his notoriety by writing his own memoirs, it seems remarkable that Ikey's biggest legacy is literary. Not only will a part of Ikey's life in England be enshrined forever in the character of Dickens' Fagin, but his life and troubles in Australia have also inspired works of fiction. Bryce Courtenay's *The Potato Factory*, one of Australia's bestselling novels, is based on Ikey's life.

Mutiny amongst the convicts at Woolwich

The prospect of transportation to Australia waxed and waned in attractiveness to convicts, as the reception of convicts waxed and waned in attractiveness to the colonies. Not only did each convict man or woman have their own personal circumstances which made departure from Britain more or less appealing, but timing could also be crucial. The same was true of the colonies. As we have already seen, in the late decades of the eighteenth century, fear of the unknown, rumours of hardship and savagery, and recent catastrophes saw some favour death at home rather than starvation or butchery abroad. However, for many, the prospect of life in Australia was radically altered by the mid-nineteenth century. Not only were the colonies fully established with most of the conveniences of Britain, but reports of the opportunity awaiting convicts at the end of their sentences (whether that be good employment, land, life in a pleasant climate, or otherwise) were common place.

For those living and labouring in misery on British hulks, the thought of making it to Australia may have been a light at the end of a long dark tunnel. There was particular fervour on the part of male convicts to make it to Australia in the early 1850s, as gold was discovered in Victoria, South Australia, a short boat ride from Van Diemen's Land. Whether they planned to abscond on arrival, or serve out the remaining years of their sentences before taking passage to the goldfields, life in Australia now offered the very real prospect of making a fortune, more than release back to their former lives in Britain could ever promise.

The growing attractiveness of life in Australia posed both the British state and the Australian colonies with a problem. Transporting convicts who went on to lead successful, affluent lives sent the wrong message about the ramifications of crime. Keeping convicts at home meant the cost and inconvenience of their care fell on the state. For the Australian colonies, the reverse was true. By 1850, Van Diemen's Land was preparing to close its shores to British convicts. The colony had been receiving increasing numbers of convicts from the 1820s, and when the transportation of convicts to New South Wales was suspended, Van Diemen's Land became the primary place of reception for British convicts. Thousands had streamed into the colony, which relied less and less on convict labour. The negatives of convict relocation began to outweigh its uses, and Van Diemen's Land looked towards a future in which it no longer operated as a British penal colony, but an independent state. Tensions between convict arrivals and Vandemonians were particularly heightened in the later years. Reports of violence and bad behaviour from recently released convicts as they prospected for gold elsewhere in the country was giving Van Diemen's Land a bad name (a name jettisoned in 1856 when the state was renamed Tasmania). Convicts were both increasingly surplus to requirements in the colony, and damaging to its reputation. Many in Van Diemen's Land believed that not only had transportation ceased to be an effective punishment, but that with an abundance of land, natural resources, a good climate, and the discovery of gold, transportation had become an attractive option. One newspaper wrote:

> Deportation to the antipodes is, in fact, considered a magnificent boon by the criminal, who is quite as aware as the honest man is, that joined to its fine climate, New South Wales now presents the additional attraction of speedy wealth in its most concentrated form to the man with strength of arm to dig, or daring enough to rob the digger.

With opposition to transportation growing in Van Diemen's Land, and transportation to Western Australia in its infancy, the British government had to be especially selective about who was chosen to sail and when. This meant a slowing rate of transportation, just as many convicts were keen to see their sentence put into action in hopes of a better life abroad. Frustration with the unfair system in which only some were sent to Australia, while many were kept in dire conditions on the hulks for their entire sentences, soon boiled over.

In January 1852, convicts aboard the *Warrior* hulk at Woolwich staged a mutiny in protest. On a Tuesday lunchtime, as the convicts arrived back at the hulk for their midday meal, a group of around 130 convicts rushed below and seized control of two of the decks. The men staged a sit-in, 'singing, cheering, and swearing; and some who had got hold of pipes and tobacco, commenced smoking'. Although the men's protest was largely peaceful, they 'refused to go to their proper places until their grievances were redressed'. *Lloyd's Weekly Newspaper* reported that the convicts:

> Complain that the Authorities have broken faith with them, as certain periods had been fixed when, if they conducted themselves well in the interval, they would be sent out of this country, and obtain tickets of leave on their arrival at their destination. The time at which several of the convicts expected they would have been sent out of the country having been exceeded.

An armed military guard was called, and the ringleaders were either placed in irons and taken to other ships, or transferred under guard to Milbank Prison. Their grievances were heard, but the authorities maintained there was little they could do as Australia was unwilling to receive large numbers of convicts. It took several months for news to filter across the sea to Australia. The colonies there, enjoying prosperity and plenty, had limited sympathy for the British law-breakers who caused unrest. The *Tasmanian Colonist* in Hobart reported:

> They regard themselves as unfairly dealt with because they are not sent out at the 'public expense' to the 'land of promise', where, furnished with a convict's passport – a Ticket-of-Leave – they may apply themselves to the pleasant task of literally 'reaping a golden harvest,' as some compensation for the sufferings they have hitherto endured ... The whole affair speaks trumpet-tounged as to the light in which the criminal classes regard transportation to Australia, and the government can have no pretence ... that their present system of transportation to the Australian Colonies, by holding out reward instead of punishment, serves but to foster crime at home, and utterly corrupt beyond redemption the streams of social life in these most important dependencies of the empire.

Almost a year to the day after the mutiny of the men on the *Warrior*, the *St Vincent* convict ship, carrying approximately 214 male convicts, left England for Van Diemen's Land, perhaps carrying some of the unnamed Woolwich mutineers. The ship arrived five months later in May 1853, and was greeted with much celebration. Not on account of the cargo it carried, but because it was the final convict ship sent from Britain to Van Diemen's Land. No doubt the convicts were treated with grudging acceptance in the knowledge that they would be the last of their kind, and heralded a new beginning for the colony. Emotions must have been mixed amongst the convicts aboard. Some may have been relieved and delighted to have finally arrived in a land which was thought to promise so much. For others aboard, transportation was no cure-all for the difficulties and disordered lives they left behind in England.

George Brittlebank was born in Yorkshire in 1828. There is very little evidence of George's family life, but it does not appear to have been a happy one. By the age of sixteen, George was living on the streets of Doncaster, making a living from theft. He was tried in 1845 for obtaining a watch by false pretences, and given six weeks' imprisonment. The following year he was convicted of a similar offence. The presiding judge warned him, 'we shall give you one more chance; but let me warn you, that if you ever appear at that bar again, there will be no alternative but to send you out of the country' before sentencing him to six months of hard labour. George did appear at the bar again in 1847 when he was convicted of obtaining cutlery by false pretences and given nine months, then again in August 1848 when he was imprisoned as a rogue and vagabond, and a month later when he was convicted of stealing clothes. For this final offence, the judge made good on his word, and sentenced George to be transported for seven years. George spent more than four years on the hulks before he boarded the *St Vincent* and was three quarters of the way through his sentence when he arrived in Van Diemen's Land.

After serving his probation in the colony, George would have ordinarily been eligible for a Ticket-of-Leave. However, being found absent from the barracks, and found guilty of misconduct several times, George only tasted freedom in 1855 at the expiration of his sentence. George never left the colony in search of gold, and remained in Hobart living a somewhat transient lifestyle. He was regularly in and out of court. Two years after the expiration of his sentence he was charged with stealing a watch but discharged. After which he amassed a number of convictions for drunkenness and disorderly behaviour, including public obscenity and insulting members of the public. He was accused, but discharged, of several other thefts. His offences became more frequent as he reached his early fifties, and work presumably became more difficult to find. In the last five years of his life, George was convicted of insulting passers by, assaulting a policeman, using obscene language in public, and being drunk and incapable. In 1885, George was found drunk and incapable in a doorway, and conveyed to the local police station. He was known to have been 'addicted to drink' for many years, and was also suspected to suffer from heart disease. After spending the night in a cell exhibiting heavy breathing, George was found dead by a police constable the next morning.

The Australian press may have been quick to present Van Diemen's Land as a place of abundance and opportunity in which convicts would be lucky to land. There would have been many convicts in Britain only too ready to believe it. George's story reminds us, however, that whatever the hopes and wishes of convicts who mutinied on the *Warrior*, or sailed on board the *St Vincent*, or were left behind in Britain, transportation to Van Diemen's Land remained a punishment to the very last. A dislocating, traumatising punishment after which there were no guarantees of fortune, happiness, or success. The misery and chaos of convict existence far outlived the convict period itself.

Conclusions

Transportation to Van Diemen's Land had been, from the arrival of the first ship of convicts, a contradictory tale for the men and women who found themselves there. Early settlers faced brutal justice in a harsh, rapidly developing, colony. Many early arrivals would have wished themselves in New South Wales instead. Yet as the colony grew and developed, some convicts had the opportunity to benefit from high employment rates, government land grants, and business opportunities in a resource rich land. Australia's gold rush in the mid-nineteenth century only furthered the life potential of many ex-convicts. Of course, none of this would compensate some convicts for the loss of friends and families and the lives they had built in Britain.

Transportation to Van Diemen's Land was full of contradictions for the British as well, as popular perceptions of life in this remote outpost of empire shifted. The dread felt by early convicts as they departed for Van Diemen's Land had turned to optimism and excitement for some in just a few decades. The early 1850s were a crisis in criminal justice and punishment for the British authorities, as the dominant punishment for serious offenders ceased to be a deterrent, with some convicts admitting that they had purposely committed their crimes with hopes of arriving in Australia. As Van Diemen's Land closed its doors to British convicts in 1853, and declared independence for the colony in 1856, the British penal estate was in flux. Modern convict prisons which would dominate the penal landscape for more than a century were on the rise, but the experiment of Australian transportation was not yet done. For fifteen years after the *St Vincent* arrived in Hobart, the British would continue to trickle convicts to Australia, at their newest, and last, penal outpost more than 2,500 miles across the country.

Chapter 5

The Hothouse of Humanity on the Swan River: Western Australia 1850–1868

The state of Western Australia takes up nearly a third of the entire Australian mainland. Much of the inner territory is made up of arid land, but along its large and beautiful coast the climate ranges from distinctly Mediterranean in the south, to tropical and wet in the north. Different from both its contemporaries in the east and the south, the settlement of Western Australia was no less problematic. The land was mineral rich, but hard to farm and inhospitable in many places. It was also one of the most remote places on earth, lacking the island chains and access to Indonesia and Malaysia which had proved such vital lifelines for the early colonists on the opposite side of the country.

European explorers had first landed on Australia's western shore in the early seventeenth century, when Dutch navigators made trips along the coast. Despite a number of visits, the earliest sailors found the coast full of dangerous reefs and shoals, and the size of the land difficult to estimate. Throughout the rest of the century, other expeditions from Europe arrived, charting the shore and scouting for potential settlement sites. By the eighteenth century, the land had been claimed by the Dutch, the French, and the English, but with the British settlement of New South Wales and then Van Diemen's Land in the early nineteenth century, it was only a matter of decades before the British took possession of the west too.

The first attempt at British settlement was officially made in 1826 at King George Sound, in the south of the state, as the authorities were concerned that a delay might lead to the territory being settled by the French. A military detachment was sent to Western Australia from New South Wales, with a handful of convicts, a doctor, and a storekeeper to establish a miniscule makeshift penal settlement. More to deter would-be colonialists from other nations than as part of a larger plan to colonise the state. However, just two years later, Captain James Stirling arrived at Fremantle and established the first permanent British settlement, the Swan River colony, in April of 1829. The penal settlement at King George Sound was withdrawn in 1831, leaving the Swan River colonists to hold the territory for Britain. Although early colonists battled with land unsuitable for agriculture, lacking supplies and in poor conditions, by 1832 more than 1,000 Europeans had settled in the colony.

Western Australia was different from both New South Wales and Van Diemen's Land by virtue of the fact that it was established as a free settlement and never intended to be a penal colony. Much of the infrastructure in Fremantle and Perth (the colony's two biggest centres) was built by and for free men and women in those early hard years. It would be almost two decades before the government ship *Scindian* arrived carrying the first seventy-five adult male convicts to settle on the Swan River, at the request of the colonists themselves. Western Australia technically had a penal depot rather than a penal colony. Thus, the experience of transportation to Western Australia was notably different from what had gone before. Yet the convicts of the *Scindian* were not the first outcasts to be sent west by the British government. Almost a decade before the convicts arrived, the British began sending juveniles from a reformatory on the Isle of Wight to begin new lives as the colony's very first 'apprentices'.

Parkhurst Boys

The British had been experimenting with alternative ways to deal with juvenile law breakers for more than a decade by the time the first Parkhurst Boy arrived in Western Australia. While young children had been sent as convicts to both New South Wales and Van Diemen's Land, by the 1830s, the British were experimenting with alternative options. From confining young boys on separate hulks from hardened adult offenders, to sending them to special training ships rather than to prison (like little George Evans in Chapter one). By the mid-century, the need to reform young offenders rather than simply punish them was gaining wider support. By the 1850s and 1860s, training ships and reformatory schools had begun to appear around the country. From 1838, Parkhurst prison on the Isle of Wight was a juvenile prison. Lacking the space to provide long term housing for large numbers of juveniles, in 1839 the Colonial Office wrote to the governor of Western Australia, asking if they would accept reformed juveniles as 'apprentices'. The boys would undertake indentured servitude, learning a trade, and eventually earning their freedom. They may have been called apprentices, but the boys were convicts in almost all but name.

The arrival of the Parkhurst Boys at the Swan River colony was the topic of some debate, as it was elsewhere. Van Diemen's Land, Victoria, Norfolk Island, and New Zealand also received more than 1,000 apprenticed boys between them, whilst South Australia refused to accept any. The labour the boys would offer, and their potential to provide important skills in the future years of the colony, was welcomed by some, whilst others fiercely objected. The apprentices would, some argued, be little more than prisoners and treated as such. Hardly a fair fate for children. Then there was the question of how such a system of emigration would be stopped once begun. By accepting even a few apprentices, fears were raised that the fragile colony could find itself awash with juvenile criminals. There was also the concern that there would be no way to determine the 'good' boys whose mistakes would be atoned for by first rate work, from the 'bad' boys, who would only serve to degrade and demoralise colonial society. Ultimately, the governor agreed to accept a small number of boys, provided that number did not exceed more than around thirty a year, and that most were under the age of fifteen.

Ultimately more than 300 Parkhurst boys were sent to Western Australia between 1842, when the *Simon Taylor* arrived with eighteen boys on board, and 1851, when the *Minden* dropped off a final batch of thirty. The boys ranged in age from eight to eighteen, and could be transported for terms of up to ten years for crimes as small as stealing bread, to burglary and highway robbery. As with any group who trod different paths to the criminal justice system and found themselves put through the process of transportation, the outcomes for the boys in Australia were unpredictable. The behaviour and success of the Parkhurst Boys once they reached the colony was mixed. George Hall, the superintendent of Parkhurst Prison, stated that he was of the opinion that:

> Many of the boys under his charge are better than many who have not been brought before a court of justice, but that the difficulties are the prejudice against them, and the danger of their being ill-treated during their apprenticeship.

This much was certainly true. Once the boys arrived, they were assigned to masters throughout the colony for the term of their sentences, who had the authority to treat and discipline the boys as they saw fit. No doubt a number of the Parkhurst apprentices were difficult charges. Many had come from dysfunctional homes back in Britain, and had been further brutalised by their experiences in the criminal justice system. They were set to work in a foreign land, miles from all they knew, and some of their experiences show that the authorities who had care of them, and the masters to whom they were assigned, neglected to remember that the boys were, all other factors aside, vulnerable children.

Allen Knight was eleven when he was tried at the Chichester Sessions for breaking and entering the house of a relative and stealing a watch and chain. He was sentenced to ten years of transportation. He arrived in the colony at the age of fourteen, and was assigned to Mr J. Wickstead as a domestic servant. Although initially it was reported that Allen 'appears a very good boy', he was returned to the Guardians (the body responsible for the assignment and wellbeing of the boys) just a few weeks later for 'neglect and impertinence'. Allen had been whipped by his master for lying and getting drunk. Allen was assigned to another master, who reported of the fourteen year old, 'well described in the book handed to me when he arrived as "cold sullen & vindictive." A most difficult boy to rule. Bad.' Allen, now assigned to farm labour, struggled to settle in his new position and was punished for insolence and idleness. He was removed again, and a Guardian noted 'placed under the strictest master I could find.' Unsurprisingly, Allen fled at the first opportunity, and was ordered by the Perth Magistrates Bench to be flogged. He was returned to his master and noted as 'incorrigible. In constant punishment.' Allen was placed in service as a sailor on board the HMC schooner *Champion*. Here he was placed under strict naval discipline. He spent two years on board, and initial reports of his conduct were good, then declining in quality. When he was sent to the hospital in Perth for an unknown ailment, he absconded again. Nothing else is known of his fate, other than a note in the Guardian's reports which states 'I have heard that he shipped on board the *Badger*, an American whaler.'

Other Parkhurst boys found to be incorrigible and uncontrollable, like Allen, suffered the same fate. John Tyne was just ten years old when he was convicted at the Old Bailey of stealing shoes from a shop and sentenced to seven years of transportation, and was only twelve when he arrived in Western Australia. Born in London, John found it difficult to settle to farm life. After a first good report, John was removed from his first master and noted to be 'A bad boy' and 'idle, lazy, lying & insolent' by his second. He was flogged and imprisoned for assaulting another boy, and imprisoned again for running away from his master. The Guardians wrote 'utterly incorrigible, only fit for a sea life'.

John was given further agricultural assignments, but sent to the Quarter Sessions for robbing his master's house, and further reported by another master 'in jail [sic] the greater part of the first half of the year. Utterly worthless.' John was placed aboard the *Champion* as a last recourse, for a term of two years in 1846 at the age of only eighteen. According to the authorities 'partly as punishment and as a last resource to reclaim him'. Initial reports of his conduct were good, but like Allen Knight, when the chance came to escape he did, and was rumoured to have also joined an American whaler. Earlier that same year, a third Parkhurst boy, John Norton, arrived on board the *Champion*. Apprenticed as a butcher in Western Australia at the age of fifteen, Norton had spent several terms in prison, and had even been sent to Rottnest Island for bad conduct before arriving on board. He, like the others, took the first opportunity to escape, as the boat passed through South Australia. These boys and more fled the system that had transported them across the world if they could, out of Australia, and out of our history.

Some simply found it difficult to adapt to their strange new surroundings and the work expected of them, or were rejected by their masters. William Beale was just eight years old when he was tried at Lewes Assize in 1840 for larceny and sentenced to be transported for seven years. He arrived in Western Australia aboard the *Shepherd* in 1843 and was discharged. William was technically no longer serving his sentence, but was instead apprenticed to a Mr F. Singleton for a period of five years as a farm labourer. He would be free in 1848, a year after the expiration of his original sentence. Just a month after his arrival, the Guardians noted that William had been 'corrected' by his master (very possibly some form of physical punishment) 'for sleeping out in the bush and neglecting his work'. William would have been just eleven or twelve at this time. Noted as being of 'very small size and deficient in strength', William was rejected by Singleton and reassigned to a Mr E. Lennard. Found to be careless and idle, as well as 'too small' for the work, he was passed on again to a Mr Robins. He received several good reports from this placement, but was suddenly dismissed by Robins for misconduct and assigned to a Mr Haughton. He absconded from Haughton's service and was placed in gaol for two months for doing so. Upon release he found himself employment with another settler on his own account. By the end of the term of his apprenticeship, William, still only seventeen, had worked off the cost of his apprenticeship, and found permanent work as a shepherd with William Bailey, for the salary of £2 a month. There are no records to suggest that William ever offended again, and he likely lived out a quiet life in rural Western Australia. Others, including apprentices who flourished in their new roles, had no guarantee of being so lucky.

Richard Andrews arrived on the same ship as William Beale, having been sentenced to transportation at the Surrey Sessions in 1839 at the age of thirteen. Upon arrival (four years into a seven-year sentence) he was apprenticed as a bricklayer to Mr A. Cornish. Over the next four years, Richard received nothing but excellent reports from his master to the Guardians. In early April 1847, when transporting a cartload of molasses for his master, the cart was upset, and Richard killed when thrown from it, breaking his neck. Both the local newspapers and his entry in the Guardians' reports noted his good record. The *Inquirer* reported 'He had borne the highest character for honesty and integrity, and is deeply lamented by his employers.' It is unknown if his family and friends back in England received notification of his death. With no next of kin in Australia, his meagre possessions and earnings were forfeit to the government.

Some of the Parkhurst boys did find success and happiness in later life. Charles Triggs had been thirteen when he was sentenced to transportation for the theft of a shawl. He arrived in Western Australia in 1847, halfway through his sentence, at the age of sixteen. He was apprenticed as a farm servant for a period of two and a half years. He served his time under two masters (the first only relinquishing Charles' services when he moved) and received unanimously good reports. Charles found work on a farm after discharge at a wage of £1 per month, and settled to life in the colony. Later in life Charles became proprietor of the Garfield Café, and was known to be 'an enthusiastic draughts player'. When he died in 1908 at the age of seventy-eight, his friends from the local club reported 'his death leaves a void hard to fill.'

For almost a decade, hundreds of children were brought to the colony as 'juvenile immigrants'. Yet the Parkhurst boys were in reality child transportees. Their experiences were similar to those of their juvenile and adult counterparts in each of Australia's penal colonies. While some went on to lead good lives in the colony, others struggled to overcome the emotional trauma of what had been done to them, whether that was the process of being shipped to Australia, the realities of being apprenticed in unfamiliar trades to unforgiving masters, or being passed from person to person like unwanted baggage during their formative years. The last major shipments of juveniles to Western Australia took place in 1851. By this time, the colony had already begun accepting adult transportees with the *Scindian* landing at Fremantle in June 1850 and more ships soon after. A primary purpose of finding alternate disposals for the Parkhurst juvenile offenders had been to keep them from free association with hardened criminals and to send them to a new environment where the good in them might flourish and the worst instincts could be trained away. However, with hundreds of adult convicts (many recidivists, and guilty of crimes of a serious nature) arriving in the colony each year, Western Australia could no longer serve such a purpose. After 1851, only two more Parkhurst boys arrived in the colony, perhaps as much by oversight as design. One came in 1853, and the final boy nine years later on the *Lincelles* in 1862.

Although separate from the convict era that followed, the reception of the Parkhurst boys might be seen as the British government laying essential groundwork for the acceptance of convicts into the colony, and testing the logistics of transportation to this new venue. The 'success' of introducing juvenile labour into the colony led to calls from Western Australians for a more substantial flow of convict labour which they had, until the 1850s, refused to accept. The change in attitude towards convict labour in the west of the country came none too soon for the British authorities who were faced with a surplus of convicts, and the imminent closure of their largest penal colony in Van Diemen's Land.

Unlike the other colonies which were founded by the arrival of convicts, or had convicts foisted upon them, Western Australia was an independent settlement and the British would have struggled to station convicts there without the consent of the Governor. Luckily for the mother country, just as the penal settlement in Van Diemen's Land was making noises about halting transportation, the Governor of Western Australia wrote and requested convicts be sent to the colony to plug the gaps of a labour shortage, and to help bolster a faltering economy. In the late 1840s, agriculturalists, merchants, and other men of stature in the colony lobbied the state to petition the British for convicts.

A tale of two halves

Although Western Australia was crying out for convict labour, the authorities had three demands when it came to the kind of convicts they would accept. The British were told that whilst some of their criminals were welcome, Western Australia would not accept any female convicts. Their labour was far less useful to the state and, if they could not assimilate, female convicts and their children might only further burden the colony after their sentences expired. The state also declined to accept any political prisoners, or serious offenders such as murderers, rapists, and those who committed life-threatening assaults. The colony was in need of a labour boost, but preferably that should come from first-time pickpockets turned honest working men, rather than political radicals who wanted to overthrow authority, or from hordes of violent, unstable or dangerous criminals.

The early penal transports to the state almost entirely adhered to these conditions – in some quarters gaining Western Australia's convicts the reputation as a 'class apart' from the rougher 'criminal class' of convicts that had been banished to the east and south in earlier years. The first condition, that no female convicts be sent to the colony, was upheld throughout the transportation period. However, almost immediately after transports started arriving, a problem became apparent. In 1851, Perth's *Inquirer* newspaper voiced concerns about the growing disproportion of men compared to women in the colony. Upon receiving their Ticket-of-Leave, convicts who could raise a certain sum (and thus prove they were capable of supporting themselves) would be entitled to have their wives and children emigrate to the colony. However, many convict men were unmarried, or never made arrangements for the emigration of their families back home in Britain. Shipping out the wives of known criminals was not, the paper felt, an adequate solution to the mass of unattached male convicts floating around the colony. Not only was the lack of female emigrants thought to risk the decline of polite society in the colony, a dearth of good free women risked the rehabilitation of ex-convicts, who would have no chance to 'settle down as quiet and inoffensive members of the community' by finding a suitable partner. For several years, some commentators still fully expected that female convicts would be introduced into the colony to redress the balance. Five years in to transportation, rumours of such a development were still rife, but no female convicts ever arrived.

Although no women would ever arrive on penal transports after the mid-1850s, a broader range of prisoners than first agreed upon began to arrive. Not only were there transports of colonial prisoners from India and Singapore, and even Canada too, but the kinds of prisoners arriving from Britain changed. Irish political prisoners were introduced to the colony on the last ship to sail from Britain in 1867, and proved to be as troublesome as the Western Australians had feared. Moreover, a notable proportion of those who ended up in Australia were habitual recidivists, violent offenders, and those serving long sentences for serious offences.

William Eaton was sentenced to be transported for life for the rape of his own daughter, Sophia. The ongoing abuse had been discovered by Sophia's concerned grandmother and, at the age of just ten, the little girl was required to give testimony at the Old Bailey. William Eaton spent the next twelve years imprisoned in England, before sailing to Fremantle on the *Clyde* in 1863. By the arrival of the last ship five years later, Western Australia had received more than one convict like William Eaton. Offences of the men stationed at Fremantle ranged from mugging, burglary, and highway robbery to rape and murder, with sentences from seven years to life. Some were first time offenders, guilty of comparatively minor crimes. Yet there were also hardened recidivists like Austin Montroe, who also offended under the names of Austin Monpock and Charles Elton, and had a criminal record stretching back a decade before he arrived in Western Australia. Austin had been lucky to escape a term of fifteen years' transportation in 1847 for larceny in a dwelling house. Austin, who was rumoured to have been transported prior to arriving in Western Australia, served his time in a succession of British convict prisons until his release on licence in 1855. Three years later, he received his third and final sentence of transportation when he was tried again for housebreaking. He received another fifteen years, and was transported aboard the *Palmerston* in 1861. Alongside William Eaton and hundreds of other serious offenders, Montroe spent the rest of his life in the colony.

A serious offender

The reluctance of the Western Australian authorities in accepting serious criminals was a precautionary measure against having a large number of incorrigible and dangerous criminals in the colony. But the precaution was largely a pointless one. With so many changes made to the material, environmental, and emotional lives of convicts, it could never be possible to predict how an offender might fare once they reached the colony. Repeat offenders might suddenly reform and lead successful, productive lives. On the other hand, those transported on their first offence might in later life turn to much more serious crimes, with nothing and no-one to lose in the colony.

On 9 July 1861, Robert Thomas Palin was executed at Perth. This Ticket-of-Leave holder's one way trip to the gallows had been secured when he was found guilty of a violent burglary at a trial in the State Supreme Court six days previously. In covering the court case and Palin's final appearance as he was launched from the gallows into eternity, the *Perth Gazette* reported, 'The career of this malefactor is said to be one of the blackest kind and there is little doubt that it would have terminated sooner or later, in the manner it did on Tuesday last.' Palin was reported to have been obstinate and impertinent almost to the last, but the Dean and Chaplain attending had given cause to think that 'if not truly penitent, he died at least much softened.'

On 29 May that year, Palin had broken in to the house of Susan Harding. After spending the night with visiting family, Harding had retired to her bedroom and was only woken when she saw the figure of Palin standing over her bed with his head and face covered by a table cloth which he had stolen from downstairs. Susan Harding asked the intruder what he wanted, to which he replied with the fanciful motto of highway men of old: 'Your money, or your life.' When Susan spoke again, he told her 'Hush! Not a word or I'll blow your brains out.'

Harding testified in court that Palin carried a pistol and put her in fear for her life. Palin was said to have told her there were six other men downstairs, and (she later hinted) that she was in danger of sexual assault. Susan Harding retrieved a pocket watch and chain from a bedside draw in compliance with Palin's demands. Palin left shortly afterwards and the Hardings raised the alarm. The burglary was clumsy and the evidence soon led to Palin. Former convicts who had known Palin, and staff from the convict establishment, notably the school master William Easton, appeared in court to testify to Palin's good conduct while under his original sentence. The testimony did him little good. The jury found him guilty and the judge sentenced him to death. One newspaper noted that whilst death for a burglary back in England might be unthinkable, 'In this colony it is necessary to have more stringent punishments than are awarded at home.' A defiant Palin stated he 'was not the first man who had been condemned to death while innocent, and that he could die but once.'

Palin's case was unusual, not only in the violent nature of his crime – and the fears it aroused in the general public – but also because his was a rare capital case. The issuing of the death sentence in a small and rather isolated colony always garnered interest and more than its fair share of newspaper column inches. What is even more unusual about Palin's case, is that until the violent robbery of Susan Harding, Palin's time in the convict establishment was exemplary. He was, to all accounts, a model convict, noted as behaving well for his entire sentence in the colony, something suggested by one newspaper to be 'often the case. Even with the most dangerous characters.'

With former good behaviour to his name and a singular serious but non-lethal conviction, Palin would not have seemed the likeliest candidate for hanging. After all, on the same day in another trial at the same Supreme Court, Michael Costello was found guilty of causing the death of a Mr John Hughes. Hughes had died from a haemorrhage in the brain a few days after a drunken fight with Costello over a bottle of alcohol. During the fight Costello had been seen to strike Hughes down and kick him, leading ultimately to his demise. Despite the court finding Costello guilty of causing Hughes' death, Costello, another former convict, was sentenced to just one year of imprisonment with hard labour.

Palin and Costello of course had different stories. Whilst the outcome of Costello's fight had been much more serious, arguably, Palin's crime, in victimising a woman, in theft, and in violating the sanctity of a private home, was worse. Palin had a record of good conduct in the colony, while Michael Costello could not boast the same. Palin's story ended abruptly at the end of a rope, whereas Costello went on to serve his time, and reoffend again. In 1874 he was convicted of burglary, and another theft in 1875 for which he was found not guilty. Just months later he received five years of penal servitude for forgery. A decade later Costello was in and out of court for drunkenness and vagrancy. Both were arguably 'bad' characters, for whom the convict system had done nothing. However, the key to their respective fates lay not in their conduct in the convict establishment, nor even out of it. Robert Palin, many contemporary reports speculated, was executed on account of the convict character he had been before ever stepping foot in Australia. The *Perth Gazette* reported:

> We presume the sentence was passed for what he did, not for any previous offences. However worthless might have been his former life it was not for those crimes that he was tried, condemned, and hung [*sic*]. If punishment is awarded for past misdeeds how many will be liable for punishment! If this is to be done let us at least be candid and inform those who are to suffer that it was not for their present misconduct, but for their past crimes that the strength of the law was exerted to its utmost.

Michael Costello was a first time offender when he arrived in Australia, sentenced to seven years' transportation at County Waterford in Ireland, for larceny. Palin, despite being less than thirty when he died, had a string of convictions to his name. Palin's execution made headlines on both sides of the world. His death, it transpired, was interpreted as a fitting end to a more than decade long tale of burglary, murder, and convictism. Robert Palin was precisely the kind of serious offender that Western Australia had sought to avoid.

Robert's first conviction was at the age of just eighteen, in March of 1851, at Maidstone in Kent. For burglary he was sentenced to be transported for ten years. Yet, like many, he never left England. Instead, Palin served time in Wakefield, Portsmouth and eventually Dartmoor prison, before being released less than halfway into his sentence in July 1855. On release he returned to his native Bromley, in Kent. In the following months Robert Palin was widely known to have committed a string of burglaries, and worse, in the local area. By December of 1855 Palin had been apprehended and placed on trial at Maidstone court not for theft, but for the murder of one Jane Beagley, the wife of a local agricultural worker.

On returning from a day's harvest work with his son in August 1855, George Beagley had found the shutters of his house closed, the curtains drawn and the door locked. After climbing through a window to gain access to the house, George found his wife, Jane, dead in her bed, having lost a great quantity of blood from several wounds on her head. A pair of tongs, the murder weapon, lay discarded on the floor, bent and covered in blood and hair. In the next room George found his elderly mother, having sustained similar injuries, clinging onto life and groaning. Her injuries were so severe that the elder Mrs Beagley was unable to give any account of what had happened. Items of clothing, money and other artefacts were missing from the house.

Palin, known to the police at this time as a convict on licence, was sought out for questioning. When stopped by the police he was found with a bundle of clothes, claiming he was on his way to London to seek work. Unbeknown to the police, the jacket, waistcoat, and trousers he carried matched the description of those belonging to Jane Beagley's son, taken in the robbery. Satisfied with his story, the police sent Palin on his way. He was later apprehended again by police in Greenwich, and identified as having possession of the trousers which belonged to Beagley's son. He claimed to have bought them from a travelling salesman shortly before leaving for London. Palin was arrested and placed on trial, but lack of evidence as to how he came by the trousers saw Palin acquitted of the murder by the jury after just two days in court.

Having foreseen that Palin would be acquitted of the Beagley murder, the authorities immediately produced a warrant for his arrest on the charge of robbing the house of Miss Jane Shepherd. The offence had occurred one week prior to the murder of Jane Beagley in what appeared to have been a burglary gone wrong. The case was heard by a magistrate and Palin was remanded in custody for trial at the Gloucester Spring Assize. Palin was found guilty of burgling Miss Shepherd's house, and sentenced to be transported for life. He waited a year and a half before he was loaded onto the *Nile*, arriving in Fremantle in 1858.

Palin had not long had his Ticket-of-Leave when he robbed Sarah Harding. The robbery of Harding, whilst traumatic for the victim, did not result in any physical harm. Nor was the value of the burglary particularly high. In other circumstances, an offence like Palin's may well have warranted ten or more years of penal servitude in the convict establishment. However, for Palin, already a serious offender and suspected murderer unwelcome in the colony, the burglary was further proof that he did not belong in Western Australia and could not be allowed to stay.

Records suggest that it may have taken several years for more serious offenders, like Robert Palin, to arrive in the colony. This slow intermingling of the 'bad' serious offenders from the latter years of the transportation period with the 'good' convict men of the early years was, it has been suggested, a matter of practicality rather than design. Despite issuing their invite, the colony was underprepared for its new convict arrivals. Until somewhere secure could be found to house them, a delay in sending the most serious, dangerous, or difficult to manage convicts may have been entirely pragmatic on the part of the British.

Prisoners without a prison

Not having envisioned a large criminal population, Fremantle found itself under-equipped to deal with its new convict masses. While there was a lock up in the town, there was no prison capable of containing hundreds of male offenders. Until the 1850s, those that had broken the colony's laws had been transported to other penal settlements (like Van Diemen's Land, or at least out of state) or hanged if the crime was thought to merit such severity. When seventy-five convicts arrived on the *Scindian* in June of 1850, expected but unannounced (rumour has it that the postal ship carrying the British government's reply that a shipment of convicts would be forthcoming was slower than the convict transport, and arrived in Fremantle after the men had already disembarked), there was nowhere for them to be placed. The first convicts were housed and kept secure in an empty wool-warehouse by the shore, as there was no alternative. They were joined a few months later by another 100 convicts on the *Hashemy*, with hundreds more scheduled to arrive the following year.

Those who had been transported relatively quickly were put to work on gang labour where poor behaviour and insubordination were met with work in heavy irons, solitary confinement and even floggings. Good behaviour and hard work earned convicts privileges and their eventual right to work elsewhere once they received their Ticket-of-Leave. Approximately a quarter of convicts had already served substantial portions of their sentences in British prisons or hulks by the time they arrived in Western Australia. These men were entitled to have their Tickets upon arrival and avoided the dreaded gang labour. Unlike earlier convict systems, Ticket-of-Leave convicts were permitted to find their own work with private employers rather than having work assigned to them. Whilst this had some benefits, convicts were not allowed to take on extra employment in their free time to earn money, as they had been able to do in other colonies. Compared to the others that had gone before, the settlement at Fremantle was small and the convicts could be closely surveyed. They were not permitted to drink, and had to adhere to a 10pm curfew. Those that flaunted the rules would find their Tickets revoked. This basic system of regulations, rewards and revocations continued to form the basis for penal servitude in the colony long after the end of the convict era.

Securing a more suitable venue for their containment until they received their Tickets was made a priority for newly arrived convicts. For the first decade of the transportation era, this saw convicts busily engaged in the construction of the colony's first convict prison at Fremantle. Fremantle Prison (Image 20), also known as the convict establishment or Fremantle Gaol, was built for convicts, by convicts, between 1852 and 1859. The ground was prepared and limestone for construction quarried on site. The first cell block was completed (along with a few service buildings and an all important tall perimeter wall) in 1855, and the convicts were moved from their waterfront lodgings into small individual cells (Image 21 & 22). This was a new kind of incarceration from previous communal convict lodgings across penal sites in Australia and the ships themselves.

Although the convicts were largely put to labour on public works, or allowed to undertake private employment once on Ticket-of-Leave, each evening they returned to sleep and eat at the prison (unless transferred out to another depot elsewhere in the colony). The small single cells and strict routine of the institution closely mirrored that in place in the convict prisons at home in England. In the confines of Fremantle Prison, escape was rendered much more difficult than it had been for convicts in previous eras, though this did not stop many from trying. Most of those who attempted to flee were foiled in their attempts and could face flogging, the restriction of rations, and solitary confinement in small windowless cells. The few that did manage to escape faced a number of new problems, not least of which was where to go. Much like those early settlers in New South Wales who attempted to abscond into the unforgiving bush, or by sea, options for Western Australia's convicts were limited.

Escaped convicts had no chance of travelling overland to colonies in the east and south of Australia. Fremantle was more than 1,000 miles from Adelaide and further still from Melbourne or Sydney. The terrain was tough, with little sustenance to forage, and escapees would have been highly reliant on the mercy of those living out in the bush, who were as likely to report them as to assist in their endeavours. Escape by boat was the most likely option, although with South Africa the nearest destination outside of Australia, this was not without substantial risk, and most would need to stow away on a commercial vessel to succeed. For many, escape meant little more than roaming the bush outside the major settlements of the colony, subsisting on whatever they could find or steal until they were recaptured, or their infamy died down enough to make escape from the colony less risky.

Despite the many obstacles and overwhelming odds against them, some did manage to escape the establishment, and as a result went on to become some of the colony's most famed convicts.

Moondyne Joe

Born in 1825, Joseph Bolitho Johns can have had little idea that the path his life would take would lead to such notoriety, and that his name would still be gracing the newspapers more than a century after his death (Image 23).

Joseph was a miner by trade, and had worked at mines in Cornwall before searching out work in Monmouthshire. Joseph, or Joe as he became known, was largely unremarkable in the eyes of history until he came to the attention of the local courts in the winter of 1848. Along with a twenty-one-year-old accomplice, William Cross, Joe had been found in possession of a number of keys, including a skeleton key, some household items, and a large amount of food. Both men claimed to have no knowledge of one another, and to have come by the goods legitimately. The food had been bought from nearby towns, and the skeleton key had never been used, Joe testified. His protestations would have been more effective had the prosecution not found, when examining his neck-tie in court, the name of its true owner, 'C. Jenkins', embroidered on the fabric. Although the court suspected Joe of robbery, with no hard proof and, more importantly, no victim, all they could do was send him to the local gaol for one month as a rogue and a vagabond.

Months after Joe's release, Richard Price, the victim of a burglary in nearby Llanelly, came forward, claiming the food items, with which Joe and his accomplice had been apprehended, belonged to him. In March of 1849, Joe was placed on trial at the Brecon Assizes for burgling Price. Already known to the court, he was found guilty and sentenced to be transported for ten years.

Joe was part of a small cohort of men in the three years between 1850 and 1853 that could have been transported to either Van Diemen's Land or Western Australia. Had he been sent to the former, an established penal colony of almost half a century with a different regime, his entire journey through the penal system may have been different. As it was, Joe was one of those selected for a voyage to the west (his accomplice was sent to Van Diemen's Land in 1852), and he arrived in Fremantle on the *Pyrenees* in April of 1853, four years into his ten year sentence.

Having served almost half of his original sentence, and with a record of good conduct behind him, Joe was granted his Ticket-of-Leave soon after arrival in the colony. He moved to Toodyay, some miles north-west of Perth, where he worked as an animal tracker. Working in the warmth and fresh air of this rural outpost of the colony must have made for a stark contrast with his years of confinement in Britain and his lifetime of work in the mines before that. Joe remained in Toodyay for eight years, well after the expiration of his sentence until, in 1861, he was suddenly arrested for the theft of a horse. Before his trial could begin, Joe broke out of Toodyay lock up. It was the first move in a decade long game of cat-and-mouse Joe would play with the police and prisons of Western Australia, for which he gained much more notoriety than he had done for his relatively mundane crimes.

Joe was recaptured and placed on trial. He was found guilty of stealing and branding a horse, although it was not clear to whom the horse belonged, and given three years of penal servitude. He was released in 1864, and moved to the Moondyne Springs settlement near Toodyay and found work as a farmer. Joe's return several times to the Moondyne Hills are what earned him the nickname of 'Moondyne Joe' by which he is still popularly known. Less than a year after his release, Joe was placed on trial at the Supreme Court for the theft and slaughter of an ox. Joe maintained his innocence of this crime for the rest of his life, but was sentenced in July of 1865 to ten years of penal servitude and returned to the convict establishment at Fremantle.

Just months later Joe absconded whilst out on assignment with a work party, and was recaptured and sentenced to spend twelve months wearing heavy irons in Fremantle Prison. In the next year, Joe made several attempts at escape, from breaking out of his irons to attempting to remove the lock on his cell by making holes in the door. He was taken on each attempt to the solitary punishment cell. On one occasion on which he was subjected to a search, the warders were surprised to find he had 'one file, one small knife with the back dentated so as to serve the purpose of a saw, one picklock, and one of the hinge hooks wrenched from his cell table' upon his person. The possession of this contraband earned him a further six months in chains. In August of 1866 Joe made a successful prison break from Fremantle. One of the glass windows from his cell was removed by the authorities in order to encourage better ventilation, and Joe seized the opportunity to squeeze through the small gap left behind.

Joe fled to the bush and met up with two other escapees. The trio perpetrated a string of armed robberies in and around Perth before they were apprehended a month after Joe's escape, almost 200 miles from Perth. For the prison break and the armed robberies, Joe received another five years on his sentence, and was taken back to Fremantle in irons. The prison authorities were enraged and embarrassed by Joe's continued success at escaping. The governor of the prison commissioned a special 'escape-proof' cell in which Joe was to be held. The cell was made from thick wood and long nails. It had only the smallest openings for light and air. There was talk of installing a ring-bolt to the floor to which Joe's chains would be fastened at all times, but such provision was never made. Joe was held in the cell, and placed on a penal diet of bread and water for more than a month, until a surgeon raised serious concerns for his health. In a concession for his wellbeing, Joe was permitted to take air and exercise by breaking rocks in the prison yard under strict supervision. After building up a quantity of rocks that partially obscured him from view one day in 1867, Joe made another escape. Reports vary from him using his stone breaking tools to tunnel through the wall to freedom, to him changing into a guard's uniform (obtained for him by another prisoner) and walking boldly out of the front gate.

At large once more, nothing further was heard of Joe until 1869. Two years after escape, having ranged around the rural settlements of the colony, living from the land when he could, and plundering when he must, Joe broke into a vineyard cellar in the Swan Valley to steal wine. By some serendipity several policemen were visiting the vineyard at the time and, recognising Joe, apprehended him. He was returned to prison, by which time the convict era had ended, but Joe was just one of the numerous recidivists from that era still being held in the colony. After two years back in prison, a sympathetic prison governor granted Joe his Ticket-of-Leave in 1871, and his Certificate of Freedom in 1873 – twenty years after his arrival on the *Pyrenees*.

Whilst Moondyne Joe's tale became something of a legend to local inhabitants, Joseph Johns passed largely out of public life after his release. For the next half century, the tale of Moondyne Joe and his many escapes tapped into narratives of brave frontiersmen and roguish bush ranging. It conjured up images of daring outlaws like Jack Donoghue and the Kelly gang, who gained notoriety in the east of the country. Joe did not enter the convict system a violent offender, but during his years on the run he did perpetrate a number of armed robberies and petty thefts to secure food, supplies, and equipment, like others who fled from the law in the colony's vast expanse. However, when we look at his offending record and his later life, there is little to suggest that Joe took to these activities with the relish for drama and glamour that has been suggested. The crimes for which he was primarily sentenced to penal servitude were animal thefts as he lived the life of a travelling agricultural labourer – an ordinary man.

After his release from prison, Joe returned to the bush, and lived for two decades near Bunbury, around 100 miles south of Perth. He did not return there as a gun-toting bushranger, a thief, or violent criminal. Joe earned money by minding sheep for local farmers, by collecting animal pelts, and later by working in a local mill, the building trade, and a shop. The remainder of his life was quiet, solitary, and, as far as records show, law abiding.

Moondyne Joe lived on in folk tales, newspaper reports, and even a successful novel (written by a fellow convict and escapee, Irish Fenian John Boyle O'Reilly). In real life, Joseph Johns, the young man from Cornwall who found himself thrust into the limelight across the world, faded back into the obscurity from which he had come. Joe died in Western Australia in 1900. His story, or a version of it, continued to be told in the Western Australian press for more than half a century. Forty years later, an old associate from Bunbury wrote to the *Western Mail*, stating:

> There has been a lot written about 'Moondyne Joe', whose real name was Joseph Bolitho Johns, by people who had neither met the man nor known him as he really was… Johns was not a man to seriously harm anyone if left alone (most of the early convicts were the same)…

In doing so he gave the ordinary man who became one of Western Australia's most famous convicts perhaps his most fitting epitaph.

Fleeing Fenians

That Western Australia receive no political prisoners in their convict transports was one of the three conditions on which the convict depot at Fremantle was established. The British authorities were true to their word until civil unrest in Ireland during the mid-to late 1860s led to panic and paranoia at home. Between 1865 and 1867 a number of republican groups attempted to raise funds, arms and men to forcefully establish a free Irish state outside of the control of the British. These efforts culminated in attempted uprisings around Ireland in the spring of 1867. The British were quick to put down the uprising, arresting many before the fighting and disruption began. Over a two-year period hundreds were arrested. The main ringleaders from the Irish Republican Brotherhood and the Fenian Brotherhood were taken to England to stand trial. Fearing escapes and violent rescue attempts for the prisoners, more than sixty Fenians were shipped to Western Australia on the *Hougoumont* in 1867. Even the most committed Irish republicans could pose little threat to the British half a world away in Australia.

Within five years of arrival, most of those transported for treason and rebellion had been pardoned, or had at least been issued a Ticket-of-Leave. Only a small number of militant Fenians remained in the convict system. The Fenians in Fremantle had not been forgotten by their comrades back home, nor by Fenians now living in America. Funds and a plan were put in place to aid the remaining convict Fenians to escape.

In April of 1876 the *Catalpa* whaling vessel dropped anchor off the west coast of Australia near the settlement of Rockingham. Unbeknown to all but a trusted few, the whaler was manned by loyal Fenians waiting to spirit six convict prisoners to freedom. A small whaling boat was despatched to shore. Six of the Fenian prisoners had been informed of the plan by Fenian agents working in the colony. Whilst on work assignment outside of the prison walls, James Wilson, Robert Cranston, Thomas Darragh, Martin Hogan, Thomas Hassett, and Michael Harrington absconded to a rendezvous point. They were picked up by a cart and driven more than ten miles to Rockingham Pier and the waiting whaleboat.

As the men took to the open water, the authorities had already been alerted to the escape. They rowed for the *Catalpa* but were delayed by a storm and damage to their boat, giving the SS *Georgette*, a government ship, a chance to make for the *Catalpa*. As the ship was in international waters, the crew were able to refuse a search by the *Georgette*, which had no jurisdiction outside of Australia. The escapees in the small whaling boat eventually made it aboard the *Catalpa*, when the *Georgette* again drew level, demanding that the prisoners be handed over, and that the ship return to Australian waters. The crew of the *Catalpa* refused. Sailing under the United States flag, they reminded the *Georgette* that any attempt to fire upon or forcefully damage the ship would be considered an act of war. The *Catalpa* and her convict cargo headed west, alone, and made port at New York City four months later in August 1876. The Fenians were free men, and remained in America for the rest of their lives. The men used their freedom to continue to advocate for the republican movement on whose account they had been transported beyond the seas, and rescued from the very same fate.

The tales of escaped convicts may have made headlines and enduring histories, but daring absconders and successful escape from the penal depot were very much the exception. As a rule, most of the British convicts served their time with little outward resistance, and remained in the colony after their release. Along with the escaping Fenians who journeyed to Australia aboard the *Hougoumont* were more than 200 other men, whose fates were a great deal less glamorous, but perhaps much more illustrative of what transportation to Western Australia could mean for a convict's life chances.

Bad men done good

There were those who found in Australia the success that had eluded their lives in Britain. Amongst the state's convict alumni was John Rowland Jones who, when his eight-year term for embezzlement expired, found employment as the Hansard Reporter for the Western Australian Government, and as the editor of the *West Australian* newspaper. Alfred Chopin arrived in the colony in his early twenties, accused of receiving stolen goods and transported for ten years in 1867. Freed two years later, Chopin became one of the earliest and most famed photographers in the colony. He was commissioned to photograph the Governor of the colony and several other notable dignitaries. Although his business eventually collapsed, Chopin's portraits have endured into the twenty-first century. His portrait of famed convict Moondyne Joe appears in this book. The paintings of convict James Walsh are displayed in the Art Gallery of Western Australia. Even the most ordinary or unsuccessful of convicts might find the opportunity to change their lives, and their luck, in Australia.

Lionel Holdsworth was born in Mauritius in 1826, the son of an army captain. By 1850 the family had settled on the Wirral, just over the Mersey river from Liverpool, a booming centre of shipping, wealth and trade during the mid-nineteenth century. Lionel began working as an agent for local businessmen. In May 1851, Lionel married Margaret Oliver, the daughter of a respectable Wirral family for whom he worked. Lionel was welcomed into the family as a partner in a new business venture: a chandler's business making ships' rope and sails. Owing to the mismanagement of this business, the partnership was dissolved due to insolvency five years later. Lionel and the Olivers, including his wife, went their separate ways, and Lionel was declared bankrupt just two years later.

Lionel moved to London, with intentions to start again in business. He did so; however, by 1864, he was bankrupt once more. Less than two years later, Lionel became embroiled in an insurance scheme, with the hopes of making back his meagre fortune. Lionel, along with Thomas Berwick and Joseph Dean, bribed the first mate of the cargo ship *Severn*, in which they all had a share, to purposefully sink her. The aim of the scheme was to claim for the loss, having insured the ship for several thousand pounds more than it was worth. The ship was 'scuttled' and the deceit discovered. Lionel and the others were put on trial at the Old Bailey and found guilty in January 1867. Holdsworth, held to be the principal architect, was sentenced to twenty years' penal servitude. He was transported on the *Hougoumont* and arrived into the colony in 1868, one of the last convicts ever to do so.

Lionel was an exemplary prisoner. He was recommended for his good conduct by the ship's surgeon, and recommended for his good conduct again by the Governor of the convict establishment. He received his Ticket-of-Leave a third of the way through his sentence in 1874, and for the next six years undertook work as a clerk, and then an accountant, in Fremantle. Lionel was given his Certificate of Freedom in January 1887.

The following year, it looked like Lionel was about to return to his former ways, when the National Bank of Australia cautioned the public against accepting promissory notes in his name, as the payment would not be honoured. The following year, however, Lionel established a new shipping business with two partners, the business being known as Lilly, Holdsworth & Barter. They first began with a pearling schooner, and by 1893 had a fleet of ships. Lionel became a well respected 'rate payer' and member of the community in Fremantle. He owned land and property, and had a second house constructed to his own design. Lionel had finally achieved the affluence and business success he had been unable to find in England. In 1899, at the age of seventy-three, having spent thirty years in the colony, the wealthy and successful Lionel began to make arrangements for the journey back to England. Lionel never made his journey, dying in Fremantle two years later at the age of seventy-five. Lionel left an estate of almost £13,000, a fortune worth approximately £1,400,000 in modern currency.

Of course, building a successful life after serving in the colony as a convict was not a simple process. It was much easier for some than others. Just as in earlier colonies, those who had enjoyed stable backgrounds, been given a good education, or who possessed an innate talent for business, would find it easier to achieve successful or affluent lives than those who did not. Those able to settle into happy family units had less chance of reoffending than those ripped from everyone they knew, unable to form new family and friendship networks. The rich and privileged who found themselves transported had a better chance of continuing to be so in the colony than those that came from poverty and disadvantage.

For every success story that came from convicts in the colonies there were hundreds of convicts who simply got by. They reformed, or at least appeared to, and went on to have lives more or less similar to those they might have lived in Britain. And for every hundred settlers who lived unremarkable lives, there would be perhaps a dozen who could not, or would not, acclimatise to the convict regime and their new environment.

The story of Mark Jeffrey is one of the more famous convict tales to filter back from Australia. The life, crimes, and times of 'big Mark', made immortal by his autobiography, paint the picture of a troubled man who managed to find a kind of equilibrium within the convict system that had dominated his life (Chapter four). His younger brother, Luke, was his partner in crime and his partner in fate. While Mark was causing trouble in the prisons and hulks of England, Luke Jeffrey progressed swiftly through the convict system. He sailed less than two years after their 1848 conviction and landed at Fremantle on the *Scindian*.

Luke's conduct record was considerably better than his brother's. Less than two years after arrival, he had earned his Ticket-of-Leave. This was, unfortunately, placed briefly in jeopardy in September 1852 when Luke was taken to court and fined ten shillings for drunkenness. Other than this minor transgression, for more than a decade, Luke was able to keep largely from trouble whilst progressing through his sentence. During the 1860s, Luke was rumoured to have taken part in numerous burglaries, similar in nature to those he had committed as a teenager in England. Luke was not convicted at the time, but later court testimony from a subsequent trial identified him as the culprit, and as a fencer of stolen goods. In 1867, as his brother Mark was leaving Port Arthur and tasting life as a free man for the first time in almost twenty years, Luke appeared in court charged with the theft of a pocket watch. Luke had sold the watch to a fellow settler called Wilson the previous year, but it had since been discovered to be the property of a Mr McIntosh, stolen in 1865. Luke could give no account of how he had come to possess the watch before selling it. He was given three months of imprisonment in place of a fine.

Like many convicts in the Australian colonies, Luke Jeffrey was an example of how convict lives intertwined with those of free settlers, other law breakers, and the long arm of the law throughout their lives. Although very often ex-convicts found themselves back in the dock on charges, they also appeared as witnesses in criminal cases. Just like George Langley in Tasmania, Luke, after his own subsequent convictions, was still considered enough a part of colonial society that his testimony was of value in criminal cases against others. In 1877, Luke was a government witness in the trial of another Fremantle man, William Bayliss, for killing Anne McGrath, the woman with whom he lived.

Luke had a partner and children, but not a stable life. He was in and out of work, in and out of court, and in a cycle of alcohol abuse. Luke's end was no happier than his brother's. In March 1883, Luke, still working in Western Australia as a sawyer, walked out to a place in the bush known as 'Robb's Swamp' and committed suicide with a shotgun. An inquest found that he had been suffering 'in a state of mental depression' for an unknown period of time. Luke had been living with Elizabeth Stinton, a local woman. The pair had cohabited for more than ten years and had three children together. According to Elizabeth, Luke had begun drinking in the week leading up to his death. One morning he told Elizabeth he was going to mend a fence, shortly before the gunshot was heard. Luke must have been quite determined to end his own life. He broke into a neighbour's tool shed, took a shotgun, and managed to shoot himself by pulling the trigger with his foot and a loop of twig. Luke left a short note:

> I cannot live any longer. My mind is loaded with more than I can bear. My last prayer is that providence will favour my children, 3 in number. May the mother live long to see them, and give them kind word in the right way, I know well what I am going to do. I am in a sound state of mind this day. LUKE JEFFREY.

He left a post script, addressed to the neighbour who he believed would find him.

> Johnny Lane you will see this and read it before you go home, and may you never have on your mind what I have on mine. Goodbye all, I shall not saw Mahogany where I am going. L. JEFFREY

Luke Jeffrey was clearly in distress when he took his own life, though the vagueness in his note left those around him, and historians, with little evidence as to the reasons behind his suicide. The year prior to his suicide, Luke had been riding a horse through Fremantle when his saddle slipped and he was thrown to the ground. He sustained a number of kicks from his startled horse, and was found to have 'sustained very severe injuries'. He was conveyed to a nearby infirmary, where newspapers reported that he made a good, but slow, recovery. The press noted 'it will be some time before he will be able to return to his work.' Luke may have been unable to cope with the financial strain caused by the loss of his ability to work for several months – especially with a partner and three young children to support. This may have been the great worry weighing on his mind that he referenced in his note. Alternately, Luke's suicide may have been the result of a longer standing unhappiness. Luke had not thrived in the colony. He may not have been regularly convicted, but there is evidence to suggest that he continued to offend. Luke was in and out of work as a sawyer for at least a decade. The job entailed hard manual labour, which Luke's suicide note indicates he intensely disliked. However, at almost sixty at the time of his death, being an unskilled ex-convict with a reputation for theft, would have made it difficult for Luke to secure other work.

Luke's life had been one of poverty and crime. His transportation did little to change the trajectory of his life and seems to have only served to isolate him from family, friends, and the familiar. Whether or not Luke's transportation extended his offending career is unclear, but by all accounts may certainly have contributed to the deep distress that led eventually to his death.

In many cases, convicts who caused trouble at home remained troubled prisoners abroad. Philip Dixon, who had caused such sensation with his repeated attempts to escape the hulks (See Chapter one) back in England, settled no better to life in the convict establishment at Fremantle. Having arrived in Western Australia in mid-1851, it took Dixon less than a year to breach establishment rules. In 1852 he was charged with being drunk at a public house in the company of those who had charge of him. He received fourteen days of solitary confinement and bread and water.

In 1855, when free settler John Hurford was murdered, Philip Dixon was implicated in having altered Hurford's will for his own benefit. He was found guilty of the forgery and sentenced to have his term of transportation extended for life. The sentence was remitted when he provided important testimony about the murder itself, leading to the conviction of the killers. He was sent to Rottnest Island (a small penal island a few miles from Fremantle, which was primarily used for the detention of Aboriginal prisoners). Fewer than six months later, in February 1856, he was found to have been 'instrumental in creating disaffection among the native convicts' of Rottnest Island and, drawing on his own previous experiences, having helped them escape. During the escape a huge fire ensued, causing considerable damage to colonial property for which Dixon was partially blamed. He escaped Rottnest, and made his way to Perth, where he posed as a member of the police before his apprehension. Dixon, a 'notorious character' even in the colony, was given three years of imprisonment in irons for his trouble. Philip Dixon appeared in south Australia two years later, causing considerable confusion as to whether he had been re-transported there by the Western Australian authorities (found too troublesome to be kept in Fremantle), or had once again escaped captivity. He was apprehended in Adelaide for committing a number of burglaries, and placed on trial.

Philip Dixon became a kind of colonial celebrity, with his transgressions making the papers in both Western Australia and his new home in the south of the country. Although still under sentence, he disappeared from all news reports after 1859, when the *Perth Inquirer and Commercial News* reported, 'A Philip Dixon has been fined in Melbourne for driving his cart over a mounted policeman, and striking the man on the head as he was falling. Is this our old friend?' Given Dixon's penchant for escape, he had perhaps finally learned the value of living by an alias, rather than the name that he had made so notorious on both sides of the world, and settled elsewhere in Australia.

Dixon's escapades became an amusing spectacle for the contemporary press and its readers, but underneath the sensationalism remains the tale of a man clashing incessantly with the institutions which tried to restrain him. A man living a solitary and transient life as he was pushed from institution to institution, and making bids for freedom around the country. We do not know what became of Philip Dixon, but as a wanted convict it is unlikely he was ever able to book passage back to England, or to have his wife or children join him in the colony.

Many names, but the same old tale

Despite the positive reputation transportation to Australia was gaining back home in England, arrival in the colonies was no guarantee of future success. The penal colony in Western Australia, like those that came before, had mixed success in reforming convicts. Some did indeed go on to lead successful lives in the colony. Others continued the spiral of punishment and recidivism they had begun in Britain, continuing to offend for decades after arrival. In some cases, a convict's interaction with the penal estate not only outlasted the short convict era of Western Australia, but continued past the federation of the colonies into the commonwealth of Australia, and into the twentieth century.

Edward Burdett was a man of many names. Born in England around 1828, by the time he was thirty, Edward was well on his way to carving out a reputation as another of London's incorrigible habitual offenders. Edward Burdett first came to the attention of the English press in 1857, when he was sentenced to four years of penal servitude for the theft of 186 yards of cotton. At the time of his trial he had been out of prison only a matter of weeks after a six-month sentence for stealing a roll of flannel from a warehouse. We do not know why Edward first turned to theft, but this early inability to remain at large for more than a few months or a year between sentences was a pattern that would recur in his life on both sides of the world.

As Edward made his way to serve his sentence in Portland prison, he left behind a wife and a young daughter, who he would not see for three years. Edward was released on New Year's Eve of 1860, but within six months, he found himself back in court on trial for the theft of a roll of valuable cloth. Under the name Peter Watkins, Edward was returned to prison on another four-year sentence. With three convictions already to his name(s) Edward was lucky to avoid a sentence of transportation. He spent three years in Dartmoor before he was released in July 1864. Just three months later, he was back in the dock of the Old Bailey, this time as Edward Carlton, charged with the theft of another roll of fabric. His luck finally ran out and he was sentenced to be transported for seven years.

By the time of his conviction, transportation to Western Australia was already waning, and the government had a large population of men undergoing penal servitude on hulks and in convict prisons. Only a small proportion of prisoners would ever be sent. Edward waited for almost half of his sentence in Portland prison before he was selected to sail on the penultimate ship to embark for the colony. The *Norwood* set off with Edward and approximately 250 other convict men in April 1867, arriving at Fremantle in July that year. Edward was processed into the convict system, and was granted his Ticket-of-Leave a year later in 1868, at which point he was free to undertake work in the colonies.

In the next four years Edward worked for six different employers as a carpenter in Fremantle and Perth. His frequent changes in employment were due in no small part to the even more regular breaches of licence conditions he committed. From disobedience, insolence, and refusing to work, to having contraband items like tobacco and watches in his possession, and theft and obtaining goods under false pretences, Edward committed fourteen infractions whilst on his Ticket-of-Leave. His infractions earned him anywhere from a few days on the punishment diet of bread and water, to twelve months of hard labour at Fremantle Prison. Each time he served a punishment, he had to convince his previous employer to take him back, or find new work. His disorderly behaviour also served to prolong his sentence by two years. He received his Certificate of Freedom in 1873, allowing him to live free in the colony or even return home to England and his, now adult, daughter Rose.

Free for the first time in almost a decade, Edward was a skilled worker with the chance to begin again in the colonies. Instead, as he had done in England, Edward reoffended in less than a year. While public order offences were relatively common in the major towns of Western Australia, often earning perpetrators a few days in a local gaol or a fine, the state authorities had less tolerance for crimes of theft and violence. Especially by recidivists and expired convicts. Receiving thousands of convicts had been necessary for the colony's failing economy but, in the post-convict era, Western Australia had no intention of becoming a lawless bandit country. For receiving jewellery obtained during a high-profile burglary, Edward was sentenced to ten years' penal servitude in January 1874. He returned to Fremantle Prison, where he stayed for five years until granted another Ticket-of-Leave in 1879. More than ten years since his first parole, Edward returned to the familiar pattern of employment and infractions which saw him change employers five times in his first year of liberty alone. The following year, 1881, Edward, still on licence, had taken to cattle raiding. With three years remaining of his former sentence as well as this new offence, Edward, who according to the newspaper was 'better known as Bombastes Furioso', was sentenced to a further fourteen years of penal servitude.

Edward returned to Fremantle Prison to begin progress through the system again. He received his next Ticket-of-Leave surprisingly early, in 1885, just four years into his sentence. In the intervening years Edward had again proved a stubborn prisoner and was noted to be idle, to refuse to work, to be insolent and difficult. Perhaps an indication as to why his Ticket was so forthcoming. As Edward stepped out into semi-freedom again, the colony was on the upturn. The discovery of gold in Western Australia saw money start to flow, and opportunities on the rise. Although Edward was not free to leave the area to prospect for himself, the value of his labour, and his carpentry skills, would have increased in value to those who planned to make the most of the mining boom. Edward worked as a carpenter for four different employers, before setting up his own business in 1886. Just a few months later, however, his Ticket-of-Leave was revoked when he was found drunk in the streets of Perth and returned to prison. It was two years before he was granted another.

Things for Edward do seem to have improved after another Ticket-of-Leave was granted in 1888, more than twenty years since his arrival in the colony, and the end of convict transportation. This sudden break in Edward's pattern of offending may have been due to a sudden personal epiphany, but is more likely to have been the result of economic abundance and opportunity following the second Western Australian gold rush in the year of his liberation, and the others that followed soon after. With money plentiful, and jobs easy to come by, Edward managed to serve out the full term of his sentence with no further infractions or offences.

Almost immediately as his former sentence expired, however, when he was truly free again, Edward was arrested on suspicion of a rash of burglaries. He and fellow ex-convict, William Burnside, had been perpetrating offences in a range of hill settlements not far from Perth. Incredibly, despite his record, and the fact that he was apprehended whilst in possession of the full range of housebreaking tools, Edward was found not guilty and released. If not, he may well have spent the rest of his life in prison.

In the later 1890s as the boom from gold discoveries settled, Edward found himself entering old age with less opportunity to work. Large numbers of young economic migrants were still flooding to the state, hoping for work and fortune, with whom Edward, approaching seventy and an ex-convict, could not compete for jobs. Like a number of older men from the convict era that were unable to settle to life in Western Australia, unmarried and with no family to care for them, Edward began to pose an increasing burden to the authorities (Image 24).

No longer agile enough to resort to the physically taxing crimes of former decades, Edward began to live a somewhat transient life, drinking, causing a public nuisance and relying on petty thefts for subsistence. Edward remained in and around Perth and Fremantle, drinking, and working when he could, using a string of aliases, including Edward Rogers, Edward Anson and Alfred Anson. As well as offending, Edward was increasingly vulnerable to victimisation, particularly at the hands of young and unscrupulous men passing through the town looking to make fast money. In 1897 he was robbed of small change whilst drunk in a Fremantle pub, in full view of the bartender, who saw two men rifling through the pockets of an intoxicated Edward.

Two years later, in 1899, Edward was in court for the offence of supplying alcohol to two Aboriginal men. It was illegal for Indigenous peoples to purchase alcohol in Australia until the second half of the twentieth century. Men like Edward could earn a good profit by taking money from Aboriginal people in return for purchasing alcohol on their behalf. This seemingly minor infraction was treated severely, due to the perceived nuisance caused by Aboriginal drinking. Edward was given a fine of £30 which he could not pay, and sentenced to one month of hard labour in default. He was given another week of imprisonment for refusing to give his details to the arresting officer.

A month of hard labour at the age of seventy-one was a serious undertaking, and for almost three years after his release, Edward was not apprehended for any significant offences. That was until 1903, when a rash of bicycle thefts and some other public order infractions saw him serve several terms – from three days, to twelve months of hard labour, in prison. Edward was, by this time in his life, reported to be completely deaf. Shortly after his release from prison in 1905, Edward was found collapsed on the veranda of a house in Perth. Noted to be 'very ill', he was taken to the hospital where he subsequently died at the age of seventy-eight. It was a sad end to one of the last convicts transported to Western Australia, a man with a string of different names and crimes, whose story was only too familiar to those that knew the convict system.

Edward's life in Australia was not only a continuation of what it might have been if he had continued to serve terms of penal servitude in England. It was similar to those of many other convicts who found it difficult to reform after sentence, to recover from the physical and mental trauma of being shipped away from all they knew, and who struggled to grow old in a place where they were little to anyone but an old convict.

Some of those shipped out to Western Australia were the most troublesome of British convicts, whom the government chose to send away rather than deal with at home. These men continued to cause trouble in the convict establishment abroad, and for many years afterwards. Although Western Australia quickly outgrew its penal settlement, that made no difference to the men abandoned there by the British state. The convicts grew old. Although new, younger, home grown, offenders began to dominate Australia's criminal justice system and penal institutions, British convicts could still be found passing in and out of the penal system on a regular basis. Like Mark Jeffrey decades before in Van Diemen's Land, some aged convicts bounced through charitable, medical, and penal institutions, relying on whatever care the state had to offer. The very last convicts in Western Australia only ceased to do so in the twentieth century, as they died as old men and their names and stories were forgotten. Until then, most prisons and gaols in the state could be relied upon to have a spattering of ex-convict prisoners at any given time.

In the same year that Edward Carlton was sent to hard labour for supplying Aboriginal men with alcohol, he was one of more than a dozen British ex-convicts committed to Fremantle Prison thirty or forty years after their transportation. Men like John Henry Venn, or Vaughan, or Bent, a convict from Liverpool, sentenced to ten years' transportation for forgery in 1861, and transported aboard the *York* the following year. A year after his original sentence expired, Venn was convicted of forging a cheque in his master's name, a man who had given him work as a cook when he was given his liberty. Venn was given a further ten years of penal servitude for the crime.

As Venn aged, like Carlton, his opportunities for work reduced, and he had no support network to rely upon. Throughout the 1890s Venn was convicted of more forgeries and obtaining by false pretences, earning himself terms of imprisonment and hard labour. In 1899 he joined Edward Carlton in Fremantle Prison, convicted of obtaining goods by false pretences. He dipped in and out of the prison system for the next four years. In 1901, Venn was convicted of fraudulently collecting money. He forged a document from a member of the Perth Hospital, claiming he was an invalid whose house and family had been destroyed in a fire, and who was soliciting charitable donations for his own recovery. He served more time at hard labour, and in the following years was repeatedly convicted of being a rogue and a vagabond. Upon conviction in 1903, the magistrates sent Venn back to prison, and recommended that he enter the 'Old Men's Home', a charitable institution for the aged and indigent. Whether Venn entered the institution or found another way to subsist in the last years of his life, he died alone in Perth Hospital in 1910 at the age of eighty-two, almost half a century after arriving in the colony.

With Venn and Carlton was sixty-seven-year-old Thomas Bone. A convict from Ireland who, alongside being regularly idle, disorderly and a vagrant, had spent the preceding five years in and out of a home for destitute men in Perth. Thomas spent time in an asylum, and had several more convictions for vagrancy before he died in Perth Hospital at the age of sixty-nine. Seventy-year-old Berkshire native Thomas Gaisford had been in the colony more than forty years when he joined the others in prison at the turn of the twentieth century, after arriving on the *Adelaide* in 1855. Gaisford struggled with alcohol abuse and convictions for drunkenness from almost the point of his arrival in the colony. Unlike the others, Gaisford did marry, but his marriage was not a happy one, and he narrowly escaped a conviction of manslaughter after beating his wife to death in 1896. He was convicted of theft a few years later, and then lived a largely transient existence, suffering a serious fall from a moving train and contracting pneumonia, before being found sleeping in a condemned building and sent to hard labour in 1904. There were many more like Bone. Men like John Hartley Bowen, who by the end of his life was estranged from his wife and children, a suspected arsonist, and convicted burglar. Irishman James Clinton, Scotsman James Hunter, Englishman George Benbow and others were British ex-convicts who continued to plight the Australian criminal justice system decades after arrival.

The end of an era

By the time the *Hougoumont* deposited a final shipment of 281 convict men in Fremantle in 1868, the colony had been operating a convict settlement for eighteen years. Although the final group of convicts, and their fellows who had arrived in the few years before, still had to serve their time, officially the system of convict transportation to Australia was at an end.

Within a decade, almost all the sentences of British convicts had expired, and those transported for life had been issued their Ticket-of-Leave. Almost 10,000 convict men, rejected from Britain, had made new lives for themselves in the colony. The convict system may have been over, the penal settlement disbanded, but the men who were its legacy lived on. While some became pillars of their communities, fathered families, and became much loved and valued friends and neighbours, others floundered. As we have seen, for decades after the last transport and into the twentieth century, ex-convicts continued to make their way around Fremantle and Perth reoffending or relying on state and charitable institutions to support them.

Australia's convict era, not only for the Western colony, but for the entire country, did not end in 1868 when the last transport arrived, nor even when the last convict gained their freedom. The end of the convict era came seventy years after the last ship when an elderly man 'as lively as a two year old' died at almost 100 years of age in 1938 (Image 25). A time within living memory.

Samuel Speed was rumoured to have been born in Birmingham in 1841 and nothing of his parents, or siblings, is known. Samuel was in his early twenties when he was tried at Oxfordshire Sessions in November 1863. Along with another man he had set fire to a haystack in a field next to a local workhouse with the intention of being arrested. Speed had been begging on the street, and with the money bought the matches he used to start the fire. Both men freely admitted the crime, and claimed they did it with the hope of receiving something to eat. They were found guilty and sentenced to seven years of penal servitude. While others served their penal servitude in Britain's convict prisons, Samuel was selected to sail to Australia. He arrived in Fremantle aboard the *Belgravia* in 1866. Samuel's Ticket-of-Leave was granted the following year, and for the next four years he made a living as a general servant in Quindalup, in the south-west of the state. He was granted his Certificate of Freedom in 1871, three years after the arrival of the final ship.

Samuel went on to live a perfectly ordinary and law abiding life, only coming to the attention of the papers a few months before his death in 1938, as he neared his centenary. By this time, old and frail, dependent on the care of attendants, Samuel's memories of transportation, like the rest of the colony's, were well faded. Amongst the few recollections of his former life a journalist reported:

> Among those unfortunates transported he recalls were men of every walk of life; doctors, lawyers, shirt-soiled gentlemen and social outcasts tipped together in the [h]ot-house of humanity that was the Swan River Colony.

Far from being ashamed of his past, Samuel's great age lent a nobility to his former convict status. To the press, and no doubt many who read his story, his life was a gratifying conformation that the system had worked.

Western Australia had taken corrupt British convicts and turned them into productive members of society. The report continued:

> During the 74 years he spent in this State, Speed's conduct was all that a reputable citizen's should be, and many people who knew him could testify to his excellent work and record. During his lifetime Speed, who was a bachelor, never smoked because as he remarked … 'I didn't like it. Besides I could always sell my tobacco rations to other prisoners.'

Despite Samuel's evident triumph over circumstances, his story was not so different from many of the convicts who did not fare so well in their new home. He never drank or smoked, which may well have kept him from trouble and helped him attain such a great age, but Samuel never married or had children either. He never regained contact with his family in England. A brother and sister back in Birmingham who he 'never heard from again' after arriving in the colony. Despite his own and other's testimony to his happy and productive life, Speed spent the last years of his life much the same as many of the ex-convicts who had lived neither happily nor productively – in the Old Men's Home at Perth. The same institution that became home to those expirees like Edward Carlton and John Henry Venn who passed in and out of the courts and prisons until they were too old or incapacitated to do so any more. A few months after the birthday that drew him to the attention of Western Australia's media, in December 1938, Samuel Speed died in the home. A report noted 'When he was buried at Karrakatta Cemetery there were only a few of his companions at the Old Men's Home present at the grave side.' Samuel Speed may not have been the last man off the last transport boat from Britain to Australia, but until his death just eighty years ago he was widely acknowledged as the last living transportee.

Samuel Speed was one of the understated success stories of the colony. After serving his sentence peacefully and gaining his freedom, he never reoffended. Samuel stayed in the colony and helped it to grow into a thriving outpost of empire. Samuel was one of the men that helped to build the Fremantle Bridge across the vast Swan River, and spent the rest of his working life at various companies around the town. Samuel was, by all accounts, an ordinary, largely unremarkable, man. Yet during his time in the colony, as a convict and a free man, he had borne witness to remarkable moments in Western Australia's history, from the escape of the notorious convict Moondyne Joe into the Banbury bush, and the Fenians across the ocean to America, to the gold rushes that saw the economy and population of Western Australia boom. He was one of the last men to experience transportation to Australia, and got to witness its end. He lived long enough to see a former penal settlement become part of the federated commonwealth of Australia. He witnessed the death of an old archaic system, a different way of life belonging to an earlier time, and the birth of a nation beyond the seas.

Conclusion

Convict transportation might seem like part of some distant history, barely recognisable in our own, often considered more civilised, age. But the days of loading convicts on board boats and sending them out of sight and out of mind is closer than we might think. As are the lessons we can still learn from the tales of the transported. The last known living convict died just eighty years prior to the printing of this book – within living memory. Moreover, some of the grandchildren and great-grandchildren of the last convicts may still be alive, and throughout Australia, the descendents of British convicts can be found in every walk of life. Transportation to Australia was one of the greatest penal experiments ever conducted by the British, and still has the power to teach us about the impact of punishment on a single life, a family, a community, and even a country.

In the space of just eighty years, the lives and fates of more than 168,000 men, women and children were altered forever. So too were the lives of their husbands, wives, brothers, sisters, children, friends, and loved ones left behind. That alone makes theirs a history worth the telling. But the history of convict transportation is more than the sum of its parts. Together, those stories of love, and loss, grief and perseverance half a world away are the story of evolving British justice and nation building too. Australia would not, and could not, have been the country it is today were it not for those eight decades of convict transportation and each of the convict men, women, and children that arrived on its shores.

Through a system of forced migration, a country largely unexplored by Europeans, intended to act primarily as a repository for the metropole's great unwashed and unwanted, grew into a thriving centre of free-settlement and economic prosperity. The roads and architecture and public spaces enjoyed by millions of tourists who visit Sydney, Perth, and Hobart each year were forged by the labour of those shipped in bondage. Men and women who later gained liberty, land, and lives they could scarcely have dreamed of back home.

When we look at the history of transportation it seems fairly self-evident that from a western perspective, the system was a success. The British Empire gained land and resources from its new colonies, and grew in size and status on their account. White European Australia gained too. Convict labour offered a cost-efficient way to build a nation, and to keep the population at a high enough level for subsistence. When the colonies were ready to move on from their years as penal settlements, to form a federation and to declare independence, the transportation era had left them with almost everything they could need. Over the twentieth century, Australia's story has been one of continued achievement, so much so that it now has one of the toughest immigration procedures in the world. The points system seeks to protect everything successive generations of Australians have built, and the considerable natural bounty their country – once considered bleak and hostile – affords them.

Yet when we look at the histories of the transported, the narrative of success seems less certain. Amongst the many thousands of individuals sent to Australia, some thrived, some simply survived, and others perished along the way. Their stories are each worth recording and remembering. Life in Australia's penal settlements was far from easy for convicts, either during or after sentence, but it did have something that life for offenders at home often lacked: opportunity. If this collection of convict histories tells us anything it is that Australia was a place in which convicts could, in certain circumstances, move past conviction. They had opportunity for employment, or to work for themselves. In the very best cases they might build businesses or own land; they could form families and seek their fortune. Fledgling Australia had, in many ways, what Britain needed to combat the root causes of crime, rather than just shipping away offenders when it was already too late. Yet, for every one convict who excelled in their Australian life, there were dozens who continued to struggle. The opportunities offered by life in Australia were matched only by the psychological, social and, at times, physical brutality that took offenders there. Convicts might not have repeated the serious crimes for which they were transported, but we do not have to look far for examples of former convicts caught up in a cycle of petty offending and public disorder which consumed large chunks of their 'free' lives. Many never fully recovered from the trauma of being torn from friends, family, and homeland, and we have little idea how their loved ones coped without them. The negative impact of convict transportation stretched across both sides of the world and could be long-lasting.

Convicts in Australia might find their lives less defined by their original offences (there were, after all, in the company of thousands of others in the same position) than they would have been in Britain. However, this did not guarantee freedom from the life-long effect of being a convict, nor the impact it might have on their children, grandchildren and beyond. The inequality that had seen many of Britain and Ireland's poorest and most vulnerable subjects shipped to Australia could be reproduced in successive generations, long after the convict era. Some of the most famed bush-rangers and offenders of the post-convict decades, like the world-famous Ned Kelly, were the children of convicts. It is only comparatively recently in Australia that finding a convict ancestor has been cause for intrigue and investigation, rather than silence and shame.

It is true too, that for all the gains made by the Australian state, and by some fortunate convicts, penal transportation to Australia changed forever the lives and culture of the indigenous population for the worse. Land was seized, resources were monopolised and racial hierarchy was installed by the British. All of which proved disadvantageous to the peoples who had roamed the continent for centuries. In this respect, the colonial legacy in Australia differed little from those which had gone before, in America, Africa, and the Indian sub-continent.

Transportation to Australia, from the First Fleet to the final ship was, at its core, a system driven by people, rather than process, and so is its history. Histories of colonial Australia are made up of histories of convicts, like the ones in this book. The practice of penal transportation when the first ships set out to Australia in 1787, and all that followed, may have been shaped by penal theorists' ideas about crime, justice, and the relationship between punishment and reform. But the reality of the convict system, and the experience of those within it, was perpetually evolving to the needs and challenges of convicts. The rigid system designed in England learned to adapt to suit the needs of the colonists and the colonies, rather than the homeland. Rules could bend and even break to give convicts the best chance at rebuilding their lives; they could even be rewritten to protect vulnerable convicts when it came to transport conditions on ships. After all, while Britain wanted to be rid of her 'criminal classes', Australia wanted to transform the criminals of the British streets and prisons into the farmers, shopkeepers, labourers, and families that the colony needed to rise up from its humble origins.

Appendix

Margaret Catchpole to Mrs Cobbold 21 January 1802:

Honred madam

With grat plusher I take up my penn to a Quaint you, my good Ladday of my saf a rivel at port Jackson new South Wales sedeny [Sydney] on the 20th Day of Desember 1801.

As I was Going to be Landed, on the Left hand of me, it put me in mind of the Cleeff – Both the housen and Lik wise the hills so as it put me in very Good spirites seeing a places so much like my owen nativ home.

It is a Grat deel moor lik englent then ever I Did expet to a seen for hear is garden stuff of all koind. Expt gosbres an currenes and appelles. The Garddenes are very Buttefull in ded all planted with geraniums and thay run up 7 and 8 foot hy.

It is a very woodey Cuntry, for of I goo out andey a Distences hear is going throw woodes for miles – But thay are very Buttefull – and very pretty Beardes.

I only wish my Good Laddey I Could send you one of these parrottes, for thay are very Buttefull, but I see so Mayny Dy on Bord it mak me so very unwilling to send you one – But if I should continner Long in this Countrey I suarteneley will send you sumthing out of this wicked Countrey – FOR I MUST SAY THIS IS THE WICKEDES PLACE I EVER WAS IN ALL MY LIFE.

The weat harvest was all most over just as I landed. I hear weat is 8 shillens pear Busshell at this time, hear is 2 Cropes in the summer, one with weat and one with indey Corn. I Cannot give you not much a count of the Countrey, not in this letter, but I will Giv you moor in the next for I niver shorll for fit yuir foodness my Food Laddey you sheow to me Befor I Left enflent – I took every thing over with me safe and thay are a Grat sarves to me in Deed.

Not that I am in such Grat trobell at present, But God oneley know how it may be for hear is maney one that have Benn heat for maney year and that have thar poor head shaved and sent up to the Coole river thear Carrey cooles from Day Light in the morning till Dark at Knight, and hald starved, but I hear that is a Going to Be put By and so it had need, for it is very crouell in ded.

Norfolk Islent is a Bad Places a nof to send aney poor Cratuer, with steel Corler on thear poor neckes, But I will tak good keear of myself from that.

I am Prettey well of at present for I was taken of the stores 2 Days after I Landed so I hav no Govment work to do, nor thay hav nothing to do with me – oneley when hear Be a general muster, then I must a peear to Leat them know I am hear – and -if I hav a mind I goo up to Parramatta, 20 miles, or to towen Gabbey, 30 mile, or to Ocberrey, 40 mile I hav to get a pass or elce I should Be taken up and put into prison – for a very Lettell will do that hear.

My Dear Good Laddey I wont to say a frat Deel moor But time will not permit for I expet the ship to sail every Day. I have Benn very Bad sinces I Com on shor, I thought I shold a Lorst my Life, But Bless Be to the Lord I am a grat Deel Better – I was Charmenley all my passed Consideren we Com over the Beay of Beakey, and wee Crost the Line very well in ded.

I was tossed a Bout very much in Ded But u shold not mind it if I was But a Coming to old englent onces more, for I Cannot say that I Lik this Contrey – no, nor niver shorll.

The Governor hav a good maney Cowes and a nother gentleman hear is a good maney horses and very smart wiskes and Leetell shay cartes and passeg Bootes

My Dear madam I must con Clud an send you moor account the next time

From your unfortuned searvant Margaret Catchpole.

Madam pray Be so koind as to Leet doctor Stebbenes hav that sid of the Letter. I hop these few scroules find you and all your Good famley well and I hop my Good ladey you writ to the furst transport ship that do Come out for I should be very glad to hear from you.

In the ssmae letter she enclosed a note for Dr Stebbenes

For Docter Stebbenes

Dear Sir

This is to a Quaint you of our saf landen at Sedney on the 20th day of December.

Wee wear all well = Barker is a live, but she was very much dritened at the rufness of the sea – she youst to very often cry out "I wish I was with my Dear mr. Stebenes for I niver shorll see Ipswich no moor" – But she is much the sam as ever.

Elesabeth Kellett luve very near to me and do very well and she is off the stores and so as we ar not driv about after work for the Govment Lik horseas – wee are free from all hard work.

Sarey Barker hav to spin for Govment and she is up on the stors But she Can Git har work don By 12 or 1 a clock if she work hard at it.

Sir pray Giv my Best respects to all my old fellear prisnors and tell them niver to say "dead Hearted" at the thoughts of coming to Boteny Bay for it is Likley you may niver see it – for it is no hapited – onely By the Blacked, the nativs of this place – thay are very saveg for thay all wais Carrey with them spears and tommeay horkes so when thay can meet wit a man thay will rob them and speer them. – I for my part do not Like them – I do not know how to Look at them – thay are such poor naked Craturs – thay behave them selves well a nof when thay Com in to my house for if not wee would Git them punneshed. Thay very often hav a grand fite with them selves 20 and 30 all to gether – and we pray to be spared. Sum of them are kild – thear is nothing said to them for killing one a nother.

The Cropes of weat is very good in this country for it perducers forteey Busshells per ackear – it is a very Bountifull place in deed for I under stand them that niver had a child in all thear lives hav sum after thay com hear.

Dear sir

Jan 21st the Blacks the natives of this places kild and Wounded 8 men and wemen and Children – 1 man they cur of his arms half way up and Brok the Bones that they Left on very much and Cut thear leages of up to thear knees and the poor man was carread in to the ospitle a Liv – But the Govener hav sent men out after them to shot every 1 thay find – so as I hop I shorll give you better a Count the next Letter

Pray Sir send me word if you know wear Dinah parker and har Child is

Sir I will Wright moor a Bout the Countrey when I wright a Gain. Tea is 22's to 20 and 15 shillenes -sugger 2 shillens to 18 and 15 pence per pound – salt beef 1 shilling per pound – mutton 2ds per pound – fifteen shillings for a par of shos – 10d for a par odf sockenes – fiv shillings for a yard of Common prent – 3d for a yard of carlaker – 3 shillinges for a pound of sop – Fish is as Chape as aney thing wee can By – But wee hav no money to trad with hear.

Pray my good sir remember me to Mrs ripshaw and tell her hear is one of Mr ripshawes own Daughters Liven up in the Countrey – But I hav no seen har – not yet.

Sir I hop you will be so koined as to writ to me By the fust ship that do Com out to Botany Bay and Drect to me at samewell rolley in the Brickfeldes No 40. Sedney.

Sir we had not one died – no not all the passeg out in so maney a wemen.

Tracing Transportees: Resources for the Reader.

There are roughly 168,000 Australian convict stories out there to discover, uncover, and recover. Whether you are looking for records of an ancestor or particular person, or simply hoping to find out more about this fascinating period of history, there is a wealth of information available. England's National Archives at Kew contain many of the original records from the Home Office and the centralised criminal justice system which tried, confined, and arranged to ship prisoners from all over Britain and Ireland to Australia. Likewise, state archives throughout Australia, particularly New South Wales, Tasmania, and Western Australia, hold a wide range of documents which recorded prisoners once they arrived. However, visiting physical archives, especially those on the other side of the world, is not always practical or preferable. We are fortunate to live in an age in which an unfathomable collection of records and information is available through the internet with just a few clicks. Many of the stories in this book were sourced in part or entirely from online repositories of historical records. Below is an introduction to some of the key sources that can help readers uncover their own tales of transportation, and suggestions for reading material for anyone who wants to know more about the process of transportation, the historical criminal justice system, or the life of the transported once they ventured beyond the seas.

The Digital Panopticon
(www.digitalpanopticon.org)

The research in this book has been greatly enhanced by the work and resources provided by the Digital Panopticon project. The Digital Panopticon traces the lives of London convicts (and many more from around the UK) as they made their way through the justice system, and experienced either imprisonment in England or transportation to Australia, between 1780–1925. The website brings together records from the Old Bailey and Founders and Survivors projects alongside a large number of new records, and information from commercial partners at Ancestry.com and Findmypast.co.uk in order to link together previously fragmentary collections of documents into 'life archives' for individual convicts. Through the Digital Panopticon website, transcriptions of an unprecedented number of documents regarding the trial, post-trial and sentencing, transportation, imprisonment and civil lives of convicts are available to view free of charge.

Tasmanian Archives and Heritage
(www.linc.tas.gov.au)

The free to access online collections provided by the Tasmanian Archives provide a first-hand history of convicts sent to Van Diemen's Land. The online collection of convict records contains ships' musters and physical descriptions of newly arriving convicts, as well as their conduct records for their time under sentence in the colony. These records tell us everything from the height and eye colour of the men and women arriving, to the labour they carried out, and when they became eligible for their Ticket-of-Leave. The collection also includes applications and permissions for convicts to marry, birth records for their children, and even in some cases records of death. The records can all be accessed via the Tasmanian Names Index and can be sorted by record time, ship of arrival, date, and more.

Old Bailey Proceedings
(www.oldbaileyonline.org)

For over ten years the Old Bailey Online has constituted one of the most important resources for those interested in crime and criminal justice in England between the seventeenth and twentieth centuries. These free to access and fully searchable trial proceedings allow an unparalleled glimpse into the courtroom, and surviving ordinary accounts can even take us all the way to the gallows. Transcriptions of cases between 1780–1867 offer the chance to take an intimate look at the crimes of those who were transported and some of their reactions to their sentences. From child pickpockets, to murderers, from famous cases to the ordinary men and women who had one day in the dock shape the rest of their lives. Through the proceedings we have the opportunity to read how offenders, prosecutors, and witnesses told the story of crime and punishment in their own words, and to find out more about some of the men and women who would become Australia's first European settlers.

Trove Digitized Newspapers
(www.trove.nla.gov.au/newspapers)

The National Library of Australia's Trove Digitized Newspapers contains more than 200,000,000 historic newspaper entries published over the last two centuries and is entirely free to access. The online archive can be keyword searched for names, ships, events, or phrases and can be restricted by date, state (colony), publication, and even article type. During the convict period, crime reportage made up a significant proportion of the printed media, and the details of convicts receiving their Ticket-of-Leave, Certificate of Freedom, or Conditional Pardon were also regularly printed. Family notices, advertisements, and letters to the editor can all hold key pieces of information which allow us to reconstruct a convict's life after their sentence expired. Australian papers also reported news about the day-to-day life in each colony, big developments in Britain and their repercussions for the empire, and news of shipwrecks, mutinies, escapes, and escapades within the convict system that rarely made an appearance in the British press.

British Newspaper Archive
(www.britishnewspaperarchive.co.uk)

The BNA is the largest digitised collection of historic newspapers available in Britain. This database (unfortunately not free to access) provides over two hundred years' worth of newspapers from across Britain and Ireland. Most of those published during the Victorian period contain weekly (if not daily) accounts of crime and punishment that can be searched for the name of an individual offender or crimes, or sentences of transportation. The papers contain articles on Britain's exploration and colonisation of Australia, and big events in each of the colonies, as well as coverage of Britain's convict population, prisons, and prison hulks. All papers can be searched by place, date, publication, and keyword.

New South Wales State Archives and Records
(www.nsw.gov.au)

The history of life in Australia's first penal colony is one of the more difficult to uncover, not least because so many of the early convict records were destroyed. Time, accident and intentional destruction has seen many convict records from New South Wales lost forever. Those looking for records of Australia's earliest transportees may well be disappointed when confronted with the sparse records of them compared to their Vandemonian and Western Australian counterparts. However, the State Archives and Records service of New South Wales has made the transcription of a number of convict records freely available online. Through the site users can access transcriptions of Early Convict Indexes which give details of convict arrivals from 1788–1801, an Index of convict arrivals, pardons, and Ticket-of-Leave issue until 1850, and applications for convict marriages.

Female Convict Research Centre
(http://www.femaleconvicts.org.au/)

The Female Convict Research Centre, based in Tasmania, is run by volunteers and provides a database of female convicts sent to Van Diemen's Land based on transcriptions of ships' records and conduct records. The FCRC also offers detail that goes past the official record – such as members' stories from descendents or elsewhere, private photographs, and information about the life of female convicts after conviction. The site also hosts a wealth of information on the provision for and treatment of women in Van Diemen's Land during the convict period. For those interested in the history of women during the 'boom' years of transportation, the FCRC can help fill in gaps left by insufficient records, provide vital background information, and help individual researchers link up with others who share their interests.

The Internet Archive
(www.archive.org)

Archive.org presents a completely open access online archive of millions of books, documents, pictures (alongside websites, music, film, and software) which can be accessed in a variety of formats. Memoirs of colonial officials, as well as convict biographies and memoirs can be found on the site, and give invaluable first-hand accounts of life in the Australian penal colonies. Search by publication title or author name to uncover the stories of men and women who experienced convict transportation in their own words.

Australian libraries and archives

A range of Australia's archives and libraries allow remote users to access both primary and secondary material via their websites. The National Library of Australia (www.nla.gov.au) and the State Library of New South Wales (www.sl.nsw.gov.au) both have extensive collections of pictures, documents, manuscripts, and more, that can be accessed and downloaded free of charge. For those looking to undertake more extensive research, the state records offices and libraries can be an invaluable first port of call for information on what collections are available, what can be accessed online, and what remains in hard copy only.

Suggested Reading

Contemporary fiction

C. Dickens, *Great Expectations* (Chapman and Hall, London, 1861).

C. Dickens, *Oliver Twist: or the Parish Boy's Progress* (Richard Bentley, London, 1838).

D. Defoe, *The Fortunes and Misfortunes of the Famous Moll Flanders* (William Rufus Chetwood, London, 1722).

M. Clarke, *For the Term of His Natural Life* (Richard Bentley and Son, London, 1875).

C. Leakley, *The Broad Arrow: Being Passages from the History of Maida Gwynnham, A Lifer* (Richard Bentley, London, 1859).

Contemporary accounts

Anon. *The Adventures, Memoirs, Former Trial, Transportation & Escapes of that notorious fence and receiver of stolen goods Isaac Solomon* (Joseph Knight, London, 1829).

G. Barrington, *A Voyage to Botany Bay* (London, 1793).

R. Cobbold, *The History of Margaret Catchpole: A Suffolk Girl* (George Barclay, London, 1846).

D. Collins, *An Account of the English Colony of New South Wales from its first settlement in January 1788 to August 1801 Vol. 2* (1804).

C. Cozens, *Adventures of a Guardsman* (Richard Bentley, London, 1848).

J. Frost, *The Horrors of Convict Life* (Holyoake & Co., London, 1856).

M. Jeffrey, *A Burglar's Life or The Stirring Adventures of the Great English Burglar Mark Jeffrey* (Tasmania, 1893).

E. B. Kelly, *Ebeneezer Beriah Kelly: An Autobiography* (John W. Steadman, Norwich, 1856).

J. Kingsmill, *Chapters on Prisons and Prisoners* (Longman, Brown, Green, and Longmans, London, 1854).

J. Martin *Memorandoms* [Memorandoms by James Martin, edited by Tim Causer] (UCL Press, London, 2017).

H. Mayhew and J. Binny, *The Criminal Prisons of London and Scenes of Prison Life* (Griffin, Bohn, and Company, London, 1862).

J. H. Vaux, *Memoirs of James Hardy Vaux, A Swindler and Thief, Now Transported to New South Wales for the Second Time, and For Life* (Whittaker, Treacher, and Arnot, London, 1830).

Modern histories of transportation and transportees

A. Brooke and D. Brandon, *Bound for Botany Bay: British Convict Voyages to Australia* (The National Archives, London, 2005).

T. Causer (eds), *Memorandums by James Martin* (UCL Press, London, 2017).

E. Christopher, *A Merciless Place: The Lost Story of Britain's Convict Disaster in Africa* (Oxford University Press, Oxford, 2010).

I. Clendinnen, *Dancing with Strangers, the true history of the meeting of the British First Fleet and the Aboriginal Australians, 1788* (Cannongate, Edinburgh, 2005).

R. Erickson and G. O'Mara, *Convicts in Western Australia 1850–1887/ Dictionary of Western Australia Volume IX* (University of Western Australia Press, WA, 1994).

T. Forbes, 'Coroners' Inquisitions on the deaths of Prisoners in the Hulks at Portsmouth England, in 1817–1827, *Journal of the History of Medicine and Allied Sciences*, 33 (1978).

L. Frost, *Abandoned Women: Scottish convicts exiled Beyond the Seas* (Allen & Unwin, NSW, 2012).

L. Frost and H. Maxwell-Stewart (eds) *Chain letters: Narrating Convict Lives* (Melbourne University Press, Melbourne, 1997).

A. W. Gill, *Convict Assignment in Western Australia: the Parkhurst 'apprentices' 1842–1851* (Blatellae Books, WA, 2009).

B. Godfrey and D. Cox 'The Last Fleet: Crime, Reformation, and Punishment in Western Australia After 1868' *The Australian and New Zealand Journal of Criminology*, 41,2 (2008).

R. Hughes, *The Fatal Shore: History of the Transportation of Convicts to Australia, 1787–1868* (The Harvill Press, London, 1987).

A. Jampoler, *Horrible Shipwreck!* (Naval Institute Press, Annapolis, 2010).

H. Johnston, *Crime in England 1815–1880: Experiencing the Criminal Justice System* (Routledge, London, 2015).

H. Maxwell-Stewart and R. Kippen, 'Sickness and Death on Male and Female Convict Voyages to Australia' in P. Baskerville and K. Inwood (eds) *Lives in Transition: Longditudinal Analysis from Historical Source* (McGill University Press, 2014).

H. Maxwell-Stewart, *Closing Hell's Gates: The death of a convict station* (Allen & Unwin, NSW, 2008).

D. Oxley, *Convict Maids: The Forced Migration of Women to Australia* (Cambridge: Cambridge University Press, 1996).

B. Smith, *A Cargo of Women: Susannah Watson & the convicts of the Princess Royal,* Second edition (Allen & Unwin, NSW, 2010).

B. Smith, *Australia's Birthstain: The Startling Legacy of the Convict Era* (Allen and Unwin, NSW, 2008).

R. Ward and L. Williams, 'Initial Views from the Digital Panopticon: Reconstructing Penal Outcomes in the 1790s' *Law and History Review* (2016).

B. Webb and S. Webb, *English Prisons under Local Government* (Longmans, London, 1922).

L. Williams and B. Godfrey, *Criminal Women 1850–1920: Researching the Lives of Britain's Female Offenders* (Pen and Sword, Barnsley, 2018).

L. Williams, *Wayward Women: Female Offending in Victorian England* (Pen and Sword, Barnsley, 2016).

Index

Ticket-of-Leave, 43, 54, 91, 92, 96, 102, 104, 116-118, 120, 122, 125, 127, 130, 134, 138, 141-42, 152-53, 157-158, 160, 161, 163, 165, 166, 171, 172, 175, 176, 187-189
Toodyay, 160.
Tothillfields, 99.
Transcription, 70, 189.
Treason, 6, 163.
Trial 3- 6, 9-10, 12-13, 16, 19, 36, 53, 56, 69, 71, 89, 95, 99, 104-105, 112-115, 119, 122, 124-27, 135-38, 153-54, 156, 160, 163, 165-67, 169, 170, 187, 191.
Tunbridge, 127-28
Typhoid, 46.

U

Uprisings, 53, 57, 163.
Uruguay, 54.

V

Vagrancy 62, 123, 142, 155, 159, 174-75
Van Diemen's Land 4, 7, 25, 35-8, 56-8, 61-63, 89, 91, 106-108, 110, 115-17, 120-60, 174, 187, 189
Vaux, James Hardy, 4, 21, 22, 24, 26, 37, 44, 45, 68, 93-105, 192
Vermin, 22-24, 46, 102, 131. *See also* Lice, Rats
Vessels, 1-2, 2, 17-21, 26-7, 33, 37, 39, 41-3, 45, 47-49, 51-2, 56, 58, 61, 63-4, 78, 100, 159, 163.
Victims, 15, 26, 37, 59, 81, 82, 95, 105, 124, 126-7, 155, 157, 159, 160, 173,
Victoria, 107, 117, 139, 147.

Violence, 2-5, 9, 11, 20, 21, 34, 42, 55, 73, 77, 80, 82, 97 112-15, 118, 124-25, 133, 138, 140, 152-154, 162, 163, 171.
Voyage, 1, 6, 11, 14, 36--53, 55-61, 63-68, 77, 79, 81, 92-3, 96, 101, 104, 127, 130-31, 160, 191-92.

W

Wakefield, 156.
War, 12, 17, 19, 28, 42, 107, 164. *See also* Napoleonic
Warwick, 32, 54.
Washing, 23, 26. *See also* Laundry
Weapons, 2, 5, 54, 156
Website, 186-89.
Western Australia, 20, 32, 35, 37-8, 42, 113, 140, 145-78, 165, 189, 192.
Westminster, 81.
Whaling, 148-49, 163-64.
Whipping, 19, 78, 96, 103, 116, 122, 148
Whitechapel, 15.
Wiltshire, 11.
Winchester, 29.
Wirral, 164-65.
Witnesses, 16, 18, 50-51, 82, 95, 105, 109, 124, 126, 167, 187
Wolverhampton, 32.
Woolwich, 20-28, 38, 59, 63, 100, 113-14, 139-41.

Y

York, 28, 30, 164, 174.
Yorkshire 36, 111, 127, 142.
Youth, 7, 33, 100, 113, 122. *See also* Boys, Juvenile